THE RAILWAY IN ENGLAND
AND WALES 1830–1914

Volume 1
The System and its Working

Volume 1
The System and
its Working

Jack Simmons THE RAILWAY
IN ENGLAND AND
WALES
1830-1914

Leicester University Press
1978

First published in 1978 by
Leicester University Press
Distributed in North America by
Humanities Press Inc., New Jersey
Copyright © Jack Simmons 1978

Designed by Douglas Martin
Set in 'Monotype' Scotch Roman
Printed and bound in Great Britain
by W & J Mackay Limited, Chatham
ISBN 0 7185 1146 8

*The publication of this book has been assisted
by a grant from the Twenty-Seven Foundation*

British Library Cataloguing in Publication Data
Simmons, Jack
The railway in England and Wales, 1830–1914.
Vol 1: The system and its working.
1. Railroads – England – History
I. Title
385'.0942   HE3018
ISBN 0–7185–1146–8

Contents

List of maps and figures

Map tipped in at back
   *The railway system in England and Wales, 1914, with inset showing the
   London area.*

List of tables

A note on some points of usage

In the spelling of place-names the general rule followed here has been to accept the practice established on the railways themselves in the Victorian age. The names of places that had passenger stations are spelt as in the *Railway Clearing House Handbook of Railway Stations*, 1904 (reprinted in 1970); Bartholomew's *Survey Gazetteer of the British Isles* (1904 edition) has been the authority for the rest. As a necessary consequence, all Welsh place-names appear here in an anglicised form: e.g. Carnarvon.

Similarly, counties are referred to throughout as they were in 1914, not in the form they have come to assume under the Local Government Act of 1972.

Metrication is overtaking Britain while this book is in progress. Here it has been ignored; but simple conversion tables in respect of currency, distance, and weight are given on page 278.

The term 'Regulation Acts' is used as a generic description of all the ten Acts passed, with slightly different titles, for the regulation of railways between 1840 and 1893.

Abbreviations

Acworth RE	Sir W. M. Acworth, *The Railways of England* (1889). Unless otherwise stated, the edition cited is the 5th, of 1900.
Ahrons BSRL	E. L. Ahrons, *The British Steam Railway Locomotive* [1927]
Ahrons LTW	E. L. Ahrons, *Locomotive and Train Working in the Latter Part of the Nineteenth Century* (6 vols, 1951–4)
Alderman	G. Alderman, *The Railway Interest* (1973)
Bagwell RCH	P. S. Bagwell, *The Railway Clearing House* (1968)
Barker and Robbins	T. C. Barker and R. M. Robbins, *History of London Transport* (2 vols, 1963–74)
BL	British Library
Bradshaw	G. Bradshaw, *Railway Guide* (1841–1961). Cf. Ottley 7950.
BRSM	G. Bradshaw, *Railway Manual, Shareholder's Guide and Official Directory* (1848–1923). Cf. Ottley 7949.
BTHR	British Transport Historical Records: Public Record Office, London
Chaloner	W. H. Chaloner, *The Social and Economic Development of Crewe* (1950)
Christiansen and Miller CR	R. Christiansen and R. W. Miller, *The Cambrian Railways* (2 vols, 1967 and n.d.)
Christiansen and Miller NSR	R. Christiansen and R. W. Miller, *The North Staffordshire Railway* (1971)
Cleveland-Stevens	E. Cleveland-Stevens, *English Railways* (1915)
Donaghy	T. J. Donaghy, *Liverpool & Manchester Railway Operations* (1972)
Dow GC	G. Dow, *Great Central* (3 vols, 1959–65)
Ellis	C. H. Ellis, *Railway Carriages in the British Isles* (1965)
Findlay	Sir G. Findlay, *The Working and Management of an English Railway* (6th edn, 1899, repr. 1976)

Foxwell and Farrer	E. Foxwell and T. C. Farrer, *Express Trains English and Foreign* (1889)
Francis	J. Francis, *A History of the English Railway* (2 vols, 1851)
Gourvish	T. R. Gourvish, *Mark Huish and the London & North Western Railway* (1972)
Helps, *Brassey*	Sir A. Helps, *Life and Labours of Mr Brassey* (1872, repr. 1969)
Irving	R. J. Irving, *The North Eastern Railway Company 1870–1914* (1976)
JTH	*The Journal of Transport History* (1953–)
Lewin I	H. G. Lewin, *Early British Railways . . . 1801–44* [1925]
Lewin II	H. G. Lewin, *The Railway Mania and its Aftermath 1845–52* (1936, repr. 1968)
LPA	Local and Personal Acts of Parliament
MacDermot	E. T. MacDermot, *History of the Great Western Railway* (2 vols., 1964 edn)
Marshall CH	C. F. D. Marshall, *Centenary History of the Liverpool & Manchester Railway* (1930)
Marshall LYR	J. Marshall, *The Lancashire & Yorkshire Railway* (3 vols, 1969–72)
Marshall SR	C. F. D. Marshall, *History of the Southern Railway* (2 vols, 1963 edn)
Mitchell and Deane	B. R. Mitchell and P. Deane, *Abstract of British Historical Statistics* (1962)
Neele	G. P. Neele, *Railway Reminiscences* (1904, repr. 1974)
Ottley	G. Ottley, *A Bibliography of British Railway History* (1966)
Parris	H. Parris, *Government and the Railways in Nineteenth-Century Britain* (1965)
PP	*Parliamentary Papers*. The pagination given is that of the set in the British Library. All are House of Commons papers, except those indicated by 'PP (HL)'.
SRO	Scottish Record Office, Edinburgh
Tomlinson	W. W. Tomlinson, *The North Eastern Railway* [1915]
VCH	*The Victoria History of the Counties of England*
Victorian City	*The Victorian City*, ed. H. J. Dyos and M. Wolff (2 vols, 1973)
Williams LSWR	R. A. Williams, *The London & South Western Railway* (2 vols published, 1968–73)

TO THE MEMORY

OF

C. L. MOWAT

AND

L. T. C. ROLT

LOVERS AND WISE STUDENTS

OF THE RAILWAY

Preface

The preparation of this book has been generously aided by two bodies, to which I am most grateful: the Leverhulme Trust, for enabling me to engage a research assistant to draw the maps that play an important part in it; and the University of Leicester, for assisting my work from its Research Fund.

I owe several personal debts. My research assistant, Mr Stephen Bowen, worked hard at the task of preparing the maps, with enthusiasm and unfailing cheerfulness. Mr Peter Stephens of the Science Museum kindly read and criticised for me a large part of the original draft, concerned with matters of technology. And Mr John Bourne helped me in the checking and correction of the proofs.

The University   J.S.
Leicester
5 December 1977

Railroad travelling is a delightful improvement of human life . . . Every thing is near, every thing is immediate – time, distance, and delay are abolished.
Sydney Smith, 1842

I have felt it my duty always to stand in opposition to every proposition of every railroad whatever.
Colonel Sibthorp, House of Commons, 5 February 1844

Here comes old Hell in Harness.
Joe Walter, Royston coachman, looking at a train, c. 1850

We who lived before railways, and survive out of the ancient world, are like Father Noah and his family out of the Ark.
Thackeray, 1860

In a hundred . . . cases . . . a railway has enriched whole districts by an augmented value of land, by new markets, and by new residents, though the shareholders who made the line never received, and never will receive, a penny of dividend.
The Economist, 1 December 1866

The pick, the Bible, and the locomotive, the sources of England's greatness.
Scroll at the Railway Jubilee at Darlington, 1875

The interests of the public and the interests of trade are safer in the hands of the State and the bodies that the State appoints . . . than they are in the hands of railway directors.
A. J. Channing, House of Commons, 11 March 1886

To my mind there is scarcely a more splendid beast in the world than a large Locomotive. . . . I cannot imagine a finer sight than the Express, with two engines, rushing down this incline at the edge of dusk.
Beatrix Potter, 1892

It is rather a difficult task in this House – and anyone who has been here long enough will realise it – to recommend any measure which seems in the slightest degree to favour railway companies.
David Lloyd George, House of Commons, 30 January 1913

Introduction

This is the first instalment of a long work, the purpose of which is to examine the consequences of railway building, the impact that the railway made on England and Wales as a whole, on local communities, and on individual men and women. Most books on the history of railways deal with them as they were, with their construction, the traffic they carried, and the way in which it was worked. The main theme here is different: not what the railway was, but what it did.

The two themes cannot, however, be separated completely. To understand the impact that the railway made, one must have a good grasp of the development of the railway system. The original intention was to supply this requirement by a preliminary essay, to be prefixed to the first instalment of the main work. But it soon became clear that this would not be enough, and the essay has grown into the present volume, standing by itself as the first of four. That it has been possible to keep it reasonably short is due chiefly to the provision of a pair of specially-drawn maps, which summarise and depict the story. These have lightened the text by relieving it of any blow-by-blow narrative of the building of railways and their extension, so as to concentrate on providing a general account of the making of the system, with particular attention to a limited number of individual lines. It is meant to be a sketch, no more; to supply what it seems necessary to know if the remainder of the work, a much more detailed study, is going to be intelligible. Though its emphasis is placed mainly on the physical expansion of the system, it has something to say about the public regulation of railways too.

These matters occupy the first five chapters. Chapters 6–10 set out some of the essentials of the railways' technology, the equipment they used and the way in which they were managed; again a necessary preliminary to an understanding of what they did, and sometimes failed to do.

The second volume, 'Town and Country', which is to consider the railways' impact on London and the provinces, is now in preparation. The third, 'Mind and Eye', will be concerned with the mental communication that the railways promoted, its reflection in the press, in literature and the arts, in the thought and imagination of the age; and with the visual impact they made on those who watched their development. The final volume will treat the community at large, the part played by railways in its social, economic, and political life.

The study is confined to England and Wales. It ought to have comprehended the whole of the British Isles; but the subject is already large enough. The railway system of England and Wales can, for most purposes, be separated from those of the rest of the United Kingdom – the railways might almost be said to have erected a new version of Hadrian's Wall between England and Scotland (cf. p. 67). Just occasionally, where some comparison or cross-reference seems to be in point, the study trespasses north of the Border or across the St George's Channel. Perhaps other people may undertake analogous investigations – they would be markedly different, and not less interesting – of the railway in Scotland and Ireland.

It might well have been desirable to take the story on from 1914 to 1947, as Mr Hamilton Ellis did with advantage in his *British Railway History*. But, here again, that would make a still larger work. The time-span adopted represents a deliberate choice. This study concerns itself with the years in which the railway achieved and maintained its dominance in the transport system. It will be for another writer to treat the changes in its role that have occurred since 1914.

1   The System Established 1830-1844

The history recounted in this book begins and ends on two particular days: 15 September 1830, when the Liverpool & Manchester Railway was formally opened; 4 August 1914, when Great Britain entered the First World War. The second of these days was, as anyone can see, outstanding in the history of the twentieth century; but the first was also of cardinal importance to the nineteenth.

The Liverpool & Manchester was by no means the first railway to be built. By the time it was opened, some 375 miles were already in operation in England and Wales, constructed under Parliamentary powers since 1801;[1] and in addition there were numerous private lines, especially in the coalfields of the North-East, the Midlands, and South Wales, whose total length it is impossible to compute.

By 1830 the great majority of these railways were made of iron, though wooden railways were still not uncommon.[2] The motive power on most of them was supplied by horses; on some by men; on others by the force of gravity. Mechanical traction, though comparatively rare, had been developed in more than one form: the stationary engine, the locomotive. The use of the stationary engine was limited, chiefly to haulage on steep inclines. The locomotive had to go a long way before it could show itself as speedy or as reliable as the horse. When the first major Parliamentary debate on a railway took place in 1825, on the second reading of the Liverpool & Manchester Company's first Bill, the most telling argument of the opposition was that, on test, the utmost speed that a locomotive had shown itself capable of achieving had been $3\frac{3}{4}$ m.p.h.[3] Since coaches were by then running on most of the chief roads of the kingdom at 9–10 m.p.h., the locomotive had still to be greatly improved before it

1. Calculation from figures given in Lewin I, 3–16.
2. M. J. T. Lewis, *Early Wooden Railways* (1970), 296.
3. *Hansard* n.s. 12 (1825) 852.

could outstrip them. Here lies the vital importance of the Rainhill trials
of 1829. They were sponsored by the Liverpool & Manchester Company,
convinced that it must find a machine that was capable of producing a
higher speed than the horse. The purpose of the trials was to decide
between the merits of the stationary engine, whose chief protagonists
were James Walker and J. U. Rastrick, and the locomotive, strenuously
advocated by the Stephensons and the Company's Secretary, Henry
Booth. The victory of the Stephensons' *Rocket* was decisive; and the
Company determined accordingly to work its line by locomotives, except
on the steep gradient up from Liverpool, where a stationary engine was
employed. Even so, it was not the first railway to be worked in this way.
The Stockton & Darlington Company had used horses, stationary engines,
and locomotives; so had the Canterbury & Whitstable, opened four
months before the Liverpool & Manchester. Mixed traction, in various
forms, was also to be found on other lines such as the Cromford & High
Peak, and the Monkland & Kirkintilloch in Scotland.

The Liverpool & Manchester Railway was designed to carry passengers
as well as goods. But in that also there was nothing new. If the business
of the existing railways was chiefly with the carriage of goods, passengers
had been conveyed, in horse-drawn carriages, on the Oystermouth
Railway in South Wales as early as 1807. The Kilmarnock & Troon, the
Stockton, and the Canterbury companies provided for them too.

Nor, finally, could the Liverpool & Manchester claim to be, in any
sense, the first public railway. None of those constructed during the
seventeenth and eighteenth centuries[4] could be called anything but
private: for the use of the promoters, that is, and the development of
their property. But when the Surrey Iron Railway was authorised in 1801
its Act stated specifically that 'all persons whomsoever shall have free
liberty to use with horses, cattle, and carriages, the roads, ways, and
passages to be made by virtue of this Act'.[5] The Company's powers were
restricted to imposing regulations for the use of the line, in order to allow
free passage on it and to prevent obstruction.[6]

These were essential provisions if a railway was to be public, open to
everybody, like a road, but at the same time orderly, without clashes
between the users. They were much elaborated in subsequent legislation,
but not essentially altered. The introduction of the locomotive, however,
brought new difficulties with it. On some railways its use was expressly

4. For these early railways cf. Lewis, *op. cit.*,; C. E. Lee, *The Evolution of Railways*
    (2nd edn, 1943); C. F. D. Marshall, *History of British Railways down to the Year
    1830* (2nd edn, 1971); R. S. Smith in *Renaissance and Modern Studies* 1 (1957) 120.
5. LPA 41 Geo. III cap. 33, sect. 65.
6. *Ibid.*, sects. 66, 70.

forbidden: as on the Newcastle & Carlisle, which secured powers in 1829 to build a line of 63 miles – the longest so far authorised – to be operated by the power of horses only. The draftsmen of the Whitby & Pickering Railway's Act in 1833 got themselves into a hopeless tangle on this point, so that by section 114 the Company was permitted to use locomotives, though forbidden to do so by section 134. At first it was envisaged that anyone should be as free to put his own engine on the railway as his own wagons. Since this could evidently be dangerous, the promoters of the Liverpool & Manchester Railway, contemplating as early as 1826 that the line would be mechanically worked throughout, secured for themselves adequate powers of control. Private owners' locomotives were not thereafter forbidden ever to work on a public railway; but if they, or the locomotives of another railway, did so, it was clearly under the direction of the owners of the line, to their timetable, at their convenience, and subject to their safety precautions.

The Liverpool & Manchester Railway was therefore, on the face of it, very little of an innovator. Almost every power it secured derived from one that had been granted to another company during the previous 30 years. It did not propose to do any single thing that had never been done by a railway before. Why then is its opening so important?

For three reasons. In the first place, though its powers were not new, they were exercised in combination on a quite new scale. All traction was mechanical from the outset; and, largely as a consequence, the Company regulated the traffic on its line more fully and minutely than any of its predecessors. The directors and their servants were not just providing a facility. They were seen to be in control of a large and complex organisation.

Secondly, though the Company was permitted to carry passengers and freight, it gave its attention at the outset chiefly to passengers. Indeed, for more than a month after its opening it conveyed passengers alone; the first train of 'merchandise' ran from Liverpool to Manchester on 4 December 1830.[7] Here was indeed an innovation. To the general astonishment it quickly began to appear that the carriage of passengers could be undertaken by a railway on as large a scale and as profitably as that of freight.

One other thing, in the nature of the case, marked off the Liverpool & Manchester Railway from all others yet built, or projected, anywhere. It linked two great commercial towns, whose needs were to an exceptional degree complementary. Manchester required, for much of its business, quicker and easier access to the sea. Liverpool's port was its life-blood; the railway helped to draw to it the trade of all south Lancashire,

7. Marshall CH, 64.

together with supplies of coal and other raw materials, for which its demand was nearly insatiable. But – once again – it was the passenger traffic that proved so valuable at first, enabling Liverpool merchants and Manchester men, for instance, each to transact a long day's business in the other town and to return home at night. Here was a mobility in commerce hardly imagined before.

There was no doubt at the time about the magnitude of this event. Not everyone welcomed it. As with the aeroplane and the hovercraft in our own day, there were those who disliked the new form of travel. Some people, looking ahead into the future, feared its implications, the changes they thought it would bring. As new railways, modelled on the Liverpool & Manchester, were projected, these prophets sounded their cautions and warnings.[8] Yet in spite of them the railway worked, and after a few teething troubles worked well. It was profitable. Not on the scale of the canals in their palmy days: but then, with that in mind, Parliament had deliberately sought to restrict the dividends the shareholders might receive, with a view to making the railway something much closer to what we should now call a public utility. (Huskisson had used this as a strong argument in supporting the Bill of 1826:[9] 'It is an especial condition that the profits upon the undertaking shall be limited always to 10%. Would the canals limit their profit to this extent – taking as they are now doing, more than 100?') Quietly but inexorably, the railway drove the coaches off the road. Its victory was evident, and famous. So famous that visitors came from all over Britain, from Europe and America to see the new organisation at work. In the 1820s there had been a pilgrimage to Stockton and Darlington. But the visitors there had been chiefly engineers, interested in methods of traction; and though some of them were important people, and learnt far-reaching lessons,[10] they were not numerous. Liverpool and Manchester – towns of infinitely greater

8. The economist J. R. McCulloch, for example, whilst admitting the magnitude of the Liverpool & Manchester Company's achievement, doubted whether 'there be many more situations in the Kingdom where it would be prudent to establish a railway': *Dictionary . . . of Commerce* (1832), 898. Six years later he had changed his mind, to recognise that the extension of railways was desirable: *Supplement* (Jan. 1839), 72.

9. *Hansard* n.s. 15 (1826) 93.

10. For example William Stinson, coalowner of Whitwick, who returned to Leicestershire from a visit to the railway filled with admiration for it, and convinced that a similar railway was absolutely required if the pits in his neighbourhood were to recover the trade they had lost with Leicester through the introduction of Derbyshire coal into the town, brought in by the Soar Navigation. The result was the Leicester & Swannington Railway. Cf. *Transactions of the Leicestershire Archaeological Society* 30 (1954) 59, 61; VCH *Leics*.iii. 110.

consequence in their own right – drew a far larger concourse. The railway had much more to show there: not only in the use it was making of the power of steam, but also in its civil engineering, in its buildings and their arrangements, in the whole complicated administration that the handling of passenger traffic on so large a scale called forth. And what the visitors saw, many of them hastened to publish: so that the new railway became celebrated at once throughout the Western world.[11]

Let us look at a few of the comments they passed, showing both what the visitors assumed and what surprised them. They give us a view of the modern railway at its birth, in terms of its first principles, set down in simple language. Some of these early accounts are well known: those of Creevey[12] and Greville,[13] for example, Crabb Robinson[14] and Fanny Kemble.[15] There are others, less familiar. Here is a visitor telling his neighbours at home in Suffolk what he thought about it:[16]

You skim along like magic. We drove to the railway office at Warrington a short mile from the town where we took our seats in a machine; for it was one continued machine although having the appearance of 3 regular coaches and three divisions of seats like those in a coffee-room – the coaches not open at the top – the seats were.

Mrs D. from having a cold was fearful of exposing herself in the open seat & therefore was in one of the coaches in no way differing from those which go with horses except that the inside is divided into six seats by elbows like an elbow chair, and numbered so that you take your place by number and get as far from the steam engine as you can – in this we proceeded 5 miles to Newton in less than 25 minutes. There we met the Train, as it is called, not Coach or Coaches, coming from Manchester to Liverpool; this is at the point called the Viaduct. We then took to this machine which had no open parts but complete handsome coaches in succession but forming only one machine each having a separate name, for instance the *Hero, March of Intellect*, &c., &c., and at the end on a platform sat a gentleman lounging at his ease in his barouche. This part we travelled about 15 or 20 miles an hour. . . .

What would you more, my good friend, of fear or danger? Answer me this. As a style of conveyance I cannot imagine anything to exceed it, if you could wholly free yourself from the idea of being blown to

11. Donaghy 145–6.
12. *The Creevey Papers*, ed. Sir H. Maxwell (1912), 545–6.
13. *Memoirs*, ed. L. Strachey and R. Fulford (1938), iii. 384–6.
14. *Diary . . . of Henry Crabb Robinson*, ed. T. Sadler (3rd edn, 1872), ii. 138–9.
15. *Record of a Girlhood* (1878), ii. 158–65.
16. W. Dalton to John Gwilt, 16 Oct. 1831: *Notes and Queries* 12th ser. 7 (1920) 461–2.

H – or hurled into the air in 1000 pieces. – However I say to you it is well worth the journey & I recommend your enjoying it.

In general, most travellers did enjoy the experience. Some time later, when the Liverpool & Manchester Railway had got more fully into its stride, Thomas Moore the poet found it 'a grand mode of travelling. . . . The motion so easy that I found I could write without any difficulty *chemin faisant*'.[17]

There were dissentients, however. 'The advantages have been a good deal over-rated', wrote one of them, 'for, prejudice apart, I think most people will allow that expedition is the only real advantage gained: the road itself is ugly, though curious and wonderful as a work of art. . . . I cannot say that I at all liked it: the speed was too great to be pleasant, and certainly it is not smoother and easier than a turnpike road. When the carriages stop or go on, a very violent jolting takes place, from the ends of the carriage jostling together'.[18]

That was fair criticism and remained valid until spring buffers and screw couplings had been evolved. But there were other visitors, as one might expect, who were less fair, or indeed obtuse. De Tocqueville was told by the French Consul at Liverpool of the foolish behaviour of some of his compatriots – engineers, inspecting the railway:

> Not so long ago M. Navier and several others came. They only wanted to stay three days; they visited the railway only, and, when some one told them a fact, M. Navier, after making some calculations, often said: 'The thing is impossible, it does not fit at all with the theory'. Those gentlemen have not left the English greatly impressed with their ability at least in practical matters.[19]

One further observation, a philosophical one, arising from another of these early visits, from George Pryme, Professor of Political Economy at Cambridge:

> On my return to Chester I visited Liverpool [in 1836] and travelled from thence, for curiosity, a few miles towards Manchester on that then novel mode of conveyance, a railroad. It seems to me extraordinary that it had not been discovered long before. When I was at

17. Diary, 7 Aug. 1835: *Memoirs . . . of Thomas Moore*, ed. Lord John Russell (1856), vii. 95–6.
18. *Notes and Queries* 4th ser. 2 (1868) 101–2.
19. A. de Tocqueville, *Journeys to England and Ireland*, ed. J. P. Mayer (1958), 113 (5 July 1835). Navier was an Engineer of the Ponts et Chaussées and a Professor in its School. A British engineer, (Sir) John Macneill, translated his treatise *On the Means of Comparing the Respective Advantages of Different Lines of Railway* in 1836. It shows Navier as a relentless theorist.

school [in 1796–7] tramways were used at Hull between the docks and warehouses, whereby one horse drawing a cart did the work of three or four. Within a mile of them were steam engines for grinding wheat, or crushing seed for oil, and yet no one till nearly 40 years afterwards thought of combining the two.[20]

He then goes on to quote Erasmus Darwin's well-known prophecy of the victorious application of steam to transport.[21]

If Pryme's comment does much less than justice to the work of Trevithick, Hedley, Hackworth, and the Stephensons, it rightly emphasises one fact: that, for whatever reasons, it was only in the Liverpool & Manchester Railway that the full potential of the locomotive was demonstrated.

And finally we must remember that that demonstration was extraordinarily sudden. We tend to see the Liverpool & Manchester Railway as evolving laboriously, building on the experience of its predecessors; and that is true. But the world at large, which knew very little of those things, became aware of the railway at a single moment of time. Looking back to that opening more than half a century later, a shrewd and reflective American remarked:

> The great peculiarity of the locomotive engine and its sequence, the railroad, as compared with other and far more important inventions, was that it burst rather than stole or crept upon the world. Its advent was in the highest degree dramatic. It was even more so than the discovery of America.[22]

The development of the new railway had its first immediate effects in Lancashire itself. It attracted traffic not only from the two great commercial centres it joined but from all the neighbouring towns:[23] so that in 1829–31 a miniature railway system had come to be planned in south Lancashire, and authorised by Parliament. This drew in one earlier railway, the Bolton & Leigh, sanctioned a year before the Liverpool & Manchester as a link between two canals. By 1838 Bolton, Preston, Wigan, and Warrington all enjoyed railway communication with Liverpool and Manchester.

20. *Autobiographic Recollections of George Pryme* (1870), 244.
21. *Economy of Vegetation*, i (4th edn, 1799), 31.
22. C. F. Adams, jr, *Railroads* (1886 edn), 3.
23. Their anxiety to link themselves with the railway was noted with satisfaction in Liverpool. By September 1829 all had put forward plans for this purpose except Wigan; and Wigan followed in October. *Liverpool Chronicle*, 12 Sept., 24 Oct. 1829.

Collectively, these railways formed what we may fairly call a system, a little less than 80 miles in length. They were built to a common gauge, and all except the Manchester & Bolton fell into the main Liverpool & Manchester line, the magnet that drew them together. These 80 miles of line were constructed by seven companies, each making a separate application to Parliament and receiving its powers under a separate Act. They did not remain separate for long. The two lines joining at Leigh were built and worked as one. The Wigan Branch Railway and the Preston & Wigan, its northward continuation, were combined into a single company, called the North Union, in 1834: the first instance of a railway amalgamation sanctioned by Parliament.

The potential of this Lancashire system grew into something greater when it became, in effect, the northern spearhead of a railway reaching up from London. In 1833 Parliament established two companies to undertake this vast enterprise: the London & Birmingham, 112 miles long, and the Grand Junction, extending from Birmingham to Warrington (78 miles). Both – but especially the London & Birmingham – encountered a fierce opposition. Once sanctioned, they were driven forward with resolute energy, the London & Birmingham under the direction of Robert Stephenson, the Grand Junction under Joseph Locke. The whole of the Grand Junction line was opened at once, on 4 July 1837; the more difficult London & Birmingham by stages. When that undertaking was completed, on 17 September 1838, a continuous line of railway had been established from London to Preston (whence a further 20 miles were already authorised, northwards to Lancaster).

By that time the country had gone through a feverish activity in the speculative promotion of railways. Something of the sort had already appeared in 1824–5; but that had been on a small scale and had also concerned canals, gas undertakings, and other utilities. The Railway Mania of 1836–7 was more properly so called.[24] In those two years 44 new companies were established in the United Kingdom – as compared with 43 set up in the whole period since the Stockton & Darlington Railway had been sanctioned in 1821.[25] But they were no more than the strong, or fortunate, survivors from a larger competition: for a total of 57 proposals, involving a capital expenditure of some £28 million, were

24. The term 'railway mania' had come into use in 1825. General Gascoyne, one of the Members for Liverpool, was using it very early in that year: T. C. Barker and J. Harris, *A Merseyside Town in the Industrial Revolution* (1959 edn), 183. By 1836 it had become so widely accepted that a country gentleman in the Isle of Wight could use it in a letter to India: C. Aspinall-Oglander, *Nunwell Symphony* (1945), 211. It is curious that the only example of the phrase given by the *Oxford English Dictionary* dates from 1903.
25. Lewin I, 186.

brought forward during these years,[26] and in the failure of many of them much capital contributed by rash investors was lost. Out of all this activity something like a national railway system began to emerge.

The London & Birmingham Railway had the same inspiriting effect as the Liverpool & Manchester. Not only did it supply communication with the industrial kingdom of Lancashire. It provided the means for a north-easterly thrust also into the Midlands, Yorkshire, and Durham. By 1840 a line diverged from it that was continuous to Leeds and to York. Indeed south of Derby there were two routes: one provided by the Birmingham & Derby Junction Company, to Hampton (about half-way between Birmingham and Coventry), the other over the Midland Counties line, to Rugby through Leicester, with a branch to Nottingham. These two railways were fierce rivals. Twice, in 1840 and again in 1842–3, they entered into a competition in lowering fares between Derby and London. At length in 1844 they came together with the North Midland, which provided the sole line from Derby to Leeds, to form a single company called the Midland Railway.

This was an historic amalgamation: not the first to be carried through, but the first to produce a great company. The Midland Railway's system amounted, when it was formed, to 180 miles. It had coherence: a centre, at Derby; a line with a connection to London, via Rugby (that via Hampton now quietly fell into desuetude); another to Birmingham and so, by means of two separate companies, to Bristol; a third to Leeds, with connections to York and beyond. The decision to amalgamate the three companies was unquestionably a wise one. The Birmingham & Derby and the Midland Counties had almost beggared each other. It was the first conspicuous example of a kind of warfare that soon became common in England and was viewed with shocked disapprobation on the Continent. The Belgian system, which was laid down in 1834 and realised in 1835–43, seemed to preclude any such possibility, being meticulously planned by the State.[27] In France careful measures were taken to the same end, by different means. In Britain, the State declining to plan or make itself directly responsible for railways, a hybrid practice grew up. Competition was permitted – sometimes deliberately encouraged, in the true spirit of *laissez faire*. It was tempered by amalgamations, until in turn those amalgamations began to raise an outcry against monopoly.

Two men may be regarded as the founders of the Midland Railway. The idea of the amalgamation seems to have been due to the engineer

26. W. T. Jackman, *Development of Transportation in Modern England* (1916), 570.
27. The Belgian system was frequently held up to Englishmen as a model for their own: cf., for instance, G. R. Porter in *Journal of the Statistical Society* 7 (1844) 177–8.

Robert Stephenson, who with his father had built the North Midland line;[28] but the task was actually carried through by a business man, George Hudson. He was a draper of York, successful in trade and enriched by a large legacy, who had begun to interest himself in railways in 1833. Under the influence of George Stephenson, whom he met in the following year, he was gradually drawn into the affairs of the North Midland, and so into those of the two squabbling companies that linked it with the London & Birmingham. He turned Robert Stephenson's idea into reality; and his reward was the chairmanship of the new organisation – for the moment the largest railway company in Britain.

Meanwhile the railway had begun to emerge in the south. London got its first in 1836 – later than Edinburgh and Dublin. This was the tiny London & Greenwich Railway, extending then only as far as Deptford, a distance of little more than three miles. By 1844 the capital was the hub of a whole wheel of railways, reaching to Colchester, Dover, Brighton, Gosport (for Portsmouth), and Southampton. Westwards there stretched another line, through Bristol to Exeter; almost as long as the one we have traced to Preston.

This last railway was different from all the others in that it was built to a much wider gauge: one of 7ft against the 4ft 8½ins that was almost universal elsewhere, on the Continent as well as in Britain.[29] I. K. Brunel, the engineer of the Great Western Railway from London to Bristol, persuaded his directors to break with what the Stephensons had made the accepted tradition in this respect; and Parliament had authorised the railway in 1835 without specifying, as it had usually done in the past, the gauge to which it was to be built.[30] Brunel considered that the Stephensons' gauge was too restrictive, that more room was needed, both for the satisfactory deployment of the locomotives' machinery and for the comfortable and economic conveyance of passengers. On both these points he was theoretically in the right – though, if the Stephenson gauge was somewhat too narrow, his may well seem extravagantly broad. It was an economic as much as a technical question: for to lay a double track of Brunel's gauge required more land; and the cost of land, for railways in Britain, was exceptionally high. All the bridges and earthworks had to be proportionately wider too. Moreover, if the full potential

28. Nine years afterwards Robert Stephenson said, 'I was the chief instigator of it': PP 1852–3, xxxviii. 123.

29. Almost, but not quite. The gauge of the Colchester line was 5ft when it was first built; and already in remote North Wales the Festiniog Railway was in operation, on a gauge of a fraction under 2ft.

30. There was one important precedent for this omission: the Act for the London & Southampton Railway, passed a year earlier, had made no stipulation about gauge.

of the broad gauge was to be realised, the bridges and tunnels would have to be not only wider but higher. In fact, rather strangely, Brunel built his line with a minimum vertical clearance only a little greater than that used by the Stephensons.

The broad gauge, then, was expensive. Largely because of its adoption, the Great Western was the most magnificent of all railways. Brunel laid it out for speed. Unfortunately, where railways were concerned his genius shone in civil rather than mechanical engineering; and the locomotives he commissioned for his company were a grotesque series of freaks, all experimental and all failures. By a delightful touch of irony, the only engines that proved reliable were supplied by Robert Stephenson & Co.: two of a quite conventional orthodox design originally ordered for the New Orleans Railway, which proved unable to pay for them, and then adapted for the 7ft gauge by their builders. The Company appointed a Locomotive Superintendent who was to make himself responsible for the machines in service: Daniel Gooch, a Northumbrian not quite 21 when he entered the Great Western's employment in 1837. It was Gooch's job to make Brunel's engines work: an ungrateful task, which brought on him the odium of their failure,[31] and in the end a hopeless one. It would have been out of the question to run any train service over the whole length of the line from London to Bristol with these machines. Gooch had therefore to set about designing new ones of his own. Brunel thoroughly concurred in this decision – meanness and jealousy were qualities omitted from his character; and Gooch was soon able to prove himself one of the outstanding practical locomotive engineers of the nineteenth century. He wisely concentrated at first on securing machines that would be reliable in service, not swift. Though Brunel had laid his line out with a view to fast running, no fast trains ran on it in regular service until 1845.

Looking back at Brunel and his broad gauge, one thing must strike us most forcibly today. It might be on its merits a better gauge than the Stephensons': but what was going to happen when the two gauges met? The answer to that question throws a good deal of light on the whole concept of a railway system in the 1830s and 1840s. It was considered a purely domestic matter. If the Great Western chose to build its railway to a different gauge from the Birmingham or Southampton lines, that was its own affair. When Brunel urged his company to adopt the 7ft gauge, he admitted this would be an inconvenience in only one respect. The line was intended to join up with the London & Birmingham at

31. G. H. Gibbs, a leading Great Western director, wrote of 'the total unfitness of Gooch for his situation' at the close of 1838: *The Birth of the Great Western Railway*, ed. J. Simmons (1971), 63.

Kensal Green and run thence to Euston. Brunel's solution to the problem thus presented was that the gauge would have to be mixed over that short distance: 'one additional rail to each railway must be laid down'.[32] In the event, for whatever reason,[33] this idea was abandoned and the Great Western constructed its own line to Paddington: so the difficulty never arose. For the rest, it was the Great Western's intention to erect a self-contained commercial kingdom. From that point of view there might even be an advantage in thus fortifying itself against the future abstraction of its traffic by a rival.

No one yet detected the importance of the question. When the Great Western Chairman and Secretary gave evidence before the Commons Committee on Railways in 1839, 244 questions were put to them. Only seven of these concerned the peculiar gauge their company had adopted. A few of the Great Western shareholders persistently questioned the wisdom of accepting the broad gauge, while the railway was being constructed. After wavering at one moment in 1838, the directors adhered to their original decision, and the line was completed in 1841 to Brunel's specification. It was extended on the 7ft gauge to Exeter in 1844.

By that time the Great Western had begun to throw off branches northward of its main line. The most important of these (originally undertaken by an independent company, which the Great Western absorbed) ran from Swindon to Gloucester and Cheltenham. Near Gloucester it joined another line, coming up from Bristol, which had been planned on the narrow gauge but altered to the broad by agreement with the Great Western. These two lines, from Swindon and Bristol, were both opened throughout on 8 July 1844, and broad-gauge trains ran on to Gloucester over them. But there they met a line from the north, opened in 1840, the Birmingham & Gloucester. It was built to the Stephenson gauge. At Gloucester, then, on that 8 July, the Battle of the Gauges was joined: a chaotic conflict in the transfer of passengers and goods. The consequences will appear shortly.

In south-eastern England the early development of the railway system offered some pointers to the future. The London & Brighton Railway was opened in 1841: a splendidly direct line, with tunnels piercing the North and South Downs rather than taking an easier, winding path through the gaps in them. Two other coastal towns that were reached early by the railway were important for the connections they offered with steamship services: Southampton and Dover. At Southampton the railway was linked with the development of a dock undertaking, and the London & Southampton (later London & South Western) Company had from the

32. For Brunel's statement of the case for the broad gauge see MacDermot, i. 17–19.
33. The explanations were various. Cf. PP 1839, x.44, 351–2, 354.

outset a finger in the steamboats' pie. But public opinion was in general opposed to the railways' extending their business on to the water; and for the time being it stopped that activity. None the less, much could be got by simple collaboration. (London and Glasgow were brought within a 24-hours' journey for the first time in 1841, by a steamship service connecting with the railways at Fleetwood and Ardrossan.) Southampton now began to rouse itself from a long lethargy. It succeeded in attracting the new Peninsular & Oriental Steamship Company to make its headquarters there in 1840. Dover's business as a packet station grew mightily after the opening of the railway from London in 1843; Folkestone came into the business too, especially after 1848, when the branch down to the harbour was completed. The South Western and the South Eastern Railways gave the electrifying touch.

Yet the railway did not have this effect everywhere. In East Anglia there was a very different tale to tell. Economically, that part of the country was going through a difficult time. The worsted manufacture of Norwich was losing a long competition with that of Yorkshire. Harwich was in full decay; the Continental packets were withdrawn from it in 1834, in favour of London.[34] A railway prosecuted with the same vigour as the London & Birmingham or the Great Western might have transformed the economic life of the East Anglian towns at this critical time. As early as 1836 the Eastern Counties Company was incorporated to build a line from London to Yarmouth, through Colchester, Ipswich, and Norwich. But it took four years for the railway to reach Brentwood (18 miles from London). After another three it got as far as Colchester (51 miles), and there it came to an end. Sickened by its evident failure the people of Yarmouth and Norwich got up their own railway, to link those towns at least. That was achieved in 1844. Further to the west, another company, the Northern & Eastern, was feeling its way with equal sloth towards Cambridge. It extended only 30 miles to Bishop's Stortford.

The lines that have just been discussed almost all pivoted upon London. But already by 1844 other towns were important centres of railway communication, particularly Birmingham and Manchester; old towns, like Rugby and Preston, were becoming notable as railway junctions; the work of establishing wholly new towns, like Crewe, which owed their very existence to the railway, had already begun. Not all the chief railways of the country ran to London. A true diagram of the system at the time would be in the form of a St Andrew's cross, with the arms extending from Gateshead to Exeter and from Lancaster to Dover, intersecting at Birmingham. And in the north there were already two railways

34. VCH *Essex*, ii. 296, 440–1.

that linked 'the eastern and western seas'. The more northerly was the Newcastle & Carlisle Railway, which had been completed in 1839 and carried on by 1843 under another company to Maryport on the coast of Cumberland. At its eastern end it was connected to the railways of County Durham, which constituted the largest – but also the least coherent – of the early local systems.[35] Further south a chain of railways had stretched since 1841 from Liverpool to Hull. In the true British manner it involved six companies, and the journey was slow. But it must be recognised that it meant piercing the Pennines, by way of George Stephenson's Manchester & Leeds Railway. And in Manchester it was able to make use of a small but significant new sort of railway, opened in 1844 after a protracted argument: a junction line, built to link the Liverpool & Manchester and the Manchester & Leeds railways, with a common station at Hunt's Bank, later christened Victoria.

Yet this was not enough: for already another east-west line was under construction, to link Sheffield with Manchester. All that remained to be completed was a second tunnel through the Pennines, even longer and more formidably difficult than Stephenson's. The Sheffield & Manchester line was in some ways an unhappy enterprise. The pessimists shook their heads and condemned it as an unnecessary project. What need could there be, they said, for another railway through the hills? Could not Sheffield be served adequately by way of Normanton and Rotherham?

The answer from Sheffield to that last question was 'no', clear and loud. The town had already been forced to accept an unsatisfactory position on a branch out of the trunk line from Derby to Leeds. It would not allow its direct line to Manchester to be abandoned. For the Sheffield cutlers, the American market was important. If there were to be railways, they needed direct access to Liverpool just as much as the clothiers of Bradford and Leeds. A route of 110 miles over the rails of four companies was an unacceptable alternative to one of 75, involving two.[36]

Such were the forces making for competition. Whatever the prudent, or interested monopolists, might say against them, they were strong, and growing stronger: especially in Early Victorian England, with abundant capital, with rapidly growing industries (themselves highly competitive) and an overseas trade that was becoming more important as every year passed, with the growth and multiplication of towns, at relatively short distances from one another.

35. For a sketch map of the system see Lewin I, 10.
36. It is fair, however, to point out that this direct line involved transhipment across Manchester. The South Junction line, extending from London Road station to the Liverpool & Manchester Railway, was not built until 1849.

All this was true of England. Wales was touched by the railway as yet very lightly. The most important undertaking that had appeared there was the Taff Vale Railway, completed in 1841 from Merthyr Tydvil to Cardiff with a branch up the Rhondda valley. The whole concern was 26 miles long, no more; but they were 26 miles of high value. Though Cardiff was already growing as a coal port, with the aid of the Glamorganshire Canal, it was a small place as yet – smaller than Swansea, less than half the size of Merthyr, which was then easily the biggest town in Wales. The building of the railway was the great turning-point in Cardiff's modern history, enabling it to outdistance its immediate neighbour and rival Newport as well as Swansea, whose railway communications were less fortunate.

The only other railway of any consequence as yet in Wales was the Llanelly, further west in Carmarthenshire. Short lines were numerous and well established in the south-east; but only a few of them were mechanically operated.

Nevertheless, a great railway question that affected Wales had already been posed: that of communication with Ireland. Telford had immeasurably improved the Holyhead road, and his work had been crowned by the Menai and Conway bridges, only four years before the opening of the Liverpool & Manchester Railway. With the successful launching and development of the trunk railways out of London, the Irish interest in Parliament naturally clamoured for the benefit of the new communication. But which port should be used as the railway terminus in Wales? Must it be Holyhead, which was not altogether satisfactory? There were two rival claimants: St George's Bay (almost exactly the place we now know as Llandudno) and Porth Dynlleyn on the Nevin peninsula.

All three were examined, together with the possible routes for railways to them, by a Committee of two, Sir Frederic Smith, R.E., and Professor Peter Barlow, appointed by the Treasury in 1839–40. Their verdict favoured Holyhead, with a railway along the north coast of Wales to Crewe, where it would fall into the Grand Junction line for Birmingham and the south. It was going to be an expensive undertaking, and a difficult line to build. It did not secure its powers until 1844, and then it went ahead slowly.

Another similar question concerned the development of railways between England and Scotland; and it was considered by the same pair of investigators, who were confronted by rival routes, along the east and west sides of England, via Newcastle and via Carlisle. In both cases railways were already built or sanctioned for a large part of the way. North of Newcastle and Lancaster there were, again, alternative and rival routes. In the event, the Committee confined its attention to those that ran through north-western England, and came out in favour of one by the Lune valley and Penrith, as against another that hugged the coast.[37] Again, the task did not begin to be undertaken until 1844, when the Lancaster & Carlisle Railway was launched, to cross the Westmorland fells. By that time plans were being pressed forward energetically for lines along the east coast too, from Newcastle to Edinburgh. 'My countrymen are *daft*', Lockhart observed to his friend Croker that Easter Monday. 'I understand they insist on two lines at once from England – one by Carlisle, tother by Newcastle'.[38]

The Lancaster & Carlisle line, and its northward continuation the Caledonian, which was authorised in the following year, were laid out by Joseph Locke. They represented a notable rejection of orthodox thinking, with their long ascents over the hills to Shap and Beattock, at inclines as steep as 1 in 75. The Stephenson tradition had been to avoid such 'up and over' construction, even at the cost of circuitous routes. Locke put his faith robustly in the developing power of the locomotive. It is strange that George Stephenson, who had fought so tenaciously for it in the 1820s, seemed now to lack confidence in its potential, remaining convinced that Locke was wrong. It is even stranger that the same should have been true of his son Robert: for he was head of the most eminent firm of locomotive manufacturers in Britain, and on his own London & Birmingham line, in this very year 1844, it had been possible to discard cable haulage up the 1 in 70 gradient out of Euston, because locomotives were now powerful enough to manage the task on their own.

The inquiries into proposals for railways to Ireland and Scotland are only two of a substantial series undertaken in 1839–44. Though much is to be said in criticism of the activities – and non-activities – of Governments, Parliament, and the civil service, they were not without their defence. On the most immediately important count of all they may be held to have succeeded: for the railways were in fact built, and quickly. By 1836, 400 miles of line were open in the United Kingdom; by 1840, almost 1,500; by 1844, over 2,000. A French historian sums up the rough, untidy virtues of the British practice: 'Notwithstanding its many deficiencies . . . this system or rather want of system enabled Great Britain to out-

37. The reports on communication with Ireland and Scotland are in PP 1840, xiv, and 1841, xxv.
38. *Notes and Queries* 187 (1944) 210. It was taken for granted that there could be only one route, even by those most closely concerned with the promotion of railways. Cf. Gladstone's clear recollection in 1888: *Hansard* 3rd ser. 325 (1888) 1400–1.

strip in the development of her railways, if not the United States, at least all the Continental nations'.[39] Government and Parliament were confronted with a wholly new phenomenon, posing technical and economic questions that could not possibly be settled except by laborious inquiry and the slow accumulation of experience. Given time, some wise answers might be found. But time was just what they lacked. It has to be remembered that the Government first called on to deal with railways in a national sense was Melbourne's, which in 1839–41 was tottering to its fall; and though Peel's administration of 1841–6 was much stronger it had a crowd of other urgent matters to consider as well as a serious depression of trade in 1841–2. The railway system emerged at the same time as Parliamentary and municipal reform, as the New Poor Law, as the first effective legislation concerning employment in factories and mines began to be passed. Given the political system, one's surprise must be not that the British Government did so little to regulate the growth of railways as that it did so much. It blundered, and it often blew hot and cold. But it made some serious attempts to grapple with these new problems, in the midst of very many others that beset it.

An energetic Committee of the House of Commons issued five reports in 1839–40, which included a mass of oddly-assembled but useful statistics. A number of the witnesses who appeared before it advocated the establishment of a Royal Commission or of a board to supervise some aspects of railway development and operation. But which aspects? There was no agreed answer here. The Liverpool & Manchester representatives, for example, desired a Royal Commission 'to ascertain whether a line is wanted and whether it is the best' – in other words a body that should have a hand in planning the future development of the railway system. Leading engineers agreed. James Walker, President of the Institution of Civil Engineers, had pressed something similar upon a Parliamentary Committee three years earlier.[40] Robert Stephenson repeatedly urged the same course. The Chairman of the London & Croydon Railway thought some such Board was inevitable as a body of arbitrators. On the other hand Joseph Pease of the Stockton & Darlington rejected the idea altogether; and so did William Reed, Secretary of the London & Southampton Company.[41]

In the end the Committee recommended that the Board of Trade

39. E. Halévy, *History of the English People*, iii (1950 edn), 276.
40. PP 1836, xxi. 259–61. The Committee rejected Walker's advice (*ibid.*, 225).
41. PP 1839, x. 32, 68–9, 156, 337, 354–5. Reed subsequently changed his mind, however, in the light of experience in France: J. Morrison, *Influence of Railway Legislation* (1848), 181.

should be made responsible for the Government's dealings with railways. This proposal was adopted, and embodied in the measure known as 'Lord Seymour's Act', passed in 1840.[42] It empowered the Board to require each company to make returns, showing the amount of traffic carried and the charges levied for its conveyance, and the accidents that occurred in working the railway. The Board was authorised to appoint inspectors, though their functions were not defined. The companies were also obliged to submit their by-laws to the Board's scrutiny and given certain powers to secure the punishment of malpractice among their servants, as well as of obstruction and trespass.

Two years later, in 1842, the Board of Trade was considerably strengthened in dealing with railways by a second Regulation Act.[43] This required companies to give notice of the intended opening of all new lines on which passengers were to be conveyed, so that they could be visited by the Board's inspectors. If it appeared that they were imperfect or incomplete, the Board was given power to prevent the opening for a period as long as a month. A fresh inspection was then to take place. Should the line still be unsatisfactory, a further postponement of the opening could be ordered.[44] This was the foundation of the State's power to act in defence of the public safety. It was a real power, backed by penalties, and feared. Its exercise in 1848, for example, in respect of the London & South Western Company's extension to Waterloo station was serious, for it resulted in depriving the shareholders of a half-year's dividend. The Board stood its ground immovably, however. The shareholders had to go without.[45] Railway companies later developed many techniques for evading the Board's injunctions. But in respect to the opening of lines they rarely set it at defiance.

Such were the first hesitant efforts at general railway legislation. They were fortunate in that they came at a moment of calm: not indeed in politics but in railway promotion. Not a single new railway company was established in England and Wales in 1840 or 1841; five only in 1842–3. Looking back nearly half a century later, Acworth remarked that in 1843 the English railway system was 'in a condition more nearly approaching a stable equilibrium than it has ever attained either before or since'.[46]

Still, many new lines, authorised in earlier years, were being brought into use. Well over 900 miles were opened in England and Wales during the years 1840–3, which almost doubled the system By the end of that

42. 3 & 4 Vict., cap. 97.
43. 5 & 6 Vict., cap. 55.
44. Sect. 6.
45. Williams LSWR, i. 159–60.
46. Acworth RE, 2.

period about two-thirds of the larger towns were already served by a railway.[47] The pause in promoting new enterprise since 1837 is easily understandable. It was natural to watch the railways that had been set on foot, and especially the long trunk lines, to scrutinise their business and the profits they made, before embarking on further endeavours of the same sort. Those who wished to go further, to set new projects going, were deterred by the tightness of money during 1841–2.

But in the course of 1843 things began to look better. The economy was becoming stronger; there was spare capital seeking profitable investment, preferably inside Britain. Three-quarters of the railways authorised were now at work. In 1842 the Stockton & Darlington was paying 15 per cent, the London & Birmingham 10 per cent; the average dividend of 36 of the companies – including all those of any importance – was 5.75 per cent.[48]

By this time railways had become attractive not only to mercantile men. Their influence was beginning to be felt, and to be seen, everywhere. In the 1830s, when they were new, landowners had been as a class their enemies. Now they had come to realise the improvement in the value of landed property that railways would bring, their potential services to marketing, to stock-raising and every branch of agriculture.

Moreover by this time the railways had begun to demonstrate their value to the country at large. They had started carrying letters for the Post Office in 1830. That business had been regulated by statute in 1838,[49] so as to give the Post Office the guarantees of service that it required if its business was to be carried on with punctuality. The railways grumbled at the burdens that this Act obliged them to assume. But in the long run they did well out of postal business: not so much in financial terms as in the proof it afforded of the service they gave to the community. The penny postage introduced in 1840 would hardly have been practicable without them, and the effects of that momentous reform began to appear almost at once.

At the same time the Government was making public use of the railways in other kinds of business too. In 1842, a year of strikes and Chartist disturbance, they conveyed troops quickly and easily from London to the north. The service they rendered was acknowledged in handsome terms; provision for its continuance was included in the Regulation Act of the same year. Again an almost unlimited future development seemed to lie before them, as instruments of the State.

The weaknesses from which the early railways had suffered were being

47. Cf. Lewin I, 140.
48. PP 1844, xi. 610.
49. 1 & 2 Vict. cap. 98.

steadily reduced or removed. Technically, they were learning from their mistakes. The bitter squabbling between small companies that had exhausted their energies and eroded their revenues was being ended by agreements to amalgamate: so that Samuel Laing, Secretary to the Railway Department of the Board of Trade, could prophesy in January 1844 that 'the principal railway communications of the Kingdom will be parcelled out into six or eight great systems'.[50]

In the light of all these considerations, most people thought the system should now expand. Though the British Government played little part directly, by promoting or financing railways,[51] it lay within its power to give the process most material encouragement, and at the same time to extend the field of its indirect regulation. It did both these things in 1844, under the aegis of a junior Minister, President of the Board of Trade in Peel's administration: W. E. Gladstone.

Investment in railways was still sluggish in the early months of 1844. For that there appeared to be a remedy. As a check to speculation, the House of Commons had included in its Standing Orders a requirement that the promoters of a new railway must, when they brought their Bill forward, deposit 10 per cent of the capital involved in it. An increasing number of people thought that this rule, introduced in 1837, had proved seriously restrictive. They pointed out that since its adoption the number of new companies sanctioned by Parliament had been extremely small: no more than 13 for the whole kingdom in the six years 1838–43. Gladstone agreed; and in February 1844 he persuaded the Commons to appoint a Select Committee to reconsider the Standing Orders of the House relating to railways, and this one in particular. The Committee quickly came to the conclusion that it needed amendment; and before the end of May the 10 per cent deposit had been halved. Looking back, wise after the event, many people attributed to this decision a large share of the initial responsibility for the wild speculation that followed.

Here was the carrot that the Government held out to railway promoters. It had also a stick for them: the much closer regulation of their affairs that it proposed, in the light of the evidence given to the Select

50. PP 1844, xi. 617.
51. It is not quite true to say that the Government gave no financial assistance to railways in Britain at this time. The Public Works Loan Commissioners made a total of 19 loans to railway companies between 1817 and 1842, totalling £490,000. The largest of these were to the Liverpool & Manchester (£100,000, 1827), the Clarence (three loans, totalling £110,000, 1832–5), the Newcastle & Carlisle (five loans, £160,000, 1833–5), and the Sheffield Ashton & Manchester (£50,000, 1842). No more loans were made to railways in England and Wales after that to the Sheffield Company. Much larger sums were advanced to railway companies in Ireland. PP 1849, xxx. 369.

Committee. Gladstone was not alone in thinking that it might be desirable for the State to take the railways over, though like all practical men who agreed with him he recognised that step could not be taken at once. It was possible to provide for it as a distant eventuality, and at the same time to secure forthwith a better service than the railways were as yet affording. Gladstone and his Committee applied themselves to both tasks; and the result of their labours was the Regulation of Railways Act of 1844.[52]

That Act[53] did not go as far as Gladstone desired. It provided the State with an option to purchase any new railway, not yet sanctioned, or any new branch of an existing railway. But the option was not to become effective for 21 years; and it was never exercised. The measure is chiefly important for what it did to regulate the facilities for travel given to the poor. It provided that the railways should be obliged to run, at the least, one train every day[54] carrying passengers at a fare not exceeding a penny a mile, to stop at every station and to travel at not less than 12 m.p.h. – a speed greater than that of the fastest coach in normal service. The passengers were to be furnished with seats and protected from the weather. The fares they paid were exempted from the passenger tax of 5 per cent levied on all others.

These famous provisions have not always been understood rightly. A penny a mile sounds to us a cheap rate of travel; and so it was by comparison with coach fares and with the rates charged by the railways for first and second-class conveyance. In relation to wages, however, it looks a little different. A good many semi-skilled or unskilled men received 10*s.* a week or less – when they were in employment. If a man with those earnings chose to make the journey between Lancashire or Yorkshire and London, that journey would cost him ten days' wages. For people living in these conditions, the Act of 1844 certainly did not introduce 'cheap trains'.

Continental railways, under the aegis of the State, were being held up as examples to England in their treatment of the poor. In Belgium, for instance, passengers paying less than a penny a mile already comprised more than half the total number carried.[55] But when comparisons were

52. *Hansard* 3rd ser. 72 (1844) 232.
53. 7 & 8 Vict., cap. 85.
54. Including Sundays (sect. 10), on those railways – by no means all – that ran Sunday trains; but on that day it applied only to 'such train each way . . . as shall stop at the greatest number of stations'.
55. A succinct account of the Belgian system, including this information, had been laid before Parliament in Laing's report of the previous January: PP 1844, xi. 621–4. Cf. also *Journal of the Statistical Society* 1 (1839) 114–15; *ibid.* 2 (1840) 50; *ibid.* 7 (1844) 177–8.

made with the system set up under the Act of 1844, it was generally forgotten that that Act also entitled each passenger to take with him 56lb of luggage free of charge. The Belgian railways made no such allowance. This was an important concession in promoting mobility in Britain. Many a poor husband and wife owned no more than a hundredweight of goods between them. If they went off to get work in another town, it was much that the railway would take those goods free.

At the same time, in July 1844, the House of Commons adopted a resolution requiring all railway Bills in the future to be submitted to a new scrutinising body, a strengthened Railway Department of the Board of Trade, which comprised five members under the chairmanship of the Board's Vice-President, Lord Dalhousie. This decision, like Gladstone's Bill, was strenuously resisted by many of the railway directors in Parliament and their friends. Their opposition revealed, for the first time, a 'railway interest'. That interest weighed heavily with the Prime Minister, Peel; and in his attitude to Gladstone's measure he seemed to pay more attention to it than to his young colleague in the Cabinet. Nevertheless, in this summer of 1844 we can sense in Parliament a willingness to accept real, if indirect, responsibility for a tightened control of the growing railway system.

Gladstone's Act can be seen both as an epilogue and as a curtain-raiser. It carried further the principle, already established by the earlier Regulation Acts, that the State had a right, and a duty, to intervene directly in the companies' management, if a broad public interest seemed to require it; and the provisions concerning cheaper travel represented the most meticulously detailed application of this principle that had yet been seen in Britain. But the Act was not made to apply retrospectively, to the companies already at work – even though, in practice, nearly all of them came to be bound by it very soon after it was passed. Though Peel's Government was rapidly engaged in extending its supervision over the processes of economic life, there were still large areas of it – like retail trade – in which the State played no significant part at all. Gladstone's Act, as it was finally passed, exemplifies the balance that, in this matter, the State had then struck. The moment at which it came into force was itself a moment of balance, of pause. In the autumn the railway world came to be convulsed by a hurricane. When that had subsided, Gladstone's Act still stood, unchanged in any important particular: effective and enforced as a regulator of practice; a mere paper programme as far as it concerned the State control of railways in Britain.

2 The Mania and its Consequences 1844-1854

The great Railway Mania did not burst on the country without warning. Shrewd observers forecast quite accurately at an early stage what was to come. In July 1844 the Deputy-Superintendent of the Bridgewater Trust stated his belief that 'from the turn events are taking, money may be raised during the next two or three years very readily, and parties may be found to undertake almost any new project, however absurd'.[1] Two months later Brunel was writing to Charles Babbage: 'There are railway projects fully equal to £100 million of capital for next year, and all the world is mad. Some will no doubt have cause to be so before the winter is over'.[2] In the spring of 1845 Francis Mewburn, the long-experienced solicitor of the Stockton & Darlington Company, prophesied how it would all end: 'I am alarmed at the number of new lines before Parliament and continuing to be brought forward. *A panic will come.* That is unquestionable; but I think it will be staved off so long as we have 15 millions of gold in the Bank of England, but so soon as a bad harvest comes then the gold will be withdrawn – accommodation of bankers decreases, instalments continue to be called for, shareholders cannot sell, there are no buyers, money is not in abundance. Hence a panic arises. *Nous verrons!'*[3] Those three observations, made by men living close to the railway world, introduce what followed.

There had been two frenzies of railway promotion in the past, in 1825 and 1836. What happened now was something much bigger in scale – though not necessarily more unhealthy than they had been for the

1. Fereday Smith to James Loch, 16 July 1844: q. F. C. Mather, *After the Canal Duke* (1970), 176.
2. L. T. C. Rolt, *Isambard Kingdom Brunel* (1957), 234.
3. Diary, Apr. 1845. Printed inaccurately in *The Larchfield Diary* (1876), 70. The text given here is taken from Mewburn's MS. in Darlington Public Library (ii. 250).

economy of the country at large.[4] We need to get an idea of the magnitude of the business, and that is not a simple matter, for no two contemporary observers, no two historians since, agree on some of the chief statistics. As the Bills flooded into Parliament from the autumn of 1844, surrounded by the illimitable penumbra of proposals that never reached Parliament at all, frantic attempts were made to analyse what the whole speculation involved.

Almost all the figures that we have for this business contain a large element of guesswork, and no research, however laborious, can now much improve them. The data remain dispersed, scattered through tens of thousands of columns of newspaper advertisements, with hundreds of prospectuses that have survived haphazardly; and even if all this evidence were assembled it would remain incomplete. The information these sources afford is full of error: necessarily so considering the desperate haste with which it had to be assembled and printed, no less than the obvious desire to mislead, to exaggerate, in order to attract the attention of prospective investors.

Certain facts do, however, confront us. In 1845 the House of Commons set up a special Committee on the Classification of Railway Bills. In the course of that session and the two following, 909 Bills relating to railways in England and Wales were examined by it. Of these, 217 came before it in 1845, 435 in 1846, and 257 in 1847.[5] Wild though some of these projects were, they were nevertheless among the stronger of those brought forward: for, in order to reach the Committee at all, it was necessary for them to have deposited plans in the Private Bill Office.

When the second wave of proposals was building up, *The Times*, which had been critical of all recent railway promotion, denounced it in a dramatic form. On 17 November 1845 it issued a supplement, listing all the railways of the United Kingdom – whether already built, under construction, or projected – and designed as a comprehensive warning of the dangers that lay ahead. It had been compiled by W. F. Spackman. He had an axe of his own to grind. He wished to see the law concerning the registration of companies made stricter and more effective, and this publication was part of his campaign to that end. But his special concern does not distort the work, and with all the qualifications just given it may be taken as the fullest compendium of the railway promotion at its height.[6]

4. For contemporary debate on this point see D. M. Evans, *The Commercial Crisis, 1847–8* (1848), 84.
5. PP 1845, x. 37–85; 1846, xiii. 17–81; 1847, xii. 9–39. It must be remembered that some of these schemes were alternatives, or dependent on others and really an integral part of them; also that some of the schemes examined in the later sessions were earlier ones re-submitted.
6. He republished it as a separate volume very soon afterwards, revised very

Spackman's analysis shows that the total capital involved in all these railways, realised and projected, for the United Kingdom as a whole was £701 million, and of this £621 million, or 88.5 per cent, was in respect of England and Wales. The total capital actually raised to this date, in shares and loans, he puts at £71 million, £65 million of it for England and Wales, or 92.5 per cent of the whole.[7]

This *exposé* was of course angrily challenged. The *Railway Times* was particularly incensed, and attacked *The Times* for manufacturing a panic. Henry Tuck, who had aided investors by producing a *Railway Shareholder's Manual*, which went through nine successive editions between 1845 and 1848, joined in assailing *The Times* in the preface to his seventh edition. 'By repeated efforts and the assistance of a few country journals', he wrote, 'it at length succeeded in creating a panic, and, within the space of a month, property worth millions became so depreciated as to be scarcely saleable at any price whatever. For this wanton destruction of property there was not the slightest pretext or excuse.' Tuck contended that the publication was vicious because it tried to include all schemes, many of them '*crude, abortive, ephemeral, and visionary*', and that such frivolous absurdities discredited those that were sound.

There of course he was right. He started out from the responsible point of view that a rapid extension of the railway system was in the national interest, and that financially the nation could encompass it. The alarm of the autumn of 1845 seriously impeded that development. But then *The Times* had been right too, for thousands of gullible investors were swarming forward, to put money into unsound, even grotesque schemes, and the whole great bubble was growing bigger daily, beyond anybody's power to control. Who was Tuck, or who were the *Railway Times* or any of the other defenders of uncurbed promotion, to draw the line between the sound and the unsound proposals? Only by looking at the frenzy as a whole could its dangerous implications be understood. The warning the newspaper uttered was well-timed and salutary. In this matter it rendered the country good service.

---

slightly, as *An Analysis of the Railway Interest of the United Kingdom*. This version is the one referred to here. It is to be noted that his analysis was taken down to 31 October. There was a further flood until 30 November, the last date for depositing plans with the Board of Trade. On that very last day alone 412 additional plans came in for railways in England and Wales: *The Times*, 3 Dec. 1845.

7. It is worth noting that Scotland was affected very much more lightly by the Railway Mania than any other part of the United Kingdom. Its share in the £701 million is no more than 3.2 per cent; in the capital raised for railways constructed, 6.2 per cent.

Nobody prepared another account of the business as detailed as Spackman's, which could claim to be more accurate. The Board of Trade produced no analysis of the projects of 1845–6 comparable with that for 1844–5. The Parliamentary Committees battled on with the task of examining them. The whole 'railway interest' – directors, managers, engineers, contractors, lawyers – laboured, some of them up to and beyond the limits of endurance. A few made great fortunes and then prudently retired to enjoy them.[8] The remainder held on, if they were determined and lucky, to achieve an assured prosperity later, or if they were unfortunate or foolish to go under.

Of the thousands of schemes put forward in 1844–7, how many were realised? Again, the question cannot be answered simply. During the three Parliamentary sessions of 1844–7, 330 railway Acts were passed, establishing new companies in England and Wales or authorising extensions and deviations of existing lines. The mileage of railway sanctioned was about 5,700.[9] The capital permitted to be raised was as follows:

TABLE 1. ACTS PASSED IN 1845–7: ENGLAND AND WALES[10]

Year	Number of Acts passed	Capital authorised		
		Shares £	Loans £	Total £
1845	79	33,572,862	11,147,947	44,720,809
1846	154	69,775,990	25,705,131	95,481,121
1847	97	15,969,539	11,451,980	27,421,519
	330	119,318,391	48,305,058	167,623,449

When the Mania was over and the country was attempting to take stock of where it stood, some laborious efforts were made to analyse what had happened. A return was laid before the House of Commons in 1851, endeavouring to show the amount of money invested in railway building down to August 1849, the paid-up capital and the loans actually raised, as distinct from the maximum capital and loans authorised in the

8. For example, the contractor Thomas Grissell, partner of Samuel Morton Peto, who retired to devote himself to Norbury Park in Surrey in 1850; or Charles Austin the lawyer, who made at the lowest estimate £40,000 by his railway work alone in 1847, broke down in health in the following year and then similarly retired to a country estate in Suffolk. Austin's fee books, in the Suffolk Record Office (50/18/3.1), would repay study from this point of view.

9. Calculation from Lewin II, chaps, iii, viii, xiii.

10. The sums are taken from the Local and Personal Acts themselves. Two reductions of capital were prescribed in 1847, amounting to £908,333 in shares and £302,200 in loans. The totals given here have been lowered by these amounts.

companies' Acts. This showed a total for the United Kingdom of £230 million, of which England and Wales contributed £187 million, £144 million in capital, £43 million in loans.[11]

Meanwhile, a more elaborate inquisition was proceeding, set on foot by the House of Lords at the instigation of Lord Brougham in May 1849. Through the Board of Trade the House asked every existing railway company in the country to supply information, to a standard pattern, concerning its capital and expenditure. Unfortunately, the companies were not told to make their returns in respect of a single uniform date. Each must therefore be taken to represent the company's current position at the moment when its return was made. The process was spread over a whole year, from 9 May 1849, when the first was completed, down to 4 May 1850, the date of the last. In the end, 120 English and Welsh companies responded. Five more disregarded the demand.[12] The credibility of the answers varies greatly. Some of the figures supplied are manifestly incomplete, or open to particular suspicion; others, like those of the London & North Western, are well ordered and extremely copious.[13] Those for the Leeds & Thirsk form a model document, a reflection of the administrative capacity of its Secretary, Samuel Smiles. The replies in the aggregate are voluminous, filling over 850 folio pages. From them, though with all the reserves that have been mentioned, some general information can be extracted.

The value of this inquiry is that it attempts to break down the companies' expenditure into costs of construction, of the purchase of land, and of plant, together with Parliamentary, legal, and engineers' charges. A broad view of the results of the inquiry emerges in this shape:

TABLE 2. FINANCIAL RETURNS FROM 93 RAILWAY COMPANIES IN ENGLAND AND WALES, 1849–50

Paid-up capital			Cost of construction	Cost of land	Parliamentary expenses and legal charges	Engineers' charges	Plant
Shares	*Loans*	*Total*	*tion*	*land*	*charges*	*charges*	*Plant*
£000	£000	£000	£000	£000	£000	£000	£000
155,841	50,138	205,979	89,173	23,254	7,565	2,908	12,315

11. PP 1851, li. 179–95.

12. The returns are in PP (HL) 1849, xvi and 1850, xv.

13. Saunders, of the Great Western, played a naughty trick. Asked to enumerate the debentures issued by his company, he did so, one by one, for 60 pages, but without adding them up: so the most important conclusion has to be worked out with tedious labour.

TABLE 3. FINANCIAL RETURNS FROM THE
LARGER RAILWAY COMPANIES, 1849–50

		Capital		
Company	*Mileage*	*Shares* £	*Loans* £	*Total* £
Eastern Counties	247	10,595,069	1,026,229	11,621,298
Great Northern	144	6,483,000	45,170	6,528,170
Great Western	231	8,611,100	5,259,018	13,970,118
Lancashire & Yorkshire	167	11,598,913	2,523,417	14,122,330
London & North Western	385	15,974,478	9,186,672	25,161,150
London & South Western	206	8,612,393	1,873,526	10,485,919
London Brighton & South Coast	158	5,974,395	1,392,938	7,367,333
Manchester Sheffield & Lincolnshire	154	4,440,420	1,100,398	5,540,818
Midland	434	13,656,473	3,137,893	16,794,366
South Eastern	146	7,111,469	1,201,227	8,312,696
York Newcastle & Berwick	191	5,687,327	833,078	6,520,400
York & North Midland	209	4,721,250	1,294,554	6,015,804

Twelve companies stand out clearly as the biggest in terms of their realised capital, standing in a group on their own; and since their returns are usually more complete and in some ways more convincing than those of many of the smaller companies (some of which had scarcely begun construction), the aggregate figures of this group are given separately. On the other hand, 27 of the companies sent in such incomplete or confused answers that they have been left out of the calculation altogether.

It would be wrong to take these figures literally. No doubt every one contained inaccuracies; some must have been guesswork, or perverted by deliberate distortion. Yet they are the best we have. We can only take them for what they are worth: as an indication of orders of magnitude, no more.

Looked at as a means of forming a railway system, the procedure adopted by the British Government and legislature in 1844–8 must seem to us now grotesque. They seldom attempted to determine a policy in relation to any part of it. They had done so, as we have seen, in 1839–40, when the trunk routes to Ireland and Scotland were examined by an expert committee. But then, with what result? The committee having reported in favour of a railway along the coast of North Wales and an improved

Cost of construction £	Cost of land £	Parliamentary expenses and legal charges £	Engineers' charges £	Plant £
4,952,299	1,275,680	413,779	214,352	822,927
2,292,627	937,273	121,508	84,755	221,875
6,960,911	1,132,964	350,408	201,909	926,929
644,504	1,287,026*	64,046*	136,220	683,101
13,202,313	3,153,225	857,528	289,698	2,075,215
2,883,091	1,002,647	166,626	63,674	528,924
4,001,837	1,097,116*	296,695*	117,857	551,789
3,333,715	556,812	367,567	110,446	351,871
9,397,344	176,458	679,393	288,282	1,714,369
5,375,366	1,458,628	558,499	116,040	524,979
2,474,526	400,029	99,072	39,118	667,152
1,998,902	547,435	92,902	92,521	399,933

* Some figures for Parliamentary and legal charges are included in those for the cost of land.

packet station at Holyhead, and this plan being embodied in the Chester & Holyhead Railway Company's Act of 1844, the rival plan for a line to Porth Dynlleyn popped up all over again that autumn. It would be hard to imagine a greater absurdity than the establishment of both these lines, side by side. Sparse as the local traffic was seen to be along the coast line of the Chester & Holyhead Railway, between Worcester and Porth Dynlleyn there would be no local traffic whatever, since that district was almost unpopulated. Yet public time and attention, and foolish investors' money, could all be wasted on reopening a question that ought surely to have been declared settled once and for all.

Again where the route to Scotland was concerned, the Commissioners reported, and the Government accepted their advice, that the West Coast line was to be preferred: yet in 1845 Parliament passed two Acts, one for the Caledonian line, the Scottish link in this chain, the other for the Newcastle & Berwick, filling the gap between the Tyne and the already-authorised North British line from Berwick to Edinburgh and so creating the second, East Coast, route that had been regarded as a superfluous extravagance shortly before.

Parliament attempted to regulate another railway matter at the same time, with very incomplete success. Among the schemes that proliferated in 1844–5 were a number for railways to be built on Brunel's broad gauge.

That gauge was well established in the south of England, where it was laid for about 300 miles. Now proposals came forward for lines that were intended, either expressly or by implication, to adopt the broad gauge, reaching northwards to Rugby and Wolverhampton, and along the coast of South Wales to Fishguard. Confronted with the first of these two plans, the Board of Trade issued a highly unfavourable report, designed one may feel to stop the nuisance at the outset. In the light of what was happening where the gauges met at Gloucester, it stated the case cogently, not only against allowing such points to multiply but even against the broad gauge itself. It pointed out, for example, that although the broad gauge was intended to facilitate high speed, the best trains on the Great Western Railway were slower than some of those on the narrow-gauge lines. The report rejected the expedient of a mixed gauge, produced by the laying of a third rail. If that showed some misapprehension,[14] the Board's general line of reasoning, applied to the situation actually in front of it, commands respect. In its view the time had come to contain the broad gauge definitively south of the Thames and Severn.

But Parliament disregarded this advice and sanctioned all the trunk lines under examination. Together with others already in progress, the prospective broad-gauge system was consequently increased to a total not far short of 700 miles, with new break-of-gauge points at Rugby, Worcester, and Wolverhampton. Among the opponents of this decision was Richard Cobden. He went on to move that a Royal Commission should be set up to consider whether a uniform gauge should be adopted for the whole country in the future and, if so, how this could be achieved. The House of Commons promptly accepted this proposal, and within a month three able Commissioners had been appointed.

They worked hard, took a great deal of evidence, and were persuaded by Brunel to conduct comparative tests of the locomotives employed on the two systems.[15] These were held between Darlington and York on the narrow gauge and between Paddington and Didcot on the broad. Since the original Board of Trade report on the matter, the Great Western had removed the ground for its remark about the slow speed of the broad gauge, by introducing and maintaining a pair of express trains between London and Exeter, covering the 194 miles, first in five and then, from May 1845, in $4\frac{1}{2}$ hours. These were the first of all long-distance express trains. The tests amply confirmed the superiority of the broad-gauge locomotives in the matter of speed, and also showed that when running fast they were economical. The Commission stated this unequivocally, adding that 'the public are mainly indebted for the present rate of speed,

14. MacDermot, i. 113.
15. Their report, and the evidence taken before them, are in PP 1846, xvi.

and the increased accommodation of the railway carriages, to the genius of Mr Brunel, and the liberality of the Great Western Railway Company'.[16] But, having paid that well-deserved tribute, their report was firmly adverse to the broad gauge. They considered the narrow gauge better adapted to goods traffic; it was cheaper in first cost; above all, for good or ill, the narrow gauge was the standard for most of the country, used on 87 per cent of the system actually opened, and where the two gauges met the nuisance experienced was intolerable. Hence the Commissioners recommended that all further railways should be built to the narrow gauge and that some 'equitable means' should be searched for, either to convert the broad gauge to the narrow or to allow narrow-gauge trains to work over broad-gauge lines.

The Board of Trade expressed itself alarmed at the suggestion of a compulsory conversion of gauge, on grounds of 'the vast expense', which it surely would be wrong either to impose upon the companies concerned or to meet out of the Exchequer. It therefore felt that the lines already being built to the broad gauge should go ahead unchanged, and hoped that a workable mixture of the gauges could be achieved on the two lines running northward into the Midlands.[17] When Parliament considered the matter, it receded even further from the strong ground the Commissioners had taken up. It rushed through a Gauge Act that summer,[18] which began by declaring that the narrow gauge should be standard for the future, but then drove a coach and six through this provision by excepting from it all railways south of the Great Western line and that of the companies that were continuing it westwards to Cornwall, as well as the South Wales Railway and its associates. Still more weakly, it provided that the standard gauge might be departed from anywhere in the country if a 'special enactment' was adopted for the purpose. That really left the whole question open, to be argued out in any case where a gauge other than 4ft 8½ins was proposed.

Very little therefore can be said to have been achieved through all this controversy and toil. The broad gauge went on extending, to reach its maximum development 20 years later, when there were some 1,040 miles of broad gauge and 887 of mixed – representing altogether about 19 per cent of the total mileage in England and Wales. The number of points at which break of gauge occurred was by then more than 30.[19]

The 20 years that followed the opening of the Liverpool & Manchester Railway were critically important in the growth of the English railway

16. PP 1846, xvi. 14–15.
17. PP 1846, xxxviii. 372–4.
18. 9 & 10 Vict., cap. 57.
19. MacDermot, i. 104.

system. Surveying them now, we are perhaps struck most of all by the lack of planning they reveal. We may well put too much naïve faith in the concept of 'planning' – our notions will doubtless seem as quaint to our successors as the Early Victorians' do to us. Still, many people thought much the same thing at the time: old-fashioned persons like the Duke of Wellington, sensibly insistent that the State should supervise and regulate the railways firmly;[20] modern men, like their own great engineer Robert Stephenson.[21] In spite of them, however, with the very few exceptions that have just been examined, the abounding develop-ment of the system in these years can hardly be said to show anything more than the pressure of competing claims, politically and economically expressed. By contrast, the steady, deliberate evolution of railway policy in Belgium or Prussia, even the wearisome debates that hampered development in France, appear commendably prudent. But then the political and economic life of Britain was different from that of all those other countries, and the railway system sprang from it. This was a world in which *laissez faire* was still a dominant principle, in which the power of the State was much less, and deliberately kept less by the jealous attention of the governing classes, in which the free forces of industrial capitalism were at this moment successful beyond all their rivals, and soaring in ambition to go further. The railway was an instrument they, ahead of all others, had created. Here was the time to reap the harvest of all that work. The spirit was competitive through and through: it was commerce against agriculture, North against South, London against the provinces, the middle classes against the aristocracy – and behind it all, Britain in competition with the rest of the world. It would have been un-thinkable to pause, consider, and calculate. Immediate action was called for, without any nice scruples or refinements of thought. Very much indeed was at stake, to be settled in the shortest possible time, against the clock. If the whole process was lamentably haphazard, there is an excitement about it, an electric energy; in the light of what was being contended for, even a certain grandeur. Only a few observers perceived that, or had the justice of mind to state it. The truth is, as two modern economic historians have remarked, that 'the struggles for power that now went on in board rooms and in Parliamentary committees were not parish squabbles but epic contests for control of the great trunk routes – a species of imperialism, no less'.[22]

20. Earl Stanhope, *Notes of Conversations with the Duke of Wellington* (World's Classics edn), 124.
21. PP 1846, xiv. 230–1; J. C. Jeaffreson, *Life of Robert Stephenson* (1864), i. 280–1, 284.
22. H. J. Dyos and D. H. Aldcroft, *British Transport* (Penguin edn, 1974), 135.

As a result of all this frenzied work, the trunk routes were finally established. By 1854 the country had what could in some respects, if not in all, be described as a railway system. Though there were still some great gaps in it, not served by any railway, most of the main lines were open, needing only to be improved later, here and there. That improvement had already begun. The main line from Euston to the North had been made up, as we have seen, by two separate railways joining (rather imperfectly) at Birmingham. For through trains to Lancashire and Scotland that involved not merely a detour but a passage through the traffic of Birmingham and the Black Country, which was rapidly growing denser. A natural improvement suggested itself, by a line running direct from Rugby to Stafford, which would also serve the sizeable towns of Nuneaton, Tamworth, and Lichfield. This Trent Valley Railway was completed in 1847 and at once became the main line. Birmingham was, in effect, relegated to a branch. But its loss was others' gain. The Trent Valley line – level, easy, and interrupted by no heavy cross-traffic – proved itself an ideally convenient by-pass. The map depicts the achievement down to 1854, and indicates what still remained to be accomplished. The total system was stated to comprise 6,114 miles, with 3,213 more authorised.[23] A railway served every town in the country larger than Weymouth. Those that had obtained a good place on the railway system were beginning to build great hopes on that for the future. Shrewsbury, having lost much of its flannel manufacture to Welshpool and Newtown, saw recovery coming through its activity as a railway centre.[24] As for Liverpool – 'there is now no town of any consequence in Great Britain', Thomas Baines observed in 1852, 'with which the port of Liverpool has not constant communication by means of railway, and scarcely one which does not add something to the commercial prosperity of the port'.[25] Table 10 (p. 271) shows something of what all this meant to the traveller, in terms of speed, the extent of the improvement on the services provided by the horse-drawn coach. For goods that had to be moved fast the trader and manufacturer now had a splendid new instrument in their hands, whether they were fish merchants in Birmingham or Manchester[26] or the ironmasters of Merthyr Tydvil.[27]

On the other hand, certain districts were as yet scantily served. Wales

23. PP 1854–5, xlviii. 11.
24. H. Pidgeon, *Memorials of Shrewsbury* (2nd edn, 1851), 259.
25. T. Baines, *History of the Commerce and Town of Liverpool* (1852), 828.
26. On Birmingham see S. Salt, *Facts and Figures* (1848), 3, and S. Smiles, *Railway Property: its Condition and Prospects* (1849), 22; on Manchester, *Journal of the Statistical Society* 9 (1846), 132.
27. W. T. Jackman, *Transportation in Modern England* (1915), 492.

provides much the largest tract of this kind. The country is framed in the trunk lines to Holyhead and Carmarthen and the line from north to south along the border, just completed in 1853–4 with the long stretch from Ludlow to Pontypool; and for the rest provided only with the small lines for mineral and slate traffic leading up into the valleys from the coast. The main line to the south-west of England stops at Plymouth; Devon contains scarcely any railway but that line, Dorset none but the one from Poole to Dorchester. There is nothing in the Isle of Wight, almost nothing in Sussex but the main line to Brighton and its offshoots running parallel with the coast; only one line along the Thames Estuary, leaving north Kent barely supplied and south Essex not at all. North Norfolk is almost a blank, and the system in Lincolnshire is sparse. In all the Pennine country north of Skipton, there is scarcely any railway; and the Newcastle & Carlisle line presents a railway frontier so absolute that it makes one think of the Roman Wall, which it paralleled and twice intersected.

Those districts were all agricultural; but there was an equally striking urban deficiency, in and around London. In 1854 the London system comprised a dozen railways, and no more. Some, like the lines to Blackwall and Greenwich, already provided a frequent service; the London & Croydon had given careful thought to the siting of its six suburban stations.[28] But the trunk lines out of King's Cross, Euston, and Paddington hardly noticed the suburban traveller at all. Each passenger arriving at Euston in 1846 had made an average journey of 64 miles.[29] The railways had in truth hardly begun to find their feet in suburban traffic anywhere in the country. There was nothing worthy of the name as yet in Birmingham, Liverpool, or Manchester. A sensibly-conceived service started at Hull in 1853 had to be withdrawn for lack of patronage.[30] On the other hand, a rare exception, the Newcastle & North Shields Company offered its passengers a half-hourly service.

There, then, are the chief gaps in the system as it was in 1854. But it is the achievement that stands out most, not its deficiencies. Of the 'Inter-City' network we use today, just over two-thirds were complete by 1854. If that does not justify the Mania in retrospect – nothing can – it gave the country, ahead of all its European neighbours, a system of railways that contributed vitally to its full industrial development.

By this time the railways of England and Wales, actually open for traffic, were in the hands of rather more than 60 independent companies,

28. PP 1839, x. 159.
29. PP 1846, xvii. 7.
30. *Regional History of the Railways of Great Britain*, ed. D. St J. Thomas *et al.* (1960–   ), iv. 45–6.

ranging from the London & North Western, with a capital of £26 million, to tiny units operating lines only a few miles long, like the Cockermouth & Workington. They varied in wealth, in efficiency, in the quality of the service they afforded, as widely as in size. In financial terms none of them had passed unscathed through the fire of the Mania; but it had been, in some ways, a refining fire, destroying the feeble and providing salutary warnings to those that went through it and survived.

The chief companies had reached their pre-eminence in two ways. Each of them comprised a great trunk line – from London to Birmingham or Bristol or Dover, from Manchester to Sheffield or from Rugby to Leeds. Then, on to the trunk lines, branches had been grafted. In some cases this had been achieved by the process of amalgamation, represented most impressively in the early 1850s by the London & North Western. That company was beyond argument the strongest of them all. For a moment, in 1852, there was talk of a much bigger combine still, bringing the North Western, the Midland, and the North Staffordshire together into one corporation. Had that been realised, the country would indeed have passed into the hands of a mammoth monopolist: a sixth of the whole of its railway system would have been in one ownership. The idea set up a general alarm that led to the appointment of a Committee of the House of Commons to consider railway amalgamation as such. It sat from December 1852 to July 1853, for most of the time under the chairman-ship of a very able young politician, Edward Cardwell; and, driven on by him, it worked hard.[31] Its fifth and final report recommended that no further amalgamations, 'except in minor or special cases', should be sanctioned.[32] The biggest of all these plans thus foundered, together with a number of smaller ones. It looked as if Parliament had decided to reverse its previous policy of complaisance towards amalgamation, to put a stop to the process for good. And yet in the very next year, 1854, it authorised a major amalgamation, creating the North Eastern Com-pany by the fusion of the York Newcastle & Berwick with the York & North Midland – two of the 12 chief companies of 1850. Though the Stockton & Darlington and several other neighbouring companies re-mained outside, and often antagonistic to the new combine, it could clearly dominate north-eastern England. At the same time something similar happened further south. The Eastern Counties had made working agreements with the East Anglian and the Norfolk companies, and in 1854 it extended them to include the Eastern Union. These were not made statutory; but Parliament took no steps to question them, or to prevent their being formed. The Eastern Counties Company thus

31. Its reports are in PP 1852–3, xxxviii. Cf. Cleveland-Stevens, 182n.
32. PP 1852–3, xxxviii. 467.

acquired what promised to become a railway monopoly in Norfolk, Suffolk, and Essex.

Again we see the confusion of railway policy in Britain – or rather the absence of any fixed policy at all. Amalgamation is condemned by a well-manned Parliamentary Committee, and in the very next year amalgamations are accepted, leading to what became the two chief railway monopolies of England, in Northumberland and Durham and in East Anglia. How can this be explained?

Chiefly as a demonstration of the political power of the railway companies. The Committee of 1852–3 wished to put a stop to amalgamation but to assist companies to enter into working arrangements with one another instead. In April 1854 Cardwell himself expounded the view he had come to take of the railway system:

If you look at the map of this country, you see it covered with railways, and your first impression is that there is a most easy and most uninterrupted transit from one extremity to the other. Examine more closely, and you will find that this is not a uniform system of railways, all under one management, and that in consequence it is divided into kingdoms, has its diplomacies and its alliances offensive and defensive, and is altogether a far more complicated affair than at first sight it appears.[33]

He thought the time had come to curb the growth of monopoly and to force the companies to collaborate more effectively, in the interests of producing a true national railway system. But the Bill he went on to introduce was opposed by the big companies fiercely, and he felt obliged to give way. The Railway and Canal Traffic Act of 1854 that emerged[34] was a severely-restricted measure, confined to requiring the companies to forward traffic from one to another without partiality or unreasonable delay and making them liable for neglect or default in the carriage of goods. Of amalgamation and working arrangements it said not a word. Cardwell made some errors of tactics in handling the Bill in the Commons; but his defeat was due mainly to the embattled railway interest, opposed in principle to any substantial restriction on the companies' freedom.[35]

If Cardwell missed his prime objective, of stopping amalgamation, the Act he did carry was not insignificant. It was indeed a limited measure. No doubt the railway politicians congratulated themselves on having checkmated a bumptious legislator. The positive principles written into

33. *Hansard* 132 (1854) 590.
34. 17 & 18 Vict., cap. 31.
35. The story is clearly told in Cleveland-Stevens, 181–204.

the Act were not spelt out clearly enough; nor did Cardwell create the machinery for ensuring their observance. That had to wait until the establishment of the Railway Commission in 1871. But its activities, and much of the laborious work of politicians and civil servants later in the century, designed to ensure that the railways provided, under private ownership, a national service, were founded in large measure upon the second and third sections of Cardwell's Act.

Only three Ministers of the Crown made any determined effort in these years to frame a railway policy: Gladstone, Dalhousie, and Cardwell. All were young at the time, Gladstone and Dalhousie in their 30s, Cardwell just turned 40. They were all Peelite Conservatives – no Whig or Liberal or High Tory made any mark in this field whatever. All three were men of consummate capacity, who afterwards left a conspicuous mark on the kingdom and the Empire. But in railway matters they were all defeated.

Gladstone and Dalhousie may well have thought that they had been sacrificed by their leader Peel, who failed to give their policies his full support. But it is characteristic both of them and of Peel that they accepted this disappointment and continued to serve him loyally, recognising that he was the umpire, who alone could assess the balance of conflicting interests, at a time of general crisis, within Parliament and in the nation at large.

In terms strictly of railways, Dalhousie may well be reckoned the most important of the three. Railways placed a greater burden on him perhaps than on any other single man during the Mania. The work that he and his few colleagues at the Board of Trade got through seems superhuman – performed too, as it was, against a barrage of public criticism and misrepresentation. It almost certainly shortened his life. Hardly was he out of office than he was sent as Governor-General to India, where he served nine gruelling years. One of the chief elements in his policy there was the establishment of a railway system, to a pattern that showed just how much he had learnt from his experience in Britain. It was a system that combined private enterprise with state control; and it began by setting a standard gauge of 5ft 6ins, faithfully applied to most main lines in the country, to its benefit ever since. As he formulated the plan and watched it move slowly into action, he must surely have felt that India was to enjoy the advantage of a railway system purged of Britain's mistakes. But he saw very little of it realised. He left India in 1856. In the next year came the Mutiny, and in 1860 he died, at the age of 48.

If all these politicians must be held, where railways were concerned, to have failed, wholly or in part, who were their triumphant adversaries? At their head stands George Hudson, whose personal triumph was short but who left behind him work that lasted.

It is not easy for us to judge him now, to appreciate him fully and fairly. Stout, forceful, perennially energetic, vulgar, and without the smallest scruple – all those epithets have been applied to him many times, and all with entire justification. As everyone could see, he built up a great empire, over which he reigned as 'the Railway King' and then crashed to ruin in 1849 when his fraudulence and mismanagement failed to sustain him. There is nothing mysterious about his personality, or about his public career at the height of his power: his occupation of the big house in Albert Gate,[36] his immense parties there, the *gaffes* of his wife, long remembered in London society as a glorious Mrs Malaprop.[37] He too was remembered, often with execration. He enters into the composition of Mr Merdle in *Little Dorrit* in 1855,[38] and his spirit still hovers above the Veneerings and their world in *Our Mutual Friend* ten years later.

Those portraits are not false. A certain tendency to whitewash and romanticise him in recent years is misplaced. He was brought down by sharp practice, much of it worthy of a small-town attorney. At the same time, moral obliquity was joined in him to great constructive power, and it is fair to say that he had a clear vision of a railway system – clearer perhaps than anybody else's in his time.[39] It was, of course, to be a system presided over by him; but since he had the drive, and in a rough and ready way the intellectual grasp that were needed, as well as a talent for spotting able young assistants and advancing them,[40] his 'reign' was in some respects beneficent.[41] If the State was prepared to take only a narrowly-restricted part in moulding the railways into a system, Hudson helped to supply its deficiencies.

He had some of the qualities most exactly required. His furious energy serviced his ambition, but both were, in part at least, controlled by an imaginative faculty, almost as quick to seize sudden opportunities as a good general's on the battlefield. Hudson was not unique in the capacity

36. Now the French Embassy.
37. *Leaves from the Note-books of Lady Dorothy Nevill* (1907), 37.
38. Cf. E. Johnson, *Charles Dickens* (1953), 888–9.
39. Spackman – certainly not, in principle, an indulgent judge – perceived this in 1845 and included it in his very fair appraisal of Hudson: *Analysis of the Railway Interest*, 8.
40. For example J. J. Allport and Matthew Kirtley.
41. But it must be recognised that his railways were run on the cheap, at the expense of every interest but that of securing dividends for his shareholders. On the North Midland this led to a wholesale reduction of staff in 1842, with a series of accidents that called down the condemnation of the Board of Trade (cf. R. M. Robbins, 'The North Midland Railway and its enginemen, 1842–3', *JTH* 4 (1959–60), 180–6). The Eastern Counties Company, of which he was chairman from 1845 to 1849, owes some of its specially evil reputation to the same cause.

for swift action, the well-timed pounce. Much quieter, less flamboyant men showed it also: his sober deputy John Ellis, for example, in the brilliant stroke by which he brought the Birmingham & Gloucester Railway into the Midland Company's net and so foiled one major extension of the broad gauge,[42] or again when he and Joseph Paxton, in the course of a chance encounter with Thomas Cook on Derby station, swept him into organising for the Midland Railway its excursion traffic to the Great Exhibition of 1851.[43] But Hudson had the gift supremely and used it boldly – in the end, recklessly. His method, quite unlike Ellis's, was as a rule to work behind the scenes and then suddenly produce a *coup de théâtre*: as with the final stage of the Midland amalgamation of 1844 and the purchase of the Great North of England Railway in the following year, an expensive deal indeed but necessary to complete the main structure of his empire in the North-East.[44]

Hudson was something of a strategist, as well as a clever tactician. The railway system he envisaged was to be achieved by the dovetailing of one small company into others to make up one large whole, an economic unit. He went a little further than that, to grasp the need for organising the supply of the materials most in demand for railway construction and maintenance. His interests stretched out into coalowning, and into glass manufacture at Sunderland, to supply the roofing materials required for his companies' stations. The large company, either self-sufficient or able to bargain from a position of strength with customers and rivals, was his ideal; and he can claim to have had a hand in the making of three such companies – the Midland, the North Eastern, and the Great Eastern – which outlived him and become great powers in the railway world down to 1922.

The example he set was quickly emulated by men who avoided the financial chicanery and imprudence that brought him down. Glyn of the London & North Western and Charles Russell of the Great Western shaped their growing companies not as soloists like Hudson but in collaboration with strong administrators. Glyn worked quite cordially with Mark Huish, a tough and masterful General Manager, during the six years that Glyn remained Chairman (1846–52), though afterwards he had his part in bringing about Huish's forced resignation.[45] Russell presided over the Great Western Company for the long span of 16 years (1839–55); Charles Saunders was its chief executive officer for much longer still, for

42. MacDermot, i. 108–9.
43. *Transactions of the Leicestershire Archaeological and Historical Society* 49 (1973–4) 27.
44. R. S. Lambert, *The Railway King* (1934), 82–8.
45. Gourvish, 54–5.

30 years from its foundation in 1833. Their relationship remained smooth throughout, a reflection of the calm temper of them both. These two companies grew more steadily than those in Hudson's empire, and they tided over with success the bad years immediately following the Mania. Both were supervised by boards containing some able and determined directors, who played a far greater part in the formation of policy than Hudson ever permitted to those of his companies, and both were served by chief officers now experienced in the management of railways, able to control the complex systems for which they were responsible.

As soon as the Mania had subsided and it became possible to raise money readily once more, new promotion started. But the business had grown much more elaborate. Although by now many railway companies – not merely the dozen biggest, but some of the smaller ones too – were surely founded and able to take the initiative, to choose what they would do next, even they were less free than they had been before 1845, for several reasons. For one thing communities, even individuals, counting up what they thought were the advantages of railway communication, came to look on it almost as a kind of right. More important, the competitive principle had now become thoroughly established. It was widely disapproved of. Samuel Smiles uttered a trenchant warning of the consequences of it in 1849: 'The idea of competition will be found in the end to be a mere delusion. It may exist for a time, but its effects upon railway property are too ruinous to allow it to be persevered in. The result arrived at will inevitably be amalgamations, or traffic arrangements for the mutual advantage of the companies concerned'.[46] John Francis wrote in 1851 that the Great Northern (whose trunk line to the north was just then being brought into use, by instalments) was 'already lowering the receipts and increasing the dissatisfaction of those lines through whose district it passes. No railway should be sanctioned which can only pay a remunerative dividend at the expense of others'.[47]

Smiles's prophecy turned out in the long run to be true, though it never became a universal rule. In the 1850s, however, free competition was still a respected principle; and it was a useful weapon in the hands of those who wished to persuade railway companies to do things they did not like. In particular, during these years following the Mania, it was often invoked to force the building of lines promoted then but since abandoned. Let us consider an example from Bedfordshire.

Two companies had been formed during the Mania with the object of

46. Smiles, *op. cit.*, 57.
47. Francis, ii. 159–60.

building a railway from Leicestershire to Hitchin, with access from there to London. One was backed mainly by the Midland Company (well established at Leicester), the other by the Great Northern, whose main line, passing through Hitchin, was sanctioned in 1846. After some fighting, the Midland project triumphed, and a Leicester & Hitchin Company was established by Act of Parliament in 1847. On the collapse of Hudson and his Midland dominion, this scheme was abandoned. But some of the landowners through whose property the line passed were determined that it should be built. Their leader was William Whitbread of Southill in Bedfordshire. The reign and fall of Hudson were nothing to him: he was set to secure the railway through his county. Early in 1852 he was one of a deputation that met the Midland board at Derby and made it clear that if the scheme were not quickly revived and realised they would turn to the Great Northern instead. The Midland Company did not at all wish to see the Great Northern at Leicester – it is a plain illustration of Francis's comment; and the result was the promotion and passing of a new Leicester & Hitchin Railway Act in 1853. The line was opened four years later.

The landowners' patience and firmness had prevailed. They considered the well-being of their whole estates was involved, as Whitbread and the Duke of Bedford proved by selling land to the Company at no more than its agricultural value, £70 an acre. Other landowners on the line were getting £300 an acre; and their agents were sighing with regret for the time, so shortly past, when they could have secured £1,000.[48]

Intelligent landowners had now come to set a high value upon railways, even in purely agricultural country. The Duke of Bedford did not like the railway for its own sake. He had objected to its passage through his estate at Oakley, not far from one of his houses, when it was first proposed; but he recognised its economic use and accepted the necessity.[49] Similar pressure was being exerted on railway companies by many landowners up and down the country. The Duke of Marlborough, Lord Redesdale, and others harassed the Oxford Worcester & Wolverhampton Railway – with every justification, for its conduct was dilatory and dishonest.[50] Lady Conyngham, having made a bargain with the East Kent Company to invest in its Dover extension, on the understanding that it would open a station close to her house at Bekesbourne, and finding herself in danger of being bilked, put the matter into her solicitors' hands;[51] the station was duly constructed, and opened with the rest of the

48. E. G. Barnes, *The Rise of the Midland Railway* (1966), 80–5, 140–4; F. G. Cockman, *The Railway Age in Bedfordshire* (1974), 108.
49. *Ibid.*, 26, 47–9.
50. MacDermot, i. 247, 264.
51. Kent Archives Office, U438/E74.

line in 1861. The railways were now glad to have landlords on their side. In the 1850s they often courted their assistance. The Cornwall Railway, for example, in the 13 years' struggle to complete its line through awkward country, persuaded landowners to accept payment, in part and even in some cases wholly, in shares.[52]

For most English railways, however, agricultural business was much less important than that which arose from industry and manufactures. If landowners could exercise pressure of this kind, how much more could coalowners, ironmasters, cotton-spinners, bankers, and merchants in every trade? In the 1830s and 1840s the railways had been conferring benefits, real or sometimes imagined, on the country and communities they served; and they were able to decide for themselves the routes they would take, subject to criticism and opposition in detail. Now they had become to some extent the victims of their own success. They had created an almost universal demand for their services, and they repeatedly found themselves obliged to construct lines they were unwilling to undertake on their merits, in particular unremunerative branches, in order to forestall a possible rival or to placate a menacing customer.

William Bridges Adams had sensibly opined in the 1830s that, while railways should be developed to handle the main arterial traffic of the nation, 'common roads must be continued where the transit is limited, and not capable of sufficient increase'.[53] That advice passed unheeded. In 1849 Sir Francis Head argued that 'a branch line must be an unprofitable concern – unless, indeed, the company be authorised to levy upon it *higher* tolls than are sufficient on the trunk line'.[54] (Here was a practice that Parliament never seriously considered.) At almost the same moment the shareholders of the North Staffordshire Company were becoming restive at the directors' promotion of a branch to Ashbourne and succeeded in getting its construction deferred until the main line was finished and in working order.[55] These were signs that danger lay ahead. It did not become fully apparent until the 1860s.

The railway companies, and those who presided over them, certainly did not now have it all their own way. The revelations of malpractice in the Mania had led to a considerable curbing of their powers. In almost every company a committee of investigation had held an inquest into what had gone on, and in many cases that had led to the displacement of

52. See the correspondence between Thomas Goode and William Rashleigh, 1852–3: Cornwall Record Office, DDR (S) 1/848, 852; and Lord Vivian to W. Langbourne, 7 Jan. 1853, AD 267/9/32.
53. W. B. Adams, *English Pleasure Carriages* (1971 edn), 291.
54. *Stokers and Pokers* (1968 edn), 149.
55. Christiansen and Miller NSR, 53.

the old directorate. Where nothing of that kind occurred, it was not necessarily a sign of virtue irreproachable. The shareholders of the Oxford Worcester & Wolverhampton Company, for example, bore with their odious chairman John Parson and his henchmen for six years on their manifestly fraudulent course. But that was a rare exception. Elsewhere palace revolutions, successful and attempted, were frequent. Rossini could have made a comic opera out of the doings of the London & South Western directorate and shareholders in the 1850s[56] – importing into it perhaps the scene at Wolverhampton in 1851 when Mr Ormsby-Gore, Chairman of the Shrewsbury & Birmingham Company, sat quietly through his shareholders' uproar reading *Household Words* and then, as it drew near his bed-time, pulled a night-cap out of his pocket, put it on his head, and composed himself to sleep.[57]

The financial operations of chairmen and directors were now much more closely watched. It was a criticism of Gladstone's Act that though its fifth section required the companies to send copies of their half-yearly accounts to the Treasury, which should be entitled to inspect their books, it made no attempt to insist on an independent audit.[58] When that idea was mentioned great railway chairmen – not only Hudson, but men of probity like Glyn, or Chaplin of the London & South Western – expressed lively indignation.[59] It was not until 1845 that even an internal audit was made compulsory by law.[60] It is fair to add that some companies had their accounts audited long before they were obliged to do so,[61] and that Glyn's had the best internal system of any, thanks largely to its efficient General Manager, Huish.[62]

As a result of the efforts of the Board of Trade and the short-lived Railway Commissioners, statistical returns were now being furnished by the companies, in such a form that some of their activities could be scrutinised by Parliament and the public. The annual *Railway Returns* begin to emerge in a rudimentary shape from 1841–2.[63] They were in many ways deficient and unsatisfactory, and they were criticised with justice.[64] Yet within their limitations they do afford us, from this time

56. Williams LSWR, i. 75–83.
57. MacDermot, i. 365–6.
58. J. Morrison, *Influence of English Railway Legislation* (1848), 22, 38.
59. Lambert, *op. cit.*, 60; Francis, ii. 7; Williams LSWR, i. 217.
60. By the Companies Clauses Act (8 Vict. cap. 16), sect. 101.
61. e.g. the Manchester & Leeds and its successor the Lancashire & Yorkshire: S. A. Broadbridge, *Studies in Railway Expansion* (1970), 40–2.
62. Gourvish, 161.
63. PP 1843, xlvii. 97–138.
64. D. Lardner, *Railway Economy* (1850), 77, 99, 104, 204. He thought the Belgian reports alone were satisfactory: *ibid.*, 517.

onwards, a continuous view of some elements in the growth of the railway system. They show us the increase of traffic. In 1854, on a system nearly 6,000 miles long, 92 million passenger journeys were made in England and Wales – half of them in the third class or in Parliamentary trains. Two years earlier, for the first time, the receipts from goods traffic exceeded those from passengers. The margin then was slight. By 1854 it had become bigger, in the proportion 54:46. The railways' total business was booming. In 1849–54 the length of miles open grew by 27 per cent; but the number of passengers carried rose by 46 per cent and receipts from goods by almost 50 per cent. Total receipts topped £17 million in 1854 (the income of the State in that year was £58.5 million), and expenditure amounted to 49 per cent of that sum. It was estimated that, taken all together, the companies were making about 3.4 per cent on their paid-up capital:[65] no lavish profit indeed, but now comparatively stable and assured, and moving upwards.

65. PP 1854–5, xlviii. 17. This figure relates to the United Kingdom as a whole.

3   Free Enterprise
1854-1876

The next 20 years, in the history of the nation, were a time of generally growing prosperity, at least in material things. There were grave set-backs, of various kinds. At the beginning the Crimean War brought more than its due share of horrors; the American Civil War affected Britain strongly, and the consequent interruption of the cotton trade hit Lancashire hard; the wars by which in 1864–70 Prussia established her primacy in Germany showed Britain her military weakness and political isolation. In the early 1870s the force of commercial and industrial competition, from the new German Empire and from the resurgent United States, made it clear that Britain no longer enjoyed the degree of leadership in the world that had been hers 20 years before. The economic crises that seemed to be cyclical at intervals of about ten years continued to occur. The crisis of 1857 had its origin in America and on the Continent of Europe. That of 1866, on the other hand, was caused in part by rashly speculative railway promotion in England and Wales.

Railway building in the later 1850s was beset with trouble. Let us turn back for a moment to the Leicester & Hitchin line. Its construction exemplifies the difficulties that railway companies faced in these years, and shows with exceptional clarity some of the makeshifts and compromises they were obliged to adopt.

The line began at Wigston, three miles south of Leicester, where it sprang away from the existing line to Rugby on a curve so sharp that it had to be re-aligned in 1973, at substantial expense. It had four ridges of hills to cross: first a low one in south Leicestershire, then two steeper ones, the southern faces of the Welland and Nene valleys in Northamptonshire, and finally another, quite gentle, south of Bedford. The original plans had envisaged considerable tunnelling. That was avoided, except for the Warden Tunnel at the southern end, half a mile long. Such economies seemed essential. The whole work was estimated to cost £1 million, even at the unusually low rate of £16,000 a mile; and when, directly after the passing of the Act in 1853, the proprietors of the Midland Company were offered the chance of taking up shares for financing the enterprise, their response was tepid. It was not until the end of the year that the money was forthcoming. Work started in April 1854 with Brassey as the main contractor. A month later Britain was at war with Russia. The whole line had therefore to be undertaken against the background of rising costs that the war inevitably produced.[1] Money was saved, both in the planning and in the execution of the line. But the result was a series of gradients steeper than was desirable, with two of the worst starting immediately from sharp curves at Market Harborough and Welling-borough. Much more than the equivalent of what was then saved must have been expended since in the heavy locomotive costs that this plan of construction involved. When the line was fully opened for passenger traffic, on 7 May 1857, the Company could congratulate itself that the work had been carried through within the original estimate; but only because the line had been built on the cheap.[2]

This is one example of a number that could be adduced to illustrate the character of railway building in these difficult years. Very few trunk lines were constructed in the later 1850s – not more than five, indeed, besides the Leicester & Hitchin. Three of them had been authorised during the Mania, back in 1845–6: the Oxford Worcester & Wolverhampton and the Cornwall, already referred to, and the Wilts Somerset & Weymouth. These three took, respectively, eight, 13, and 11 years to complete. The other two were both incorporated in 1854.

The East Suffolk, designed to link Ipswich with Lowestoft and Yarmouth, was laid out on the same principle as the Leicester & Hitchin. Like the Cornwall, it ran parallel with the coast, across the grain of the country. No expensive cuttings or embankments could be afforded; and in consequence its gradient profile resembles the temperature chart of a patient tossing in fever.

The same was true, on a larger scale, of the last of these lines, the Salisbury & Yeovil, with its continuation to Exeter. It was the outcome of a long battle with the established London & South Western Company, many of whose proprietors wished to see a quite different railway built into the West Country, continuing the existing line from Dorchester through Bridport to Exeter. As in Bedfordshire, so in Hampshire and

1. The prices of minerals (iron, copper, tin, lead, and coal) rose by 44 per cent in 1852–4; of Scottish pig-iron by 76 per cent: Mitchell and Deane, 474, 493.
2. The construction of the line is described in E. G. Barnes, *Rise of the Midland Railway* (1966), chap. 7. It can be followed in detail in the minutes of the Leicester & Hitchin Construction Committee, BTHR RAIL 491 1/298.

Wiltshire, landowners combined to force the South Western to make its first move in this direction, by building from Basingstoke to Salisbury. That section was completed in 1857. When the big company refused to go beyond, landowners further west formed the Salisbury & Yeovil Company. Its efforts to raise money were at first ludicrously unsuccessful, and its shares were freely given away;[3] but it held on, and as it moved towards completing its line the South Western was persuaded to continue it from Yeovil to Exeter. The railway reached Gillingham in 1859 and Exeter in 1860. The promoters got their reward, and much more. The railway was worked by the South Western, under agreement, at an exceptionally favourable rate. As time went on, the South Western grew more and more anxious to purchase it. The Salisbury & Yeovil proprietors shrewdly held out, until at length in 1878 they secured £260 of South Western stock (which then stood at 133) for every £100 of their own.[4] They were among the most fortunate railway proprietors in British history.

The South Western's eagerness to buy the line is easily explained. The Salisbury & Yeovil had become a component of its new main line to the West Country. Once that had happened, the South Western seized the opportunity, reorientated itself away from its earlier preoccupation with Surrey, Hampshire, and Dorset, setting its sights on Devon and ultimately Cornwall. The completion of the line brought the narrow gauge to Exeter, by a route much hillier indeed than the original line of the Great Western, but 20 miles shorter. The result was a stiff competition, which lasted for half a century, until it was virtually ended by agreement between the two companies in 1910.[5]

Before 1854 the competitive principle had been well understood by railway managers and proprietors; but it had been more of a threat than a realised force. Although there had been intense competition here and there it had not lasted long and had been terminated either by agreement, to unite or to divide the spoils, or by the withdrawal of one of the competitors. When the Great Western completed its line to Birmingham in 1852, it began with a gallant show of rivalling the London & North Western for the traffic from London, with expresses making the journey (17 miles longer by the Great Western route) in a quarter of an hour less. They figured in the timetables for three months, no more. Then the Great

3. Williams *LSWR*, i. 75.
4. L. H. Ruegg, *The Story of a Railway* (1878), 56. This is one of the few really good accounts of the promotion of a railway company written by someone who took part in it.
5. Cf. J. Simmons, 'South Western *v.* Great Western: railway competition in Devon and Cornwall': *JTH* 4 (1959–60) 13–36.

Western gave the competition up as hopeless; the trains were slowed down by 25 per cent, and the field left in its rival's occupation.

The map of the system in 1854 shows very few truly competitive routes. There were two or three over short distances – from London to Windsor, from Birmingham to Wolverhampton; and there was competition between Manchester and Leeds. Two trunk lines, however, both recently completed, offered the possibility of competition in the future. One, obviously, was the Great Northern, which had already begun to compete with its established rival the Midland for the traffic between London, the east Midlands, and the North. In this year 1854 Parliament allowed the Great Northern to absorb the Ambergate Company,[6] so giving it a route from London to Nottingham via Grantham two miles shorter than the Midland's and entirely under its own control, whereas the Midland had to make use of the London & North Western system for two-thirds of the distance, south of Rugby. To Sheffield, again, the Great Northern's route was shorter and more convenient; and behind Sheffield lay Manchester, also accessible from Retford. The collaboration of the Manchester Sheffield & Lincolnshire Company was necessary here, and that was for the present withheld, through pressure exerted on it by the London & North Western, which was determined to retain its own monopoly of the Manchester-London traffic. But as in all political relations, alliances and enmities might change. They did so in this case in 1857, when the Sheffield Company deserted its former ally and agreed with the Great Northern to run a joint service from Manchester to King's Cross. The distance here was greater, and the road involved a climb to nearly 1,000ft over the Pennines between Manchester and Sheffield. The allies' trains could not equal the North Western's in speed, but they were punctual and reckoned comfortable, which made them true competitors nevertheless. The North Western reacted – literally – with violence, designed to deter passengers at London Road station in Manchester from using the new route; but that could be no more than a furious gesture. The competition had arrived, and it was there for good.

It was soon taken further. In 1862 the Midland Company, the most ambitious empire-builder of all railways in the Mid-Victorian age, set itself to develop a route of its own to Manchester, from Derby through the Peak District, to join the Sheffield Company's system at New Mills and so proceed by means of running powers. That was completed in 1867, and with the opening of the line from Bedford to St Pancras in the following year there were three express routes from London to Manchester, in lively competition.

6. Properly – but cumbrously – the Ambergate Nottingham & Boston & Eastern Junction Railway.

To Leeds and York the Great Northern's route was easier than the Midland's; even more clearly, to every place beyond. No wonder the Midland, seeing all this valuable traffic pass more and more to its rival, sought to improve its own route to London. Unless it did that, it would lose most of the southward business of the large towns between Bradford and Nottingham to the Great Northern, as well as the coal traffic from South Yorkshire, Derbyshire, and Nottinghamshire, just beginning to break decisively into the London market. Its London extension had become a necessity to it.

Another important line, finished in 1853, on the other side of the country, was also potentially competitive: the Shrewsbury & Hereford, designed to join up at Hereford with a new line – still being built, but opened at the beginning of 1854 – from Newport and Pontypool. Hitherto the whole of the traffic from the North of England to South Wales and the West had passed over the Midland line through Birmingham and Gloucester. Here was the possibility of a major new cross-country route. It was already shorter between some points – for example, Manchester and Newport; and if a direct line were built over the easy country from Crewe to Shrewsbury it would become 20 miles shorter still.[7] The Shrewsbury & Hereford Company began life modestly; it was worked by the contractor who had built it, Thomas Brassey. He ran the line on a shoestring, and that was acceptable as long as it was merely a local railway serving the Welsh Marches. But in the later 1850s the South Wales coal trade leapt forward, and the large railway companies began to interest themselves in securing a share of it. The London & North Western, in particular, was anxious to challenge what might become a monopoly of the Great Western, much strengthened by agreements the Great Western reached in 1861–2 for amalgamation with the West Midland and the South Wales companies. The London & North Western considered absorbing the Shrewsbury & Hereford. Then it arrived at a treaty with the Great Western, providing that they should take it over jointly. So it passed into their keeping, to be used for the development of the interests of them both, chiefly at the expense of their common rival the Midland.

This story is highly characteristic of the years we are now considering: years in which small companies, many of them launched during the Mania and built in the difficult times that followed, came to be absorbed by larger ones, to form the elements of great railway systems. The network as a whole virtually doubled in length during these years, from about 6,000 miles to 12,000. But in doing so, it to some extent changed its nature. The movement towards amalgamation was accelerated. The

7. Shorter, that is, by comparison with the existing route from Manchester, through Warrington and Chester.

major companies of England and Wales, as they eventually became, had all begun to emerge. In these years they notably extended their predominance, their power in the railway world, and in so doing they went a good deal further towards creating what could be described, not just on a map but in reality, as a national railway system.

Of the two amalgamations brought into being in 1854, the creation of the North Eastern Railway by the fusion of the York & North Midland, the Leeds Northern, and the York Newcastle & Berwick companies was much the more important. This was an outright amalgamation, based on an agreement reached privately in 1853 and made absolute by Parliament in the following year. With small exceptions, the new North Eastern Company included the whole railway system of Yorkshire east of Leeds and of Co. Durham south of Darlington. It had a great main line, about 175 miles long, running north and south between Normanton and Berwick-on-Tweed. But the two chief east-west lines, the Newcastle & Carlisle and the Stockton & Darlington, remained independent; and that was a source of anxiety to the new company, for either of them might ally with other railways, perhaps hostile, to break into the territory it dominated. At first the danger came mainly from the Newcastle & Carlisle, which linked up with the London & North Western, a company always anxious to extend its interests into the far North-East; but after 1856 a similar threat grew, with the building of the South Durham & Lancashire Union Railway, a continuation of the Stockton & Darlington westwards, over Stainmore, to Tebay on the London & North Western main line up to Scotland. These threats of possible 'invasions' made the North Eastern anxious to come to terms with the two independent companies. But their men tended to dislike the North Eastern Railway;[8] and this step, if it were taken, would really mean the establishment of a territorial monopoly. So the first attempt made by the North Eastern to amalgamate with the Newcastle & Carlisle failed in Parliament in 1861. It had, however, reached a working agreement privately with the Stockton & Darlington Company in 1860; and in 1862–3 the three companies were fused at last.

These measures were steadily opposed by the London & North

---

8. Francis Mewburn (the venerable solicitor of the Stockton & Darlington Company) called it 'the most unpopular and most unaccommodating line in the Kingdom': *Memoir of F. MacNay by his Son* (1867), 68. When the amalgamation with the Stockton & Darlington came, it was looked on with no enthusiasm by Joseph Pease or by Mewburn himself: Larchfield Diary (MS. in Darlington Public Library), 186.

Western and also by the North British, a Scottish company bent at this moment on extending itself southward. The Border was an important barrier in the development of the British railway system. The English and Scottish companies exchanged traffic and collaborated in running through services; they inevitably met head-on at such historic points as Berwick and Carlisle. But, with one insignificant exception,[9] no English company crossed over into Scotland; and, ignoring the short distances of English ground that had to be traversed to reach Berwick and Carlisle, only one Scottish company penetrated south of the Border. That was the North British, which, not content with opening a line from Edinburgh through Hawick to Carlisle in 1857, set itself, by means of subsidiaries, to run westwards to the Cumberland coast at Silloth, and on the east side far into Northumberland, joining up with the English railway system both at Hexham and at Morpeth. At Morpeth (which it reached by the Wansbeck Railway in 1865) it allied itself with the one company of substance in Northumberland that was still independent of the North Eastern, the Blyth & Tyne, and so attained running powers into New-castle. Here was no great threat to the North Eastern, however; for the lines of the North British and its allies were circuitous and had to cross long stretches of almost empty country. Altogether one may say that the Border retained many of the characteristics of a frontier, thrust across the British railway system, even in the peaceful nineteenth century.

The line over Stainmore, just mentioned, was not built primarily to serve the bare countryside it traversed, but to carry a two-way freight traffic: in iron ore from Furness to Teesside, and in coke from Durham to the ironworks of Cumbria. These were boom years in the northern iron trade. The railways played their part in creating that prosperity and shared in the gains. The Furness Railway paid an average dividend of 7.3 per cent on its Ordinary shares for nearly 30 years (1854–82), attaining a maximum of 10 per cent in 1864–6 and 1871–2. As for the North Eastern, it paid almost 8 per cent from 1870 to 1883, reaching its peak in 1873 at $9\frac{1}{4}$.

That prosperity was not secured by the exploitation of the monopoly the North Eastern Company achieved in 1854–63. It could fairly be reckoned among the most efficient in England, treating its customers liberally and providing them, in general, with a good service. If the traders of Hull were already criticising it, theirs was in many ways a special case. The North Eastern had a difficult task to satisfy the demands of Tyne, Wear, Tees, and Humber, which were often clamorously discord-ant. As a monopolist, it was always particularly exposed to attack from

9. The exception was the Kelso branch of the North Eastern Railway, which penetrated rather less than 4 miles into Scotland.

one or other of these interests; but it held the balance between them and earned, in normal times, their gratitude.

The other combination brought into being in 1854 was in almost every respect different. It was a working agreement only between three weak companies, very unlike the powerful trio that came together to form the North Eastern: the Eastern Counties, the Eastern Union, and the Norfolk, which provided between them most of the railway system in Norfolk, Suffolk, and Essex.

The Eastern Counties Company was much the largest of the three. It had never been strong. Hudson had failed to make it efficient; it was the feeblest part of his railway kingdom, and its weakness helped to bring about his fall. Since his departure it had staggered from one folly and malpractice to another, exposed by shareholders' committees of investigation in 1849 and 1855 and lit up by the fireworks of angry pamphleteers,[10] headed by the joyous Mr Ancell, with his donkey racing the train at Bethnal Green.[11] The jokes seemed good enough to spectators, but they were bad ones for the shareholders and perhaps worse still for those who lived in the country the Eastern Counties Company was supposed to serve.

That country was almost entirely agricultural, given over largely to corn-growing, with the east-coast fisheries as a useful complement in its economy. At a time when the population of England as a whole was rising fast, in this large tract it was falling.[12] The life seemed to be draining away from it. As an obvious addition to its other economic misfortunes, perhaps in part accountable for them, stood the Eastern Counties Railway. No other continued to be wracked by dissension, after the Mania was over, in the same degree as this one.

Its difficulties sprang in part, clearly enough, from its relationship to the neighbouring companies with which it had to divide the traffic of the eastern counties: all of them dependent for access to London on its line. Their disputes were notorious, and since none of them was able to make a satisfactory living it was natural to think that they would do better to unite. On the other hand, some of those concerned urged a move in the opposite direction, to break up the limited combine of 1854, releasing the Eastern Union from an oppressive bondage.[13]

But these companies formed a single system: that was a fact, not to be

10. Ottley (5811–36) lists 26 such publications relating to the Company and the adjacent lines associated with it, issued in 1849–61. One of them, *The Eastern Counties Railway. Why does it not Pay?* (1859), ran into at least seven editions (Ottley 5833).

11. He adopted the pseudonym George Hoy: Ottley 5829.

12. It fell in Norfolk, Suffolk, and Cambridgeshire in 1851–61.

13. Cf. *A Word or two about 'E.U.'* . . . *By an Old Acquaintance* (1860): Ottley 5835.

gone back on. Somehow they must be made to operate successfully as one. The wiser elements in their management saw this and determined to work to that end. The result was the full combination of the three companies, to form the new Great Eastern Railway in 1862. It was a step fraught, very plainly, with risk. All that an Act of Parliament could do was to establish a framework for a new administration, and to give it a legal validity. It was for the administrators to make it work, to the reasonable satisfaction if not to the profit of the shareholders and of the country it served.

The creation of the North Eastern and Great Eastern companies seemed to open the way to further projects of the same kind. Several were attempted in the succeeding years, and all failed. The most notable of these was the plan to fuse the London & North Western Railway with the Lancashire & Yorkshire in 1871, which would have given the combine as complete a control of Lancashire as the North Eastern enjoyed in its sphere. This led directly to a Parliamentary inquiry into railway amalgamation in general. Again, as in 1853, the verdict was adverse. That particular scheme was abandoned and no others, aimed similarly at setting up a large monopoly, were put forward for a good many years to come. Only one more, indeed, was ever achieved before 1914.

There was another kind of amalgamation: what was sometimes called the 'end-on' type, uniting two or more companies with continuous main lines into one. The London & North Western secured permission to absorb in this way the Chester & Holyhead Company in 1859; the Great Western brought in the West Midland and the South Wales companies, on the same principle, in 1862–3, and the four that continued its line westwards from Bristol to Penzance in 1876.[14] Even here, however, such projected unions were not always realised. The Midland and the Glasgow & South Western railways (whose systems were to be joined, by a railway already sanctioned, at Carlisle) made three separate attempts at amalgamation in 1867, 1872, and 1873. All were approved by the shareholders of both companies, and all were rejected by Parliament. In this case some allowance must be made for the antipathy felt by Scotsmen towards a threatened English invasion. Had the attempt succeeded, the Midland Company's board might well have felt that it had broken down the Pyrenees.

One territorial monopoly enjoyed by a railway company was ended in

14. This was the date at which Parliament approved the practical amalgamation of all five undertakings, and the dissolution of one of them, the Bristol & Exeter. The others were formally dissolved at various times subsequently; the West Cornwall maintained a nominal existence until 1947. MacDermot, ii. 95, 132, 152, 154, 165.

these years: that exercised by the South Eastern in Kent. It was the only railway there, and by 1854 it served every important place in the county except Sevenoaks and the towns at the mouth of the Medway. It also controlled the whole of the Continental traffic through Dover and Folkestone (whose harbour it had purchased outright in 1843). The sole defect in this happy system was the approach of its main line to London, by the roundabout route through Redhill, where it fell into the main line from Brighton – a conjunction that bred endless disputes and delays to trains from that point northwards. For this there was an obvious remedy in the building of an independent line up from Tonbridge through Sevenoaks. That would be a costly enterprise, the line having to pierce the North Downs; it would clearly have to be undertaken when the Company felt able to afford it. Meanwhile, there seemed to be no pressure of competition forcing it to act quickly.

But in truth it was there, a cloud no bigger than a man's hand. In 1853 an East Kent Railway had been authorised, to build a line from Strood through Chatham to Canterbury. Two years later it got powers to extend to Dover. The South Eastern already served Strood, and it regarded the new line simply as an eastward extension of its own. Soon the East Kent's ambitions soared higher. In 1856 it tried to secure access to London under its own control. That effort failed, but it succeeded two years later. By 1861 it had turned itself into a London Chatham & Dover Railway, with a line fully open and exactly described by that title. It was a serious matter for the South Eastern, which had despised the East Kent as an insignificant rural concern, even refusing an offer the little company made to sell out to it. Now it was too late to retrieve that mistake. The South Eastern found its monopoly broken, and the Chatham Company's line was nine miles shorter to Dover than its own circuitous route via Redhill. At once it felt obliged to make the direct line to Tonbridge, for which it secured powers in 1862. That cost, before it was completed seven years later, £1 million. It was the shareholders in the two companies, and the unfortunate people of Kent, who suffered most in consequence. The companies wasted their money on a ludicrous rivalry, to provide double services to every town of any importance in the county except Folkestone; with the result that neither of them could afford any service that was decent. The planning and development of the English railway system appear at their most deplorable in Kent.

The largest deficiencies in the railway system of 1854 were in the northern Pennines, Devon and Cornwall, and inland Wales.

The South Durham & Lancashire Union Railway, already mentioned, crossed the Pennines from east to west. Its line, opened in 1860, joined the London & North Western's at Tebay, and a branch was added in 1862 from Kirkby Stephen to Penrith. The only trunk route north and south was provided by the North Western main line, until the Midland Company opened its Settle & Carlisle line in 1876. None of these railways was undertaken to secure the agricultural business of the district, which was small. The Tebay and Penrith lines were designed primarily for mineral traffic; the Settle & Carlisle was part of a new trunk route from London to Scotland. Two other small lines were also developed to serve the district: one up Wensleydale from Northallerton to Hawes, the other from Clapham in Yorkshire to Low Gill, $4\frac{1}{4}$ miles south of Tebay on the London & North Western main line. At that the system remained complete, though numerous other attempts were made, especially to secure a line running from Skipton to the industrial North East. These efforts had begun during the Mania, with such projects as the Northumberland & Lancashire Junction and the Manchester Liverpool & Great North of England Union railways. Twenty years later came the North of England Union project (1865);[15] then the Skipton & North Eastern Junction of 1884, which aroused justified indignation by proposing to cross the Swale on a brick bridge, 80ft high, immediately over Aysgarth Force;[16] and finally the Yorkshire Dales Railway, which was under discussion for four years from 1890, designed to run up Wharfedale and then down Coverdale to Richmond and Darlington.[17] The ambitions that lay behind these repeated attempts were never satisfied, though they help to account for the willingness of the North Eastern to support the extension of the line up Wensleydale in 1870–8, an unattractive economic proposition in its own right.

The system was extended substantially in the far south-western counties during these years. The Cornwall Railway managed to complete the Saltash Bridge and its line westwards to Truro in 1859, whence the West Cornwall Railway (which had been opened seven years earlier) carried the route on to Penzance. In the same year 1859 a branch line was opened from the South Devon Railway east of Plymouth to Tavistock; it was built by an independent company, which the larger one subsequently absorbed. Six years later another small company extended the line just across the Cornish border to Launceston. At the time this was only one in a series of branches thrown off the South Devon main line to small

15. Prospectuses of all these schemes are in the North Yorkshire Record Office, Northallerton: ZOP.
16. Cf. the pamphlet *The Railway Vandal at Aysgarth Force* (same Office, Z57/29). This disgraceful scheme will be considered in Vol. III.
17. Papers in same Office: ZRF/4/2/2.

country towns, characteristic of these years everywhere in England; others were the extension of the existing line from Torquay to Kingswear, for Dartmouth (1859–64), followed by the Moretonhampstead, Brixham, and Ashburton branches in 1866–71. Presently, however, the Plymouth-Tavistock-Launceston line acquired an unlooked-for importance, when the London & South Western, anxious to extend westwards from Exeter and so to compete for the traffic to and from Plymouth, secured powers to build a railway round the northern edge of Dartmoor through Okehampton, to join the Launceston branch at Lydford and so allow its trains by the exercise of running powers to reach Plymouth. This line was completed in 1876. It had been strongly opposed by the South Devon Company and the whole Great Western interest, defending the broad gauge against an invasion of the narrow, but on that very account the new line had been welcomed and assisted by some people in Devon who disliked the old companies' conservatism and their leisurely ways. Sir John St Aubyn even went so far as to give the South Western Company valuable land in Devonport, free of charge, to induce it to come in and serve the town.[18] So in 1876 Plymouth ceased to live under a monopoly. The new line west of Exeter was not a satisfactory one: running powers were never a good substitute for independent control, and here they had to be exercised over a line that was itself hostile. Still, the South Western had thrown its hat into the ring. Before long it began to consider ways of improving its access to Plymouth and of extending its competition into Cornwall.

There, much of the field was still open. Four branch lines connecting with the Cornwall Railway had been thrown off, but three of them (to Looe, Fowey, and Falmouth) ran southward. Only one, the line to Newquay opened for passenger traffic in 1876, went the other way. For the rest, North Cornwall remained entirely empty, its only other railhead far away at Launceston.

In 1854 the Principality of Wales was framed on three sides by railways, but scarcely penetrated by them at all. There had been a busy promotion of schemes for railways to serve central Wales and the west coast during the Mania. There were, for example, three projects for lines to run from Birmingham to Aberystwyth, by different routes, together with others coming up from Gloucester and Newport.[19] Nothing whatever emerged

18. *Western Daily Mercury*, 18 May 1876.
19. H. Tuck, *Railway Shareholder's Manual* (8th edn, 1847), 358, 350, 367. A map of the chief lines proposed between 1837 and 1855 appears in Christiansen and Miller CR, i. 15.

from all these imposing plans, or from any of the others put forward at that time. But the progress of the north-south line along the border had its influence. The Shrewsbury & Chester Railway threw off a short branch to Oswestry, opened in 1848. Five years later Parliament rejected another attempt to build a railway across the country to Aberystwyth, but it authorised the construction of a line in Montgomeryshire, to run from Llanidloes to Newtown. After six years' struggle, this was opened in 1859.

That end was not achieved by the shareholders unaided. The contractor for the railway was a local man, David Davies, and he took a partner, Thomas Savin. They were building the Vale of Clwyd Railway, from Rhyl to Denbigh, at the same time. There they were associated with Henry Robertson, who was engineer of the Shrewsbury & Chester Railway and of others radiating out from Shrewsbury. Davies and Savin agreed to take up all the unissued Llanidloes & Newtown shares, finish the line, and then work it on a lease. The lease was written into a supplementary Act of 1859.[20]

Meanwhile another railway was making equally slow progress from Newtown to Oswestry. The Company displaced one firm of contractors by another, and the second went bankrupt. Thereupon Davies and Savin stepped in, with an offer similar to that which had enabled the earlier line to be completed, and the Company accepted it, though the two chief landowners on its board resigned in protest. Again Parliament sanctioned the arrangement, and the line was completed at last in 1861; another, running out of it near Welshpool to Shrewsbury, followed the next year. By that time a westward extension to Machynlleth was nearly completed and another, running on to Aberystwyth, authorised. Aberystwyth was at length linked with Oswestry and Shrewsbury, by a line made by four different companies, in 1864.

During these operations Davies and Savin quarrelled. Davies was a man of strong common sense, and sound judgment coloured by caution; Savin a speculator. To Davies the first task was to make the existing railway system work. Savin became involved in ambitious plans for further extension from Machynlleth, not only to Aberystwyth but also northwards along the shore of Cardigan Bay. He was not interested in railways alone, but also in the building of hotels, to turn the coastal villages into watering-places. In 1860 Davies dissolved his partnership with Savin, turning his attention henceforth more and more away from railways to coal-mining, to become one of the greatest figures in that world: Dai Davies the Ocean.[21] Savin remained in railway business. From

20. LPA 22 & 23 Vict. cap. 30, sect. 16.
21. Cf. the admirable biography of him: I. Thomas, *Top Sawyer* (1938).

his base at Oswestry he promoted, built, and worked a disconnected series of lines stretching from Newport to Carnarvon and Denbigh.[22] By the earlier 1860s he had become more than a contractor. He had assisted these struggling companies by accepting payment for his work in shares, and by entering into agreements to undertake the operation of the lines when they were completed. It became a necessary part of Savin's activities that he should secure boards of directors, and officers in the companies, subservient to him, and that led him into much further quarrelling.

Through all these storms Savin drove on. Having completed the line to Aberystwyth, he made a beginning with the section north of the Dovey estuary. But his resources were now becoming over-stretched. In February 1866 he suspended payment. It was the end of his career as a railway promoter, though he continued actively in public life at Oswestry (he had been mayor of the town in 1862), with substantial interests in coal-mines and quarries near by. He died, quietly enough, in 1889; his personal estate amounted to £105.

As for the railways in which he had been engaged, they had to shift as best they could. In 1864 all the separate companies responsible for the route from Oswestry to Machynlleth came together to form the Cambrian Railways; and in the following year this amalgamated company engulfed the coast lines too. But very large claims were outstanding against it for land not paid for, and its creditors took it to court. Meanwhile the northern stretch of the coast line, though far advanced, lay unused – except, it is said, by trains run surreptitiously at night, when the creditors' baliffs were believed to be asleep.[23] The whole line up to Pwllheli, including the long viaduct across the estuary at Barmouth, was not opened until 1867.

Aberystwyth and all the coast to the north of it thus secured a railway to England. In the same year the completion of two short lines gave it, at least on paper, communication with the rest of Wales. One ran from Afon Wen, a little east of Pwllheli, to Carnarvon, and so to Bangor and the main line to Chester. The other had a more complex story: the Manchester & Milford Railway.

This concern cuts a ludicrous figure in history, first because of its grandiose title. It never proposed to build a railway from Manchester to Milford Haven; all it set out to do was to drive a fairly direct south-westerly route across mid-Wales by means of a line about 50 miles long from Llanidloes to Pencader, where it was to join the Carmarthen & Cardigan Railway, authorised in 1854. Economically, such an enterprise

22. They are indicated on the map in Christiansen and Miller CR i. 75.
23. *Ibid.*, 67–8.

could not be promising, though its prospects were no worse than those of some other lines promoted and built in these years. What put it into the realm of the absurd was the topography of the country it proposed to cross. The Cambrian line had sensibly followed river valleys, mounting only one watershed. The Manchester & Milford ran right across the grain of the country southwards from Pantmawr, demanding two tunnels, 1½ miles long between them, and a viaduct on piers intended, so it was said, to be 280ft high. Here we are in the world of fantasy. By 1863 the Company's shareholders had paid up less than £8,000 towards the authorised capital of £666,000. In the end the Company abandoned this hopeless line through the hills, to run instead from Aberystwyth to Pencader. There it duly joined the Carmarthen & Cardigan Railway – a much murkier undertaking, which was in the hands of a receiver from 1864 to 1878.[24]

Three other long lines of railway communication in Wales were also completed in these years. One ran westward from Ruabon, on the Great Western Railway from Birmingham to Chester, to Dolgelley, where it joined the Cambrian. Forty-five miles long, it was the work of four separate companies and opened in stages from 1862 to 1868. From the outset it was an appanage of the Great Western. The other two lines formed a St Andrew's cross intersecting not far from Builth. The Mid-Wales ran from Llanidloes to Talyllyn, connecting there with the Brecon & Merthyr Railway. It was opened in 1864 and had a hard struggle to keep going at all; the Cambrian agreed to work it in 1888. Crossing this line was the Central Wales, which realised the idea represented by the Manchester & Milford, of a more or less direct route from the Midlands and the north of England to south-west Wales. It ran from Craven Arms, on the Shrewsbury & Hereford Railway, to Llandovery, whence it was continued by the lines of other companies to Carmarthen, Llanelly, and Swansea. The system thus described, nearly 120 miles long, was opened in 1858–67.[25] It owed its completion to the strong support of the London & North Western. That company purchased the whole of it in 1871 save the 11-mile stretch between Llandovery and Llandilo, which it divided with the Great Western.

Those two large English companies played a substantial part in the making of railways in Wales. Generally they were rivals, especially in the coal and iron traffic of Monmouthshire, which the North Western broke into from Abergavenny. Both of them tried at various times, but without success, to gain control of the Cambrian. The Midland Company also

24. The history of these two companies is compendiously summarised in
    MacDermot, ii. 178–81, 229–30.
25. The 6½ miles from Pontardulais to Llanelly had been opened in 1839.

developed Welsh interests, on a smaller scale. Ever since the 1840s it had supported projects for railways running westwards across the border. It subscribed to the Worcester & Hereford Railway and helped to work it when it was opened in 1859–60. Then in 1869 it stepped in to control the Hereford Hay & Brecon Company; five years later, by means of an alliance with the Neath & Brecon, its trains were running through to its own station in Swansea.

A very large part of the Welsh railway system was thus opened in the years 1858–68. The means by which this was achieved were often questionable, or indeed fraudulent beyond question, and much of what was done proved unremunerative, bitterly disappointing to shareholders in the companies concerned. But much of the work was carried through in entire good faith, from a genuine belief that the railway was an essential element in the life even of remote rural communities. What must strike us most, looking back over the story now, is the tenacity of these Welshmen in the Mid-Victorian age, their energy and determination in overcoming all the obstacles in their path. They did not create a wisely-planned railway system in their country, any more than Englishmen did, or Scotsmen. But they did build a large rural network with undaunted vigour and a remarkable turn of speed.

The fraudulent promotion and financing of railways was by no means peculiar to Wales. It had many parallels elsewhere. In the early 1860s there was another general boom in railway promotion, especially in and around London (see pp. 120–2) but in other parts of the country too. It was the fourth and last of the 'manias', and it differed from all its predecessors both in character and in outcome.

Partly as a consequence of the Mania of the 1840s, the range of investment in companies of all kinds had very greatly increased, facilitated by legislation in 1855–62, which much extended the principle of limited liability. Capital became once more freely available from about 1860, and a good deal of it flowed into railways. Much of this investment arose not directly, from the purchase of shares by individual investors, but indirectly, by other means. Insurance companies, now rapidly growing larger, were sometimes willing to invest in railway development; finance companies had now appeared, one of the chief purposes of which was to make capital available where there would otherwise have been difficulty in raising it. And frequently railway directors found help in the construction of their undertakings from contractors, who came forward to invest in them.

As a simple illustration of the process, consider the Sheffield Chesterfield & Staffordshire Railway, promoted in 1863–4. It was a grandiose scheme for building a line 36 miles long, with a capital of £1,100,000. Of that sum a contractor, William Field, undertook to provide £800,000, on condition that £300,000 was locally found in Sheffield. In the end, despite many brave speeches, no more than £10,000 was actually forthcoming there. Meanwhile, if any progress was to be made, a deposit had to be lodged with Parliament, and that was provided by a loan from another party, without any direct interest in Sheffield or in the railway at all: the General Insurance Company. This last transaction was private, but inevitably soon came to light. A Committee of the House of Commons then investigated the whole business. It held that the deposit had been irregularly raised, in contravention of the Standing Orders of the House, and the scheme was thrown out.[26]

Who was William Field, and why should he have been apparently willing to invest so heavily in such a project himself? He had been an associate of Thomas Brassey – sometimes his partner in a contract, sometimes his agent, sometimes both – on and off since 1846. He also worked with Henry Robertson in north-eastern Wales.[27] It is most unlikely that he possessed the enormous sum of £800,000 himself at this time; much more probable that he relied on borrowing it if the need actually arose. He was only one of many contractors who were doing the same sort of thing in the early 1860s. What brought them into this dubious business at all?

It had not been unknown for them in the 1840s to assist railway companies whose works they had undertaken by accepting payment in bonds. Brassey did this for the Great Northern and the North Staffordshire railways in 1848.[28] In the 1850s the practice became common, and extended much more widely, under the leadership of the big men in the business. Brassey put up most of the capital for the Bideford Extension line, for example, Peto did the same for the Chipping Norton Railway; both were completed and opened in 1855. They were small feeders to main lines, on which the same contractors were at work. Already, however, they had begun to move into other divisions of the business, on a larger scale. The London Tilbury & Southend Railway was built by the partnership of Peto Brassey & Betts in 1852–4, and on its completion they undertook to work it, paying 6 per cent on the capital.

These big contractors needed to keep their labour and management

26. The investigation is in PP 1864, x. 903–21. For further details of the affair see *Victorian City*, i. 287–8.
27. Some of Field's activities in 1846–68 can be traced in Helps, *Brassey*, 162–6.
28. *JTH* 3 (1957–8) 46. In this article, 'Railway contractors and the finance of railway development in Britain', Mr Harold Pollins first opened up the subject.

forces, and their plant, employed. When the great work of construction arising from the Mania of the 1840s was finished, that presented some difficulties to them. They could move into work abroad, or into different branches of contracting; and they did both these things in a large way. But they knew there was much more railway work to be done at home, and they needed to be able to tender for it and execute it as soon as the opportunity arose. To invest in the promotion of further railways, on condition that they secured the contracts for them, seemed to be a useful device to this end.[29]

In the 1860s a much larger range of people than ever before had come to be interested in the promotion of railways, for a wide diversity of reasons. Only a few of those who have just been mentioned had any real or lasting interest in fostering railways themselves. The great promotion that now followed was obviously an affair of middlemen. It has to be seen in its context. It played a substantial part in the changing attitude towards money in general that is evident in mid-Victorian Britain. The public rise and fall of Hudson in the 1840s had set a spectacular example. John Sadleir provided another in the 1850s, arising partly from railways but chiefly from Irish banking; Dickens acknowledged that he drew Mr Merdle in *Little Dorrit* largely from him – doing so while Sadleir was still alive, just before his suicide in 1856. Then came Albert Grant (*né* Gottheimer), mixed up notoriously in all kinds of fraudulent companies and yet retaining his public prominence: M.P. for Kidderminster from 1865 to 1868 and re-elected there in 1874, the munificent donor of Leicester Square to the people of London. These were all figures in national life. There were others in the provinces, like Ralph Ward Jackson, who might be called the creator of modern Hartlepool. Old-fashioned persons detested these people, less for their moral depravity than for the corruption that emanated from them. Dickens assailed them again in *Our Mutual Friend*. Here he is, writing in 1864:

As is well known to the wise in this generation, traffic in shares is the one thing we have to do with in this world. Have no antecedents, no established character, no cultivation, no ideas, no manners; have Shares. . . . O mighty Shares! To set those blazing images so high, and to call us smaller vermin, as under the influence of henbane or opium, to cry out, night and day, 'Relieve us of our money, scatter it for us, buy us and sell us, ruin us, only we beseech ye take rank among the powers of the earth, and fatten on us!'[30]

29. Brassey and his partners repeatedly accepted payment for parts of their work on the Leicester & Hitchin line in shares: cf. BTHR RAIL 491 1/298, ff. 66, 103.
30. *Our Mutual Friend*, chap. 10 (Penguin edn, 159–60).

Trollope went even further. Returning from a long absence abroad in 1872, he was appalled by the spectacle of London society in the grip, as he thought it, of a despicable lust for money, and he sat down to write a long, powerful, and fierce novel on the theme: *The Way We Live Now*, published in 1874–5. The central figure in the book, Augustus Melmotte, has elements in him both of Hudson (recently dead) and of Baron Grant – though the railway promotion he engages in is not in England but in America. Trollope allowed afterwards, in his *Autobiography*, that the indictment was too sweeping; but he continued to attack commercial fraudulence and the social corruption it brought with it.

Here, as usual, the novelists were reflecting their readers' thoughts. At the heart of them all stood Black Friday, 11 May 1866: a grim date in the history of the time, when the discounting house of Overend Gurney crashed with liabilities of £10 million, incurred through dealing in unsound shares, of railway companies in particular.[31] The collapse had been foreseen at least since the previous February by those who really knew the state of the firm;[32] but to the general public the disaster seemed astounding. It brought with it immediate and obvious consequences for the railway world. Sir Samuel Morton Peto and his partner Edward Ladd Betts went bankrupt; and they were, after Brassey, the biggest railway contractors in Britain. The fortunes of Brassey himself quivered in the storm;[33] but he rode it out, calm and tenacious – though even he was thought to have lost £1 million at the time.[34] Three important English railway companies also failed: the London Chatham & Dover, the Great Eastern, and the London Brighton & South Coast.

Their cases were different. The Chatham's was disgraceful beyond redemption. It had been a rickety concern from the start, and the competition it embarked on with the South Eastern was ruinous. But the Company rushed on its fate by recklessly over-issuing debentures, in a manner that left even hardened observers gasping. In financial terms it never made more than a feeble recovery from the disaster of 1866, at least until its working union with its rival in 1899 (p. 961).

31. See P. L. Cottrell, 'Railway finance and the crisis of 1866', *JTH* n.s. 3 (1975–6) 20–40.
32. Cf. *Economist* 24 (1866) 553. Among many others, George Rae, General Manager of the North & South Wales Bank, seeing some of the bills held by the firm, withdrew his deposit from them shortly before their collapse. He suffered no loss and was thus able to stand behind David Davies, who would otherwise have been destroyed too. Thomas, *op. cit.*, 82.
33. See Helps, *Brassey*, 145–9.
34. That still allowed him to leave £3,200,000 when he died in 1871: one of the greatest fortunes of the Victorian age, and made primarily out of railway contracting.

The Great Eastern also paid for the follies of its past. In 1864 it had secured powers for the extension of its line into the City of London at Liverpool Street: a most necessary improvement, but a very expensive one. Its recovery from a long history of malpractice and quarrelling had been slow; too slow to permit it to withstand the troubles that now broke. So it too, for a few months in 1867, passed into the hands of a receiver.

Neither the Chatham Company nor the Great Eastern had ever been truly prosperous. The Brighton Company had been so, for a long time, in a high degree. But its affairs had been unwisely directed in the early 1860s, and it came to grief with the rest. Having paid a steady 6 per cent from 1856 to 1862, it paid nothing at all in 1867 and an aggregate of less than 2 per cent in the three years 1868–70. It did not fully recover financially until 1875.

The impression made by the crisis of 1866 was powerful and lasting. Trollope's later novels, from *The Prime Minister* onwards, continue to reflect that feeling faithfully. Sir John Rennie – an old man, but still full of work – retired from the engineering profession in disgust forthwith.[35] Railway investment, which had seemed for 15 years past so sound and simple, changed its character in the eyes of the public. Most of those who in 1866 owned shares, through purchase or inheritance, not for speculation but to furnish an income, were obliged to retain them. All but the very best could be sold only at a loss; a great many could hardly be sold at all.[36] The Mania of the 1840s had taught an elementary lesson about railway investment, as gambling, which anybody could learn. That of the 1860s, though it was also caused in part by speculation, was – the *Economist* insisted on it from the beginning – 'a *credit* panic';[37] and, in the broadest sense, the credit of the railways never wholly recovered from these troubles. When Lewis Carroll said of the Snark in 1876 that 'you may threaten its life with a railway share', he condensed a great deal into a single phrase. But it was more than a business of shares. This financial crisis was quickly succeeded by a crisis of confidence of a different sort: of confidence in the technical management of railways, by their directors, officers, and staff. Major accidents multiplied, some of them dramatically appalling. Two of them occurred in tunnels: at Clayton on the Brighton main line in 1861, and at Welwyn on the Great Northern, exactly a month after the Black Friday of 1866. In the first of these,

35. *Autobiography* (1875), 455.
36. On 12 May 1866 the shares of only nine English and two Welsh companies stood at a premium – the Taff Vale much the highest, at 141¼: *Economist* 24 (1866) 577. They all retained their value, hardly shaken, throughout the rest of that disastrous year.
37. *Ibid.*, 581.

excursion trains were involved; in the second, three freight trains, which turned the tunnel into a furnace. Then came a third, in which fire also played a dreadful part: the Irish Mail disaster at Abergele in 1868. Among the passengers in that train were the Duchess of Abercorn and the Marquess of Hamilton; Lord and Lady Farnham were killed. Regardless of wealth or class, all were exposed alike to the railways' malpractices.

Nor could it be said that it was the poorest railways, those that were most unsound financially, that were the most dangerous. On the contrary, the one that had the worst record for accidents in these years was the London & North Western – so bad indeed that the Chief Inspecting Officer of the Board of Trade, departing from an established rule of refraining from direct comparisons of performance, felt pressed to draw attention to its bad eminence in 1870, when nearly one-third of all accidents reported on in the United Kingdom took place on that one railway.[38] The Queen, in her indignation, spoke for her subjects, drawing the attention of Gladstone's Government in 1872 to 'the very *alarming and increasing insecurity* of the Railroads'.[39] The Government took some action, in the Regulation Act of 1871, which gave the Board of Trade the power to make more stringent inquiry into accidents; two years later it called for an annual return from the companies to indicate the provision they were making for securing public safety.

Part of these troubles arose, it was clear, from the use of poor or obsolete equipment. Were the directors and shareholders therefore reaping their profits at the expense of their passengers? Where the Lancashire & Yorkshire was concerned, that judgment, in these years, was largely justified; and all that prevented its accidents from being more disastrous than they were was the parsimony that forbade it to run any trains at all that could be described, even on paper, as fast. With the North Western and the North Eastern the explanation was different, more complex and morally less discreditable. Still, the record stood.

At the same time it was coming to be established that accidents were caused in part by the long hours that many railwaymen worked. Complaints on this subject began to be heard with increasing insistence in the 1860s. It was brought before the notice of the House of Commons in 1862, when certain companies were named as notorious in this respect: the Lancashire & Yorkshire (here again), the Great Western, the Midland, and the Manchester Sheffield & Lincolnshire.[40] Nothing happened in consequence then. But the complaint was not stilled.

---

38. PP 1871, lx. 113.
39. *Letters of Queen Victoria*, 2nd ser. ii (1926), 276–8.
40. *Hansard* 3rd ser. 168 (1862) 660–71.

The railways were now moving into a new phase of their history. In the 1830s and 1840s they had been things of wonder. Then they had arrived at a position of secure strength, courted and admired as the instruments of progress, indeed its very symbol. The Mania had been an aberration, deplorable no doubt but all part of the explosion that had given the country its railway system. In the late 1860s, however, the estimation in which they were held began to change again. The rush of promotion in the early part of the decade was not an heroic struggle to build necessary lines of communication. It was very plainly a business of making money; and making it, only too often, by fraudulent means. The crash of 1866 discredited railways more than any other group of enterprises. It was followed by revelations of mismanagement extending beyond finance to the conduct of the railways themselves. At the same time manufacturers and traders in Britain were coming to find the battle with their foreign competitors harder and for this, searching for scapegoats, they tended to blame the railways for what appeared to be their high rates and charges.

All these things formed a conjunction, of opinions hostile to the railways and to those who directed and managed them. It found effective, indeed formidable, political expression at the same moment. The second Reform Act had been passed in 1867, making the electorate for the first time in Britain a truly popular one. The railways' shortcomings and misdemeanours provided an opportunity for politicians, of both the great parties, to busy themselves and acquire popularity with several sections of the community: the traders, the working classes, even to some extent the traditional electorate. The Regulation Acts of 1871 and 1873, passed by the strong Liberal administration that the Reform Act had put into power, showed the new mood beyond any mistake. Henceforward the railways were to conduct their business under more searching public scrutiny. They now moved over to stand on the defensive.

Competition and Government Regulation 1876-1914

On 1 May 1876 the Midland Company opened its Settle & Carlisle line, creating a third trunk route between England and Scotland. The date is a landmark. The railway looked backwards into the past; but also, in at least one respect, pointed to the future.

It stood at the end of a long succession. Physically, it was the last main line in England to be constructed by the traditional methods, by the brawn of navvies unaided in any great measure by mechanical equipment. The next large lines to be built were undertaken with mechanical excavators. Even with their help, the work could at times prove very difficult. But the Settle & Carlisle line traversed a mountainous and unpeopled country, ravaged by blizzards in winter. On its 72 miles the only intermediate towns were Kirby Stephen and Appleby, with a population between them of not much more than 5,000. The simple tablet in the church of Chapel-le-Dale commemorating the men who died in the construction of the railway between Settle and Dent Head is an epitaph on an age and a way of life.

The materials these men handled, too, were wholly traditional: timber, iron, stone quarried in the surrounding hills, bricks brought up by rail from Staffordshire and elsewhere in the Midlands. All in all, the railway differed in no essential respect from those that had been built in Robert Stephenson's time.

It may also be seen as one of the last and most spectacular products of the British competitive system. Another was to come, a dinosaur: the Manchester Sheffield & Lincolnshire's London extension of the 1890s. But the Settle & Carlisle enterprise exemplified the force of competition in a double sense. For the undertaking owed its completion not merely to the original resolve of the Midland Railway to extend its share in the traffic to Scotland but also to the determination of its allies, the Lancashire & Yorkshire and North British companies, to hold it to its bargain when in 1867–8, hard pressed financially, it tried to abandon the undertaking. The railway epitomised the relationship of the companies with one another, not only their enmities and rivalries but their uneasy alliances too.

Finally it may be said that the Settle & Carlisle line represented almost the last effort, on a large scale, to provide railway service to remote agricultural communities. Not quite the last: there was still some more to be done in this way in Yorkshire, Norfolk, and Cornwall. The railway was primarily intended to carry through trains; but some attention was also given to the local traffic that might be developed in the district.[1]

So this enterprise stood at or near the end of a succession. There is, however, one important respect in which the railway looked forward, not back. It was the first to be built in England for a two-class structure of passenger traffic, pursuant to decisions taken by the Midland Company in 1872 and 1874, and the first whose express trains were equipped from the start with bogie vehicles and Pullman and sleeping cars (cf. pp. 195–7). A Midland Scotch express of 1876 belongs firmly to the modern world; those of its West Coast and East Coast rivals were still, one might say, medieval. The Midland Company could not provide the shortest route from London to Edinburgh and Glasgow. Instead, it set out to attract custom by superior service. Here was the new sort of competition that came to characterise the later Victorian age and its Edwardian successor; and it was trumpeted forth by the first expresses running over the brand-new line from St Pancras (its opulent hotel almost completed) to Glasgow, with its brand-new station on St Enoch Square.

In the same year two important changes also occurred in the south of England: the enlargement of the Great Western Railway by amalgamation (p. 69); and – balancing that, tempering monopoly – the opening of the London & South Western line to Plymouth.

With 2,000 route miles, the new Great Western Company became the largest in Britain. Though it and its old allies were regarded by many people in the West Country with affection and pride, there were others who felt differently. The distinctive element of these railways was Brunel's broad gauge. Whatever the merits of that system in engineering terms might be, by this time it was clearly on the way out. The Great Western Company had been steadily abandoning it north of the Thames since 1868. A great operation in 1872 had removed the broad gauge altogether from over 300 miles of the line in Gloucestershire and South Wales; 190 miles more went two years later in the country between Reading, Bristol, and Weymouth.[2] By 1876, therefore, the broad gauge

1. Cf. D. Jenkinson, *Rails in the Fells* (1973), 47–51.
2. For details of this conversion – a considerable administrative and engineering feat – see MacDermot, ii, chap. ii and 310–12.

survived in the four south-western counties alone.[3] As if to emphasise that singularity, one new piece of broad-gauge line was actually being built at this moment: the branch to St Ives in Cornwall – the last line ever constructed anywhere on the 7ft gauge.

No wonder some people in these counties thought their railway service antediluvian. Alert travellers became increasingly apt to note that much of the broad-gauge rolling-stock was down-at-heel, proclaiming that the Company did not intend to replace it. And to complete the picture as it appeared to these critically-minded folk, the whole corporation was presided over by Daniel Gooch, the one surviving giant from the railways' heroic age.

If this view of the Great Western Company in the late 1870s was understandable, it was not quite fair. Gooch was no aged mummy – he was only in his early 60s; when he died, still occupying the chair in 1889, no more than 73. Though conservatively-minded and cautious, he was still equal to overcoming formidable difficulty, as he had done in his early days with the Great Western locomotives, or in the 1860s as chairman of the company laying the Atlantic cable. His caution was needed at the time by the Great Western, which had narrowly escaped bankruptcy in 1866 and was in financial trouble for most of the 1870s. On the credit side it should be remembered that the Severn Tunnel (cf. p. 162) owed much to his firm resolution, never to be discouraged. There was good as well as bad in the Company's services, too. Unlike some of its fellows, notably the London & North Western, it steadily developed the use of an effective continuous brake, from experiments first conducted in 1876. And even its venerable carriages were sometimes renewed or replaced. It put its first sleeping cars into service between London and Plymouth in 1877 and then, recognising their imperfections, a second pair, so much improved that they could be considered the best running anywhere in Britain at the time, four years later.

The railway industry in the mid 1870s, looked at as a whole, is no bad reflection of the state of Mid-Victorian England: living on its past achievements, looking back on them with well-founded pride but also with a dangerous complacency; content to go on in the same way, disregarding some important developments from abroad, yet also capable of throwing up new ideas, adopting new practices and taking them ahead faster than other people. We are not looking here simply at a watershed, where everything before has been climbing upward to improvement and there is nothing ahead but a decline, for there were some new triumphs still to come. But the 40 years preceding the First World War represent

3. With the trifling exception of the Faringdon branch in Berkshire ($3\frac{1}{4}$ miles long), converted to narrow gauge in 1878.

for the railways an increasingly stiff battle with opponents and competitors, in which the weapons forged by preceding generations are growing obsolete and the outlook of those in control tends to become more defensive, less quick to seize new opportunities and develop them experimentally.

In the later 1860s, several companies had devoted capital and energy to building new lines whose chief purpose was to improve their trunk routes rather than to tap wholly new business: strategic lines, they may be called. The South Eastern's new line to Tonbridge is an outstanding example. Two others appeared on the North Eastern, one from Doncaster to York in 1871, the other from Ferryhill through Durham to Gateshead, completed in the following year. The idea was carried further in the next decade. The Lancashire & Yorkshire determined to engage, in a fully competitive fashion, in the lucrative traffic between Manchester and Liverpool, and for this purpose built a new line avoiding Bolton and Wigan. When it was completed in 1889, though its route between the two cities remained longer and more difficult than those of its rivals, it could offer a train service equally attractive. The Midland acquired in 1880 what was in large measure a new route from London to the north diverging from its established main line at Kettering, running to Nottingham and thence to the Erewash valley at Trowell. This was a good stroke. Taken in conjunction with its new route through Sheffield, opened in 1870, it allowed the Company to claim that it offered the best service between the chief towns of the east Midlands and the West Riding, Manchester, and London. In Hampshire the London & South Western, observing the brisk development of Bournemouth, set about providing it with a direct line from London and Southampton, in place of the existing one, which meandered through Ringwood. It was opened in 1888. In the 1860s and early 1870s Bournemouth had grown, one might say in spite of the railways, which visited rather than served it. Now, with through carriages to and from the Midlands and the North of England by the Somerset & Dorset line and a service to London in less than three hours, it began to owe a real debt to the railways, and to repay it by the traffic it brought them.

The principal undertaking of this kind in eastern England was designed chiefly to facilitate the conveyance not of passengers but of freight, and especially coal. In 1863 the Great Eastern Company had begun a tenacious effort to secure direct access to Yorkshire, with its mineral traffic and the manufactures of the West Riding. It sought powers to build a line from March to Spalding and to move on from there over the Great

Northern. The Great Northern resisted the proposal, which would have allowed the Great Eastern to abstract a good deal of the coal conveyed up its own main line through Newark to London. The Bill was rejected; whereupon the Great Eastern returned in the next session (assisted by an insurance company, which undertook to provide half the capital) with a much more ambitious plan for a line of its own, 108 miles in length, from Cambridgeshire to Yorkshire, where it would join the West Riding & Grimsby Company's line from Wakefield to the Humber. No plan for any one railway so long had been seriously considered by Parliament since the Great Northern's own had been sanctioned in 1846. This 'Great Eastern Northern Junction' scheme envisaged a new kind of railway: one laid out entirely for cheapness. To this end it was to be virtually level, having no gradient steeper than 1 in 400, and to leave on one side Peterborough, Sleaford, Lincoln, and Doncaster, serving them by branches in order to avoid purchasing much expensive land in their neighbourhood. The promoters claimed that they would be able to work trains two-thirds as heavy again as the Great Northern's, and they undertook to charge the derisory rate of no more than $\frac{1}{4}d$. a mile on each ton of coal they carried. So across the Trent Basin, the flat country of Lincolnshire, and the Fens, the coal of South Yorkshire was to be conveyed at a steady 15 m.p.h. to East Anglia and London.

At first the railway was intended to convey no passengers at all, only coal. Presently the carriage of passengers was provided for – at exceptionally low fares since they would travel slowly, in accordance with the general scheme of management of the line. The project was supported by leading railway engineers – Bidder, Hawkshaw, Fowler, and Gooch. All that was not enough, however. The examination of the Bill occupied 25 sittings of a Commons Committee, and in the end it pronounced against the proposal.

The idea was renewed, in varying forms, in 1865 and 1871, and again failed. By the mid-1870s conditions had changed. The Great Northern was now anxious to relieve its own overcrowded main line. At length in 1878–9 a fresh arrangement was arrived at, accepted by itself, by the Great Eastern, and by Parliament: for the construction of a new line from Spalding through Sleaford to Lincoln, at the expense of the two companies, and for their joint ownership of the whole system (including lines already in existence) from Huntingdon through St Ives and March to Doncaster.[4]

The Spalding-Lincoln line was opened in 1882, and it did something

4. This complicated story is told clearly, and very fairly, in C. H. Grinling, *History of the Great Northern Railway 1845–1902* (1903), 205–11, 224–6, 233–4, 244–55, 315–16, 318–20, 324–32.

for both the companies that promoted it. It gave the Great Eastern a fairly straight and easy route up from Yorkshire, marred only by bottle-necks at Doncaster and Lincoln. That allowed the coal to be handled easily, and also offered a chance to extend the carriage of Yorkshire manufactures, and of travellers, to the Continent by way of Harwich. For the Great Northern this was a political victory, removing a trouble-some enmity on its eastern flank. But the new loop line could also be regarded as useful in itself. If it was 13 miles longer between Huntingdon and Doncaster, its length was offset by more favourable gradients. It helped to give the Great Northern Company a respite from the task, otherwise threatening it, of quadrupling its main line to accommodate a relentlessly increasing traffic. It did not solve that problem, however: the London traffic carried by the new line had still to pass over the old one south of Hitchin, through nine tunnels. By one means or another, four tracks would have to be provided on this section, to cope not only with the long-distance trains but also with those from the fast-growing northern suburbs of London. Prosperous though the Company was, the bill for that work, when it had to be undertaken, would be alarming.

This contest began as a struggle over the conveyance of coal, and that was a powerful element in it throughout the 20 years of its course. No wonder: for coal production was rising very fast. In England and Wales it doubled in 1855–75, and had more than doubled again by 1913:

TABLE 4. COAL PRODUCTION IN ENGLAND
AND WALES, 1855–1913[5]

(millions of tons)

1855	57	1890	157
1865[6]	86	1895	161
1870	96	1900	192
1875	115	1905	200
1880	129	1910	223
1885	138	1913	245

The railways' part in carrying this traffic grew more than proportion-ately. Coal influenced very powerfully, it even dominated, the thinking of some companies; most clearly those in South Wales. Production there was increasing almost without a check. In the late 1860s it was 50 per cent greater in quantity than it had been ten years earlier; another

---

5. Source: Mitchell and Deane, 115–16.

6. No figure can be given for 1860 since the volume of production in the South Wales coalfield is unknown for that year.

increase occurred in the 1880s of the same order. In 1913 for the first time it outstripped that of any other coalfield in Britain – a pre-eminence it maintained until 1925.

The coal was concentrated chiefly within Monmouthshire and Glamorgan. It was handled locally by the Monmouthshire, Taff Vale, and Llanelly companies; each independent of its neighbours, and all in strenuous rivalry with them. Two main lines served the district, both incorporated into the Great Western in 1863: the South Wales Railway, running parallel with the coast eastwards to Gloucester, and so to London; the Newport Abergavenny & Hereford, skirting the edge of the coalfield and running north and south.

The larger part of the coal was taken away by sea, through Cardiff and the other ports; the more so because the South Wales Railway was broad-gauge, whereas all the local lines (as well as the Newport Abergavenny & Hereford) were narrow. Pressure from the coal interests, to end this inconvenience, was largely responsible for the Great Western's decision to abandon the broad gauge in South Wales, implemented in 1872.[7]

In east Glamorgan the Taff Vale Company was strongly entrenched. In the 1850s it enjoyed a monopoly in the Rhondda valleys – whose steam-coal was just then beginning to be exploited – and it had a working agreement with the Marquess of Bute, who owned the docks at Cardiff. But when the accommodation there was extended by the construction of the East Dock in 1859, the Marquess allied himself with the Rhymney Railway, a new competitor, and the Taff Vale Company did not secure access to it until 1866. As a reprisal, the Taff Vale revived an earlier scheme for developing a new coal port further west, which emerged as Penarth Dock in 1865, served by a railway under the Taff Vale's control. Within 20 years Penarth was handling nearly 3 million tons of coal a year.

But all this was not enough. In 1871 the Rhymney Company opened its own separate line into Cardiff. It then busied itself with extensions northward (partly in conjunction with the Great Western), bringing it first into the Aberdare valley and then, in 1886, up to Dowlais and Merthyr, the Taff Vale's original preserve. What was much more alarming, not to the Taff Vale Company alone but to the entire coal industry, was the growing congestion of the docks at Cardiff and of the railways leading to them. For this both the Bute Trustees and the Taff Vale Company were to blame. Neither of them extended their facilities in step with the expansion of the coal trade. The coal was delayed intolerably in transit to the docks; siding accommodation was totally inadequate; so

7. MacDermot, ii. 25.

was the provision for unloading and for handling the ships. Trains were said often to stand seven or eight hours without moving. The coalowners' pressure produced little effect. The Bute Trustees extended their accommodation once only, when they opened the Roath Basin in 1874; but though they took powers in that year to add its much more expensive complement, the Roath Dock, they refused to exercise them, in the belief that the production of coal was already reaching its maximum. That proved a grave error. The railway company and the dock owners felt the strength of their position and determined to move at their own pace. But the pace was too much like that of the coal trains themselves. The coalowners would stand it no longer, and in 1883 they promoted a scheme for a railway down to an entirely new port, south-west of Cardiff, at Barry. Contested tooth and nail by the established interests, the Bill was defeated; but it was revived in the following year and passed, con-stituting the Barry Dock & Railways Company.[8]

So far the story is of a not uncommon kind: the promotion of a new railway in close proximity to an older one, to afford facilities evidently necessary, and not being rendered. The Midland Company had done the same thing in London in the early 1860s. But the sequel to the construc-tion of the Barry Railway is unique. Enormous as the coal traffic of Glamorgan had become, nobody could have predicted with confidence, when the railway and the docks were opened in 1888–9, that the enter-prise would succeed. If it did, that could surely be only by beggaring its rivals. For a time that seemed to be happening. The Taff Vale Company was desperately beset. Another new railway was built to siphon off part of its traffic to Newport. That was finished in 1886 and followed by the Rhondda & Swansea Bay line, piercing the hills in 1890 to carry the coal to yet other ports, Port Talbot, Briton Ferry, and Swansea. All this expressed itself in the Taff Vale Company's accounts. Between 1888 and 1891 its revenue fell off by a third. But the Barry Company prospered notably. Then, as the new arrangements settled down, the full truth began to appear: that all these railway companies, and all these ports, could live off the coal traffic and go on growing rich together. In the early years of the new century the tide began to turn for the Taff Vale, and its Ordinary shares were back to paying an average dividend of nearly 4 per cent. Those of the Rhymney yielded almost twice as much. As for the Barry Company, its financial success appeared dazzling. In 1898 its shares never stood lower than 254 in the market. The price fell in the more difficult times that followed, but in 1913 they were still not quoted below 162, and over the years 1893–1913 the average dividend they paid

8. Its title was changed to 'the Barry Railway' in 1891.

was well over 9 per cent. This prosperity may not have been altogether genuine.[9] But it accurately reflected the long-continuing wealth of the South Wales coal trade.

Two other railway companies appeared in the 1880s and 1890s, both ambitious and heavily capitalised. The Hull & Barnsley Railway, like the Barry, was set on foot as a protest against a monopoly: the monopoly exercised by the North Eastern Railway in Hull. The case was less straightforward than at Cardiff, the monopolist's failure less self-evident. The real burden of Hull's complaint was not so much against the inadequacy of the railway facilities afforded by the North Eastern; it was the favour that company was alleged to show to other ports at Hull's expense, and especially to its own port of Hartlepool.[10] The argument became very bitter, an emotional affair involving the Corporation of Hull. There was strong feeling against railway companies elsewhere, at Bristol and Southampton, for example, at one time at Blackpool. But none of it had the intensity, or bore the same communal character as the hatred of Hull for the North Eastern.

Other railway companies were near at hand on the south side of the Humber. The Manchester Sheffield & Lincolnshire had done much for Grimsby, which was also served by the Great Northern; the Lancashire & Yorkshire was at Goole. The London & North Western and the Midland were not very far away. The natural thing therefore was for the aggrieved citizens to attract one of these companies to the town. Having made several efforts of this kind, which failed, they turned to promoting a railway of their own.

Like the Barry Company, the Hull & Barnsley proposed to build a dock as well as a railway. It achieved both in 1885, but at ruinous expense. The railway cost £59,000 a mile, which made it one of the most costly ever built in Britain.[11] It never reached Barnsley, but it joined up with the Midland at Cudworth and with the Sheffield Company at Wath. It had to cross the East Riding Wolds, and the Drewton cutting, 2 miles long through treacherous chalk, proved extravagantly expensive. The railway took five years to construct (1880–5), and soon after its opening the Company was bankrupt. Three years later it managed to regain solvency. By 1896 it was able to pay a modest dividend. In the

9. Certainly the Company did not plough back enough of its high profits into renewing its plant. The condition of its locomotives had become deplorable by 1910. See the papers of John Conacher, who was brought in first as a consultant and then, in that year, as Managing Director, to remedy the deficiencies in the Company's administration: SRO, BR/SPC/9/3.
10. See D. Brooke, 'The struggle between Hull and the North Eastern Railway': *JTH* n.s. 1 (1971–2) 220–37.
11. *The Hull & Barnsley Railway*, ed. K. Hoole, i (1972), 15.

end it came to terms with its rival the North Eastern (to the anger of many people in Hull), and on that basis it even attained a certain degree of prosperity.

The other large new company of the late Victorian age avoided the bankruptcy court, but proved itself a pretentious and feeble failure. This was the Lancashire Derbyshire & East Coast Railway, which proposed to build a new line across the breadth of England from Warrington to Sutton-on-Sea. The capital authorised by its Act of 1891 was £5 million, but it never raised anything like half that sum; the line it actually constructed, and opened in 1896–7, ran only from Chesterfield to a point west of Lincoln. After an unprosperous independent life, it was bought up by its neighbour the Great Central Railway in 1906.

That title 'Great Central' is a new one. The enterprise it represented arose out of the building of the one new trunk line of these years: the London extension of the Manchester Sheffield & Lincolnshire Railway. Like the Midland line to St Pancras, this was an attempt to give a provincial railway a share of the London traffic. But the motives lying behind its construction were different. In the 1850s the Midland had suffered evident and intolerable delays in the conveyance of its traffic, by two other companies, to London. About 1860 the traffic, in coal and passengers, was increasing so impressively that there was clear justification for a third trunk railway line. Twenty-five years later, when the plan began to be considered by the Sheffield Company's board, traffic was indeed growing still. The established companies were all engaged in providing themselves, by one means or another, with four tracks instead of two to carry their trains up to London. The Great Northern had its joint line with the Great Eastern, which provided it with an alternative route for much of the way. The Midland widened its line piecemeal until it had four parallel tracks for the first 75 miles out of London and then, by means of two routes, four tracks on into Yorkshire. The North Western quadrupled its line from London to Roade and then built a new loop serving Northampton and avoiding Kilsby Tunnel, which gave it four tracks to Rugby.

Here then was good evidence, from the three companies already engaged in the traffic between London, the Midlands, and the North, that they expected it still to grow larger. The protagonists of the Sheffield Company's extension made much of it. But the argument was two-edged: for these established companies had already embarked on extending their facilities and would therefore be able to handle the additional traffic well in advance of the time when a new company could hope to break into it.

The plan owed its main driving force to the Company's chairman, Sir

Edward Watkin, a megalomaniac and a gambler.[12] He was also chairman of the Metropolitan and the South Eastern railways, as well as of the company for building the Channel Tunnel, which was then being actively prosecuted. His idea was to extend the Sheffield line from Annesley (not far from Mansfield) down to north Buckinghamshire, where it would join with the Metropolitan and make use of its line, to save much of the heavy capital expenditure involved in approaching London. The Metropolitan was already linked with the South Eastern system, which could then take the Manchester and Sheffield trains on to Dover and to the Tunnel when it was built. The 'Manchester to Paris' notion was visionary and foolish, a flashy advertising slogan, no more.

On calculations such as these, Watkin managed to persuade his colleagues to accept the plan. (One wonders how he did it. He must have had some strangely compelling power with business men who would have reckoned themselves hard-headed.) The project went forward to Parliament in 1891, was defeated at its first attempt and then succeeded in the following year. Its Act, passed in 1893, provided for the building of 95 miles of new railway by means of a capital of £6,200,000. The line was planned to pass through two large towns, Nottingham and Leicester, and two smaller ones of some importance, Loughborough and Rugby. But all of these were well served by existing railways; the largest place on which the new undertaking conferred the benefit of railway communication for the first time was Lutterworth, whose population was 1,800. In Nottingham two tunnels were required (as well as a huge station, built jointly with the Great Northern Company, costing over £1 million); the railway strode over Leicester on a viaduct three-quarters of a mile long. There were expensive works at Rugby, crossing over the Oxford Canal and the London & North Western Railway, and then the Catesby Tunnel, boring through the Northamptonshire uplands for nearly $1\frac{3}{4}$ miles.

Considered as a work of engineering the railway was of great interest: a late masterpiece, showing very clearly how the lessons of the past had been profitably learnt. It was laid out for high speed, with easy curves and a moderate ruling gradient of 1 in 264; in the whole of its length there was only one level crossing; almost all the new stations, except the largest, were designed to a common pattern, comprising a single island platform; the bridges throughout were built either of Staffordshire engineering bricks or of steel. By a piece of extraordinary good fortune the whole progress of the undertaking was meticulously recorded by a Leicester photographer, S. W. A. Newton, whose work enables us to

12. For a discussion of its origins see H. Pollins, 'The last main railway line to London': *JTH* 4 (1959–60) 85–95.

watch the entire process from the laying out of the line to the passage of its first trains.[13]

Looked at in these ways, the railway was a magnificent enterprise. But as an element in the country's system it was a superfluity; conceivable, by this date, in no other country in the world except perhaps the United States. Long ago the initials 'MSL' were held to signify not 'Manchester Sheffield & Lincolnshire' but 'Money Sunk and Lost'. The financial performance of the new Great Central was far worse. It never paid any dividend on its Ordinary stocks. Its lavishly appointed new trains were poorly filled. And at the same time its existence served to depress the revenues of the established companies with which it competed, especially the Midland, but the London & North Western and the Great Northern too.

One short branch from the new line did, however, afford the means of providing a useful service, hardly supplied before. This was the $8\frac{1}{4}$-mile line from Woodford to the Great Western Railway at Banbury (opened in 1900), which gave access to Oxford, Reading, and so either to the south-east of England by way of Redhill or to Southampton by Basingstoke. There was also the Banbury & Cheltenham Direct Railway (scarcely 'direct' until certain small improvements had been made in 1906). By means of this Woodford-Banbury line new cross-country passenger services were established from the North of England to Kent, Hampshire, and South Wales; and they offered useful routes for freight traffic besides.

Much was done, indeed, in these years to improve cross-country services in general. A number of these were made possible by the opening of substantial new railways, like the Great Northern & Great Eastern Joint line through Lincolnshire, or the Severn Tunnel, which afforded the means of providing new services from the North to the West of England and from Cardiff to Southampton. Sometimes only a new junction was needed for the purpose, with a short loop line. The West Curve at Didcot, for example, and the loop east of Temple Meads station in Bristol,[14] two pieces of line making up less than a mile between them, were both put in during 1886, to allow traffic to flow eastwards from South Wales and the Severn Tunnel. Other useful lines, which might also be very short, enabled through trains to by-pass towns which they had previously had to enter and then leave in reverse. Spalding (by-passed

13. Newton's negatives are now in the Leicestershire Record Office, Leicester. A liberal selection from them is reproduced, with a good commentary, in L. T. C. Rolt, *The Making of a Railway* (1971). The construction of the line is described in Dow GC, vol. ii.
14. From Dr Day's Bridge Junction to North Somerset Junction.

like this in 1894 on the line from Bourn to Lynn) is one example. Another, also in Lincolnshire, is provided by the Kirkstead & Little Steeping line, opened in 1913 with five stations, serving a sparsely-populated agricultural territory but intended primarily to act as a direct route enabling trains from the east Midlands to cut out Boston on their way to the coast.

In-and-out exercises of this kind are common enough on the Continent, where in so many great cities all the main railways converge on one central terminus. In Britain they were unusual. The North Eastern Company had two that were outstanding. The tangle of junctions at York, with main lines approaching its small terminal station from seven directions, produced a discreditable and dangerous confusion. Everyone who did business there complained of it loudly.[15] Nothing short of a thorough reconstruction would do; and that was at length achieved, when the present impressive station was completed in 1877. For those who use it today, moving easily round its great curve, it is hard to realise what a splendid improvement it represented. This job so admirably done, there remained a still more complicated and expensive task for the North Eastern, at Newcastle. Every train travelling from King's Cross to Edinburgh had to enter the Central station there over the High Level Bridge from the east and then reverse. There was no room for loops to be built. North of the station lay the densely-packed centre of the city; immediately to the south of it, the steep gorge of the Tyne. The only solution was the building of a second high-level bridge to the west. By the beginning of the twentieth century it had become an inescapable necessity. It was completed in 1906.

Other sorts of by-pass were built in these years for a different purpose: to solve problems of overcrowding and to eliminate circuitous detours. The main line from London to Brighton had never been the sole property of the London Brighton & South Coast Railway. The South Eastern Company owned the section from Coulsdon to Redhill, where its lines branched away east and west, to Tonbridge and Guildford; and the two companies were constantly at odds. The straightforward remedy would have been to build two more tracks, side by side with the existing pair. But that would not have produced harmony between the two squabbling companies. So the London Brighton & South Coast felt compelled to undertake its own line, avoiding Redhill, a bottleneck in itself: an expensive work, which had to slice and bore its way through the North Downs. When it was completed in 1900 it gave the Company what it needed, and Brighton a somewhat improved train service.

15. Cf. accident reports in PP 1872, lii. 344 and 1874, lviii. 736–7.

Its uncomfortable neighbour the South Eastern entered at last in 1899 into a partnership with the London Chatham & Dover Company. The new Managing Committee quickly began rationalising the service. The London Chatham & Dover's ridiculous independent station at Ashford was closed directly the fusion took place; the South Eastern's even more ridiculous line at Chatham followed in 1911. One opportunity arose from the vicious and wasteful muddle. The multiplication of lines running up into the six terminal stations of the two companies in London offered a feast of alternative routes, with only a little new construction of spurs and connecting lines. The South Eastern & Chatham management started to undertake this useful task, putting in for example in 1902–4 junctions south of Chislehurst to allow trains from the old Chatham line to work up to Charing Cross. Its funds were severely limited, but what it began its successor, the Southern Railway, carried much further in the 1920s and 1930s, in the service of a long-overdue electrification.

Among the new lines built in these years to shorten circuitous routes the most important were undertaken by the Great Western Railway. Its many critics said that 'GWR' stood for 'Great Way Round', and the gibe was just. Its trains ran from London to Exeter via Bristol, to South Wales via Gloucester, to Birmingham via Oxford. The Severn Tunnel was built as a contribution towards reducing one of these detours, but even when it was finished it shortened the distance between London and Cardiff by only 16 miles, since the trains had still to travel via Bristol. The full benefit could not arise until a direct line had been built westwards from Swindon to the Tunnel. This was undertaken in 1896 and opened in 1903, bringing a further reduction of 9 miles in the distance and being laid out for high speed the whole way, whereas the previous route involved a slow passage through Bath and Bristol. With this new line in progress, the Great Western Company made up its mind to invest in the development of a port at Fishguard, in order to provide a greatly improved service to the south of Ireland. That was introduced in 1906. But a greater prize lay beyond. In the summer of 1909 the Cunard Company began to use Fishguard as a port of call for its liners from America. It continued to do so, several times a month, until 1914. Three or four special trains were required to service each of the great ships on its arrival. A new line, $10\frac{1}{2}$ miles long, was opened in 1912–13, to carry this traffic clear of Swansea.

At the same time the Great Western was similarly improving its route to Somerset, Devon, and Cornwall. The means to this end were obvious. Ever since 1862 it had had a line running up the Kennet valley from Reading to Devizes. All that was needed was another branching out of this one somewhere west of Hungerford to Westbury, where it could join another existing line to Weymouth, branching out of that again when it turned south at Castle Cary and running over the marshes to Taunton: a total of less than 30 miles of new construction. Proposals just of this sort had been sanctioned by Parliament in 1848 and again in 1883, but they had not been implemented, and the line up the Kennet valley remained a rural backwater until 1900, when it came to form part of a new main line to Westbury and then, six years later, to Taunton. At last the Great Western had a route from London to Exeter of virtually the same length as that of its rival the London & South Western, and designed for high speed. The long competition between the two companies for this traffic now turned decisively in its favour.

The Great Western also shortened its main line to Birmingham and the North by nearly 19 miles with a new line through High Wycombe. The southern part of this was built in collaboration with the Great Central Company; the northern part, from a point near Princes Risborough to Aynho, outside Banbury, by the Great Western alone. The whole was completed in 1910. Since the new line was two miles shorter from London to Birmingham than the old-established London & North Western route, it was highly competitive, and both companies settled down to provide a liberal service to a standard time of two hours.

Collectively, these Great Western lines, all opened in less than 15 years, have often been described just as 'cut-offs'. But they were something bigger than that expression implies. Their aggregate length was about 155 miles. They traversed lightly-populated country. Each of the new lines served one town only: Chipping Sodbury (whose population was 1,177 in 1901), Somerton (population 1,797), and Bicester (population 3,023).[16] All were expensive undertakings in terms of their engineering. It is impossible to say, on the evidence we have, how far they justified the expenditure they entailed.

The railways that have been discussed so far, built between 1876 and 1914, make up a total length of about 660 miles. But that is less than one-fifth of the new mileage brought into use in England and Wales during these years. What accounts for the very large remainder?

Some of it comprises short lines and extensions, further minute improvements of the system, too small to justify recording. But two other kinds of railway were also constructed in these years, and they have been little examined so far: suburban railways into and out of London and the large provincial towns; and rural branches.

16. This statement disregards, of course, towns like Westbury and High Wycombe, served by already established railways that became part of the new routes.

The extensions of the London suburban system will fall to be considered in the next chapter. Let us look here at what was going on in the provinces, in Liverpool, Manchester, and Birmingham.

In the 1870s Liverpool, with half-a-million people, was the biggest provincial city in England, bigger even than Manchester-cum-Salford. Its growth had owed much to the railway: to its own original railway to Manchester and to the trunk lines that had grown out of that. Nearer home, railways had played their part in the city's local growth. By the mid-1870s its suburban system extended northwards to Southport and Ormskirk, and eastwards at least as far as Garston. Across the Mersey, the development of the Wirral peninsula as a Liverpool dormitory had begun, with railways bringing their commuters to the ferries at Seacombe and Birkenhead.

But as the number of these commuters grew, the ferries became less and less adequate. They were crowded and uncomfortable, especially in the frequent rain; in fog their passage was dangerous. And briskly though they were managed, they were slow. A tunnel under the river carrying a railway was the obvious remedy, and it was afforded by the opening of the Mersey Railway in 1886. The tunnel's approaches were steep, with a gradient at the Liverpool end as stiff as 1 in 27. The whole line was worked by steam, on the precedent set by the Metropolitan Railway in London, and the ventilation was hopelessly insufficient. Financially, the railway was a disaster. The company went bankrupt in 1887 and remained so until 1901; in 1902 its receipts still did not equal its expenditure. It carried fewer passengers than the Woodside Ferry, with which it chiefly competed.[17] But electrification, in 1903, released its full potential. Within two years it was doing more business than the ferry, and it went on to become a vital element in the development of Merseyside. In Birkenhead it made connection with a system of lines grouped together as the Wirral Railway in 1891, stretching up to the top of the Peninsula at New Brighton and through the quiet countryside to the east and south. The Wirral was very far from being a well-managed railway, however, and it played a restricted part in suburban development before 1914. It too was transformed eventually by electrification.

The growth of the port of Liverpool in these years was astounding. In the half-century following 1857 the volume of its business approximately trebled. By 1906 the members of the Liverpool Steamship Owners' Association possessed, between them, 22 per cent of the entire steam tonnage of the world. The system of docks in Liverpool itself (excluding Birkenhead) stretched north and south continuously for more than 8 miles. Communication between them was difficult through over-

17. G. W. Parkin, *The Mersey Railway* (n.d.), 17–20.

crowded streets. A railway for the docks seemed desirable, but it had to be of a kind new to Britain: an elevated railway on the model of those that had long been at work in New York and other cities in the United States. It was first proposed in 1877 but not completed until 1893. Then it was a pioneer: the first elevated railway anywhere to be operated by electricity. The example it set in that matter was soon widely followed – though not in England, where it remained the sole elevated railway of any kind ever to be built.

Liverpool, then, experimented boldly with the railway. The system in Manchester was different: entirely conventional, built up piecemeal, stopping timidly short of realising the railway's capabilities. Passenger traffic came to be based on three terminal stations: Victoria and Exchange (adjacent and communicating, and so virtually one), for traffic to Liverpool, all over Lancashire, and north-eastwards across the Pennines; London Road,[18] for Sheffield and the North Western line to London; and Central, a new building modelled on St Pancras, brought into use in 1880 for the trains of the Cheshire Lines Railway and the Midland service to London. A sort of circular line connecting these stations was built, but it was imperfectly integrated and carried no continuous service. Passengers had to make their way from one station to another through the streets. The Manchester South Junction & Altrincham line, opened in 1849, did serve in some senses, however, as an urban railway, running westwards from London Road[19] to Knott Mill & Deansgate station before veering to the south into Cheshire; and it certainly did much to make Sale and Altrincham into middle-class suburbs. The same must be said, emphatically, of the district to the south, Withington and Didsbury, much developed in the 1870s and 1880s, and next to them Burnage, an early attempt at a garden suburb, built in 1907–10 and then sadly left unfinished. Further out, Wilmslow and Alderley Edge have a history similar to Altrincham's.

A railway suburb of a different kind developed east of the city: Gorton, with Longsight adjoining. This was a whole district given over largely to the railway industry: to the big depots of the London & North Western and Manchester Sheffield & Lincolnshire companies, whose lines traversed it, to the Sheffield Company's locomotive works, to Beyer Peacock's factory for building locomotives and Ashbury's for carriages and wagons. This represented a concentration of railway plant, by the companies and manufacturers together, that was unique in England.

18. This was the arrangement that emerged in the 1880s. For the long history of ill-feeling that lay behind it see J. R. Kellett, *The Impact of Railways on Victorian Cities* (1969), 170–1.
19. Now known as Piccadilly.

The Manchester railway system developed earlier than that of Liverpool, where the physical difficulties to be overcome were much greater. Then, after the completion of the line into Central station in 1880, it changed scarcely at all. Manchester watched electrification in Liverpool, Newcastle, and London, but secured no benefit of that kind until the Lancashire & Yorkshire Company's line to Bury was converted in 1916. As for an underground railway, the idea was never seriously entertained until the 1950s.

The third great city, Birmingham, treated its railways, once again, in a different fashion. As early as 1852 it had acquired a pair of main-line stations – the London & North Western's New Street and the Great Western's Snow Hill – much better situated than those in any other large English town, including London.[20] Not only were they truly central, and so convenient; they were both below ground level, their lines approaching them in tunnels, and they therefore disturbed the surface life as little as possible. They had too a third merit, uncovenanted. The construction of them both, but especially of New Street, involved a great slum clearance. The railways were thus an agency in producing one of the classic achievements of the century in urban replanning.

So the traveller who came into Birmingham from London or Manchester arrived at once in the heart of the city. Many people who lived closer in found the journey more difficult. The railways made very little effort to cater for suburban traffic until the Mid-Victorian age was well advanced. A map of Birmingham of the 1860s shows the railway system as almost an irrelevance to suburban development. There were only seven stations within the whole borough, in addition to New Street and Snow Hill. One of these was at the north-eastern boundary, three lay on the lines to Wolverhampton; the other three were in the south-east, at Bordesley and on the Midland line from Bristol to Derby. That was the third main line serving the town, and it deposited its passengers most inconveniently a long mile away from the centre. The south-western quarter, towards Edgbaston and Harborne, was traversed by no railways whatever.

All this changed in the 1870s. The Harborne Railway built its little line in connection with the London & North Western in 1874, and that helped to develop the place as a suburb. The Birmingham West Suburban Railway was opened in 1876, branching out of the Midland line at King's Norton, running in by Selly Oak and skirting the prosperous quarter of Edgbaston. The railway was planned for the service and development of suburbs. Presently it came to serve another purpose too. It had been promoted with the active support of the Midland Railway. That company

20. For the establishment of these stations see Kellett, *op. cit.*, 127–43.

decided to make use of it as a main line, running its trains, by agreement with the London & North Western, into New Street station. So in 1885 the West Suburban Railway became part of one of the country's chief main lines. But it continued to fulfil its original purpose; and it made a considerable contribution to a venture quite unthought of when it was built – the Cadburys' factory and garden village of Bournville.

Yet in spite of these efforts, the railways' part in the growth of western Birmingham proved relatively small.[21] No more new lines were built, then or later. The villages further out, King's Norton and Northfield, must have owed their growth in part to their convenient train service into New Street. But the real developer, in transport terms, in Birmingham was not the railway, it was the tram: the steam tram in the 1880s, its electric successor 20 years later.

Further out, however, beyond the convenient distance for a tram journey, the railway did a good deal more. Sutton Coldfield was turned into a dormitory town for Birmingham by the creation of the Sutton Coldfield Railway, a branch line for which the capital was raised locally. It was opened in 1862 and worked by the North Western. On the south-eastern side, also well away from the centre, suburban communities grew up along the Great Western line – Acocks Green, Solihull, Dorridge. And, in the same country, the Birmingham & North Warwickshire line of the Great Western, long planned but not opened until 1908, was deliberately designed to induce suburban development, with five 'platforms' or halts, cheaply built in advance of the arrival of the communities expected to grow up around them. The line provided a new route to Stratford-upon-Avon and did something to make that historic place, too, into a dormitory town.

Such were the patterns of suburban growth associated with railway building in the three largest towns outside London. No generalisations will serve to describe what happened at the same time in other towns that also had substantial suburbs. Some examples may however be given, to indicate types of development differing from those that have so far been considered.

Newcastle had what Manchester seemed to have striven for at one time but never attained, a system based on a circular line: not envisaged as such, but put together piecemeal. It was a town with the advantage, to passengers, of a single main-line station, and from that station the service set out, along the north bank of the river to Tynemouth, then up to Whitley Bay and back again by Gosforth. The southern section, parallel with the river, began to suffer severely from the competition of electric trams in 1902. The North Eastern Company met it by electrifying the

21. *Ibid.*, 148–9.

line in 1904, thereby recovering much of the traffic it had lost. Whitley Bay owed its development, simultaneously as a seaside resort and as a residential suburb of Newcastle, almost entirely to the railway.

This line had a long history as a suburban developer. Even before electrification, there were 55 trains a day from Newcastle to Tynemouth: a frequency of service to be found nowhere else in the provinces except on the two urban railways of Liverpool.

All the railways so far discussed were financed in the usual English way, entirely by private capital. There was at least one, however, that was paid for in part by a town's ratepayers. This was the Nottingham Suburban Railway, a line 3¾ miles long traversing a district on the north-eastern side of the town, almost empty but just beginning to become populated. It was promoted in 1885 by a group of business men. The Town Council helped them by a grant towards meeting the Parliamentary expenses of the scheme, and by the terms of the railway's Act of 1886 it was authorised to accept payment for land required by the railway in the form of shares in the Company. The line was opened three years later. Though never profitable, it certainly fulfilled something of the social purpose the Town Council had in mind.

In this last case the railway was acting as the harbinger of suburban development. It did so in many other places too. The Loop Line through the Potteries is a good example. It was projected as early as 1847, to serve the eastern side of the Vale of Etruria, but it came to nothing then. A branch was opened as far as Hanley in 1864, and the whole scheme revived, on a slightly different basis, in the following year. A long struggle followed. The North Staffordshire Company sought to abandon the undertaking in 1868, but the local opposition was too strong. It was fully realised at last in 1875.[22]

By the later years of the nineteenth century most railway companies, other than the Great Eastern and the southern lines into London, were coming to look on suburban traffic with disfavour. It was difficult to work, with its two peak hours – sometimes four, where the line was used extensively in the lunch-hour[23] – and the revenue it brought in, from season-ticket holders travelling at a cut price and in rapidly-increasing numbers,[24] was not commensurate with the costs of its operation. On top of that came the mounting competition of buses and trams: not negligible even when they were horse-drawn, serious when they went over to steam or cable traction, formidable when they turned to electricity.

From 1903 onwards many lines of this sort made experiments with

22. Christiansen and Miller NSR, 77–81.
23. *Ibid.*, 199.
24. The total for England and Wales rose from 450,000 in 1880 to 674,000 in 1912.

steam railcars (cf. p. 185), calling at little halts as well as established stations. The Great Western, which went furthest into this business, set up 112 halts, chiefly on suburban lines and in rural areas, in 1904–14.[25]

The process is strikingly exemplified in and around Plymouth. Two companies were at work there, the Great Western and the London & South Western, often in rivalry with one another and always with the municipal tramways, which began to be electrified in 1899. The railways established some 40 stations and halts in the Plymouth district. They made suburbs of places 15 miles out and more, like Yelverton and Tavistock. They did much to weld together the long-warring 'Three Towns' of Plymouth, Devonport, and Stonehouse, and to bind into their fabric places as far apart as Turnchapel and Saltash. If a genuine City of Plymouth emerged, not merely a paper creation, that was owing in large measure to the railways, and especially to their energetic efforts between 1890 and 1914.

So the suburban system grew greatly during these closing years, in length and in the sophistication of its working. Rural lines multiplied and were extended also, to a degree that must surprise us. Looking back over the list of lines closed in the 1950s and 1960s, one notes how many of them were built in these years; how many, that is, were added to the system late and failed to appear viable under the stringent examination, and in the changed society, of our time.

A very large proportion of the mileage of railway constructed in the years we are considering comprised rural branch lines that became a liability, or were never in any financial sense an asset. What then led their promoters to undertake them? Here is one of the large questions to which this whole work is addressed, and no full answer to it can be offered now. We are concerned at present with the system, not with the forces that went to its making. But one or two things may be said on this matter, as a prelude to a brief examination of the extension of railways in rural England and Wales during these years.

First, branch lines were often not built in any real expectation that they would be profitable, or even pay their way. The motives were apt to be different. Within the British competitive system, many of them were undertaken for strategic reasons, to occupy ground that might otherwise fall to a rival; or to placate a district, or an influential set of customers.

It has also to be remembered that these years coincided exactly with the decline of British agriculture, when politicians and the country at

25. MacDermot, ii. 224.

large were necessarily concerned with the troubles confronting rural districts, social as well as economic, and anxious therefore to encourage the improvement in services and amenity that railway extension might bring.

It was only in the very last years of this period that the railways began to face any serious new competition in rural transport. If motor buses, driven by steam or petrol, began plying in England in 1899,[26] they showed themselves erratic in service, and financially unsuccessful, compared with the familiar, dependable tram. The motor lorry was little better. In 1913 there were still only 39,000 motor buses and taxis in the whole of Great Britain, 64,000 motor goods vehicles.[27] As the railways began to face the new competition, they believed it would indeed be a long time before the motor bus established itself effectively in rural England. Might it not go the same way as the steam carriage of the 1830s? And even if it did not, the railways had anyway taken a share in it themselves from 1903 onwards.

One other thing must be said. It is wrong to suppose that all the late rural railways were unprofitable. Some earned, even in these years, a satisfactory revenue. The Easingwold Railway provides a good example, clear beyond mistake since it was an entirely independent company, whose accounts can be scrutinised. It was no more than a single line, $2\frac{1}{4}$ miles long, running from Alne on the main York-Darlington line to Easingwold, and opened in 1891. For the next eight years it paid no dividend, then 3 per cent, then 4 per cent from 1905 down to the War.[28] No general conclusion, of course, ought to be drawn from this one case. But the Company was in no way exceptional save in being so small (its railway among the shortest ever built as an independent concern) and therefore, one might suppose, so vulnerable. Its simple surviving records[29] show that it was possible still to build a railway in the 1890s, offering an adequate service to a lightly-populated district, and at the same time to make a modest profit.

With these considerations in mind, let us look at the growth of the rural system between 1876 and 1914.

Very few long lines were built. Apart from those that have already been mentioned, the most extensive new system was that of the London & South Western Company in Devon and north Cornwall. This comprised one line from Lydford to the south, opened in 1890 and giving the Company much improved access to Plymouth, and another striking

26. J. Hibbs, *History of British Bus Services* (1968), 43.
27. Mitchell and Deane, 230.
28. BRSM 1915, 60; K. E. Hartley, *The Easingwold Railway* (1970), 34.
29. North Yorkshire Record Office, Northallerton: ZSH.

westwards from Okehampton to Bude and Padstow, a total of 80 miles in all, completed in 1899. The Cornish line traversed a country that had hitherto been entirely untouched by railways except by the little Bodmin & Wadebridge line, which was not connected to the main system until 1888. The Padstow fisheries and the Delabole quarries offered profitable traffic, and the whole Cornish coast was beginning to be sought after by holiday-makers; but the line was a long thin thread, and a sparse train service always proved adequate for its needs.

One other system, of comparable length, was constructed through east Leicestershire, partly by the Great Northern and partly by that company and the London & North Western together. This ran from Market Harborough to Newark, with a branch to Leicester. It traversed good agricultural country – hunting country too, which caused its promoters some difficulty; but its prime purpose was to enable the two companies interested to compete with the Midland. The new line provided an alternative route from Leicester to the West Riding of Yorkshire, a matter of industrial importance to both districts, for their products were to some extent complementary. It also gave the Great Northern access, for the first time, to Northampton; and it enabled coal from Nottingham-shire and Derbyshire to be distributed more easily over the London & North Western system. It did something else too, establishing com-munication between Leicester and the other east Midlands towns and the resorts on the coast of Lincolnshire. Moreover, the northern part of the country served by this railway was rich in ironstone, little exploited as yet. There was thus a sound case to be made for this undertaking, on its merits, even though it traversed a very thinly-peopled countryside. But it was realised chiefly because it seemed to benefit the two companies competitively, against their long-established rival. The north-south line was opened in 1878–9, the Leicester branch in 1883. Their expectations were in part fulfilled. The ironstone was worked, on a large scale, and the coal traffic from Nottingham; the Leicester excursion traffic was heavy in summer-time. But the ordinary passenger business remained light – lighter still perhaps as the population of the district fell;[30] and the traffic in West Riding woollens was hardly valuable enough to compensate for that deficiency.

All the longer lines built in these years, even if they passed through agricultural country, were either competitive or had some expectation of industrial traffic. Thus the Bala-Festiniog line (22 miles long, opened in 1882–3) was aimed primarily at serving the Festiniog slate quarries. A new main line was built, piecemeal, across Norfolk from Lynn to Yar-mouth and Norwich in 1879–83. In 1893 it became part of a 'Midland &

30. VCH *Leics.* iii. 152.

Great Northern Joint Railway' which in the hands of those two companies challenged the Great Eastern's monopoly in East Anglia. The
Didcot Newbury & Southampton line, opened in 1882–91, was a *protégé*
of the Great Western Company, which desired access to Southampton,
encouraged by interests in the town that resented the London & South
Western's unassailed monopoly there. The Great Western made some
show of its patronage, eventually running through carriages between
Paddington and Southampton via Newbury (can anybody have used
them, to make the whole of that journey?) and others between Southampton and York. But, strolling over the empty Berkshire Downs and then
through rural Hampshire, the line was manifestly a loser.

So, rather similarly, was the Midland & South Western Junction
Railway, lying further west: a combination of two projects into a single
company, which retained its independence until 1922. As its name
suggests, its purpose was to strengthen the links between the Midland and
the London & South Western Companies. They were strong already
through their joint ownership of the Somerset & Dorset Railway, directed
towards Bournemouth; here the aim was to improve the communications
of Southampton. In this they were attacking the Great Western, which
controlled the long-established route from Southampton to Birmingham
and the North West, via Basingstoke and Oxford. With some reason, for
it was very circuitous. The new line, via Andover and Cheltenham,
offered Southampton a route to Birmingham 10 miles shorter than the
old one – though to Manchester the distance was almost exactly the same,
since beyond Birmingham the Midland Company's route, via Derby, was
circuitous too.

This railway did not pass into the joint ownership of the two large
companies, as the Somerset & Dorset had done. It struggled ahead on its
own, and the struggle was severe. It never became a profitable railway –
in 1913 expenditure was 72.4 per cent of traffic receipts;[31] it too ran
across much empty downland, offering little traffic, and the long-distance
services it carried were run on the account of its large neighbours, not on
its own. Still, it would be hard to contend that it should never have been
built.

Such were some of the longer rural lines – main lines, they might be
called – constructed in these years. Many others were undertaken, to fill
in some of the remaining gaps in the system: the line running from
Scarborough through Whitby to Middlesbrough, for instance (opened in
1883–5), the Great Eastern's from Wroxham to County School in Norfolk
(1879–82) and from Bury St Edmunds to Thetford (1876), the Brighton's

31. BRSM 1915, 263.

from Chichester to Midhurst (1881). The Worcester Bromyard & Leo-minster line represented a protracted effort, to which it would be hard to find a parallel. Promoted in 1861, it was opened in four instalments in 1874–97. So it took 36 years to complete this line, 24 miles long. It did little for the town of Bromyard when it got there in 1877, and much less than nothing for its shareholders.[32]

Lines of this kind were often constructed as 'light railways': railways built with a light track on which no axle load was to exceed 8 tons, and no train travel faster than 25 m.p.h. That was the definition laid down in the Regulation of Railways Act of 1868.[33] Very little use was then made of the device. Among the few lines that were built under the terms of that Act was the Culm Valley Railway to Hemyock in East Devon, which was opened in 1876. The Tramways Act of 1870 was also used occasionally for the same purpose. Britain therefore moved slowly in this matter, but she made one technical contribution to light railway develop-ment of great importance: the successful application of mechanical power to the narrow-gauge Festiniog Railway in North Wales, which was demonstrated in 1863–70. That achievement was studied by foreign visitors,[34] and it played a considerable part in their decisions to keep the cost of constructing railways down, in poor or sparsely-peopled country, by adopting a narrow gauge.

In the 1870s and 1880s the French went ahead with the building of light railways in rural districts, on the principle that they should be publicly financed, partly by the State and partly by local authorities. They were quickly followed by the Belgians, who developed the most successful general system of light railways to be found anywhere, with over 2,600 miles in operation by 1914.[35]

Nothing of the kind happened in Britain, and for that there was a good political reason. Outside the incorporated towns, local authorities had no revenue at their disposal until the creation of the county councils in 1888, and then few of them had any money to spare for new ventures like light railways. Nor indeed had they the power to spend money in this way, even if they desired to do so. But in 1896 a Light Railways Act was passed,[36] setting up a Commission with the duty of encouraging proposals for railways of this kind, and giving power to local authorities to work

32. See *Bromyard in Local History*, ed. J. G. Hillaby and E. D. Pearson (1970), 3, 107. When the Great Western took over the local company in 1888 its share-holders received 10s. in cash for each of their £10 shares: MacDermot, ii. 50.
33. 31 & 32 Vict. cap. 119, sect. 28.
34. Cf. J. I. C. Boyd, *The Festiniog Railway* (1956–9), i. 107–8.
35. W. J. K. Davies, *Light Railways* (1964), 111. This is the most useful modern work on the subject, and these paragraphs are much indebted to it.
36. 59 & 60 Vict. cap. 48.

light railways themselves or to assist them financially. Loans might also be made from the Treasury for the purpose, even outright grants in the case of railways designed to benefit agriculture or fisheries.

All this was impressive. But the results were generally disappointing in Great Britain – in Ireland the story of light railways is rather different. The first line to be completed on the conditions of 1896 was the Basingstoke & Alton, which was worked by the London & South Western Company as a minor branch. Some others that followed were entirely independent, or remained so for a time: the Lambourn Valley, opened in 1898 but taken over by the Great Western in 1905; in Shropshire the Cleobury Mortimer & Ditton Priors (1908), which continued on its own until 1923; the Nidd Valley, built to service the construction of a dam for Bradford Corporation but carrying passengers from its opening in 1907 until 1929. Several narrow-gauge lines were built in this way: the Vale of Rheidol, the Welshpool & Llanfair, and the Leek & Manifold in Staffordshire.

Some of the purely agricultural light railways and tramways proved useful, even profitable: the Wisbech & Upwell line and the Benwick branch did a good deal for the development of the fruit and vegetable traffic of Cambridgeshire. But very few of these undertakings could show any adequate return on the capital invested in them. Some were hopeless from the start. A pathetic example is the Mid-Suffolk Light Railway, authorised in 1899 as a system of lines in that district, which had suffered as severely as any in the country from the collapse of arable farming. The idea was not foolish. Communications there were totally inadequate, and the plan provided for modest lines to link up at four points with those of the Great Eastern Railway from Ipswich to Norwich and Lowestoft. Only a part of one of these lines was built, in effect a dead-end branch from Haughley to Laxfield. It began to carry freight in 1904, and passengers in 1908. By then it was bankrupt, and so it remained. It became part of the London & North Eastern Railway, and was eventually nationalised. Strangely, it remained open until 1952.

One last class of lines remains to be considered: branches designed to serve small towns hitherto left off the system, whether provided by main-line companies or by local undertakings, which they leased and worked. They were especially numerous in the south-west of England. Eight towns there were newly served in this way between 1877 and 1898: Abbotsbury, Helston, Highworth, Kingsbridge, Malmesbury, Princetown, Tetbury, and Yealmpton. In 1903 Lyme Regis secured a light railway from Axminster. In Kent, Hawkhurst, New Romney, and Westerham got branch lines in 1881–1903; Tenterden came to be served by the Kent & East Sussex Light Railway in 1903. In Wales Cardigan, promised a railway in 1862, achieved it at last in 1886. Such lines went on being built until the very eve of the First World War. The light railway from Lampeter to the little port of Aberayron was an attempt (intended to embrace New Quay also) to open up to holiday-makers the quiet southern shores of Cardigan Bay. It was opened in 1911. Next year came one in North Wales: the very steep branch up to Holywell in Flintshire. Holywell was – and is – a sizeable town, which, but for its situation, would doubtless have been served long before. And finally, in the flat countryside of Essex, came the little line from Elsenham to Thaxted, which began its unprosperous career in 1913.

A question will have occurred to anybody who has read so far and is at all acquainted with the problems and policies of railways today. Were any of the evidently unprofitable lines built during the Victorian age closed before 1914? How far did the companies try to disembarrass themselves of liabilities of this kind, and with what success?

A useful modern investigation enables that question to be answered, in part, at once.[37] It confines itself to lines on which passengers were conveyed: necessarily so, for the evidence is insufficient to allow those open only for goods traffic to be included. If we disregard very small sections of railway (under a mile in length) and those that were replaced by others running parallel to them but on another alignment, it appears that the total mileage closed to passengers in England and Wales before 1914 was about 400. Of that total, about 190 miles were reopened to public traffic at a subsequent date within this period. So that some 210 miles were altogether abandoned for passenger service: an infinitesimal fraction – 1.3 per cent – of the whole system. The longest of all these lines individually was the Cromford & High Peak Railway in Derbyshire (31 miles, $2\frac{1}{2}$ of which were re-used subsequently), closed in 1877. Only five of the other lines were 10 miles or more in length. They are so few, and therefore so curious, that they are worth listing:

Chesterford – Six Mile Bottom (Cambridgeshire)	1850
Stratford-upon-Avon – Shipston-on-Stour (Warwickshire)	1859
Washington – Pelton (Co. Durham)	1869
Towcester – Ravenstone Wood Junction (Northamptonshire)	1893
Denaby – Wrangbrook Junction (Yorkshire: West Riding)	1903

Some other more substantial stretches of line were closed to passengers,

37. M. D. Greville and J. Spence, *Closed Passenger Lines of Great Britain, 1827–1947* (2nd edn, 1974).

but subsequently reopened. The system (if it may be called that) of the Potteries Shrewsbury & North Wales Company (20 miles), one of the 'contractors' lines' of the 1860s, is a striking example. Part of it was shut down only four months after it was opened in 1866, and all of it was closed from 1880 to 1904. Further south on the Welsh Marches, the Golden Valley Railway (18¾ miles) was equally unfortunate in the 1880s and 1890s, though reopened by the Great Western in 1901.[38] In the English Midlands the East & West Junction Railway, running from Northamptonshire across to Stratford-upon-Avon (33 miles) was opened in 1871 and closed for nearly eight years (1877–85).

The amount of line closed down, then, whether temporarily or permanently, was insignificant. But that cannot imply that all other lines were profitable. Some that remained open were, very evidently, not. The Bishop's Castle Railway Company, for example, became insolvent in 1866 and remained so for the rest of its life until it was shut down at last in – amazing date! – 1935. Yet through all those years its trains still toddled to and fro between Bishop's Castle and Craven Arms. There were many other rural lines that plainly did not pay. Why then were they not shut down?

In the heyday of railway development the State had stipulated that once a railway had secured an Act of Parliament authorising its construction, it might not be abandoned without Parliament's leave.[39] The land on which the railway was built had been acquired by compulsory purchase, sometimes from reluctant vendors, and its coming had set up many expectations that ought not lightly to be disappointed. If a company had undertaken a losing speculation, that was its own affair and it must pay the price.

This measure was applied only to railways projected or begun, but not opened. The notion of closing down a railway because it had proved itself not to succeed lay beyond its scope; and it remained beyond the scope of thought of the age. The trifling examples that have been adduced were so unimportant that they disturbed nobody. So the legal power to close an existing line went almost unquestioned. It was once raised in Parliament, when in 1907 a Gloucestershire Member sought to forbid any railway to withdraw a service without the sanction of the Board of Trade; and then he was put off by a promise to investigate any case he might choose to bring before the Board's notice.[40]

38. It is entitled to posthumous consolation in having called forth what is probably the most perfect history of a British railway company yet written: C. L. Mowat, *The Golden Valley Railway* (1964).
39. Abandonment of Railways Act, 1850: 13 & 14 Vict. cap. 83.
40. *Hansard* 4th ser. 170 (1907) 1428.

It must, moreover, be remembered that even a weak branch line fed some traffic into the main line it joined. It could be what is called a loss-leader today. To abandon it might involve local unpopularity, which would do the company no good. And such a line might fall into the hands of a competitor. Better to keep control, even by maintaining it at some expense.

But above all one is bound to feel that railways of this kind remained open because no one examined, in strict accountancy, the losses they entailed. The matter deserves much more investigation than it has yet received.[41] It must be said straight away that the evidence is very insufficient. Taking the documentation as it now stands, in the British Transport Historical Records (and here we may consider them all, in Edinburgh as well as in London), one is often at a loss to comprehend how the Victorian railways managed their business. It is true that the greater part of their financial records have been lost, or destroyed. No doubt the officers had better means of assessing the profitability of the different parts of the system than we have, on the basis of the surviving documents alone. There are, for example, no long runs of the traffic books that must have been kept, on all well-conducted railways, at individual stations. It seems indeed that only two such sets of records survive, showing the receipts and working costs of every individual station on a large system: those for the Midland[42] and the Glasgow & South Western[43] Companies – in unison on this matter from 1876 onwards, anticipating an amalgamation that did not come.

A still more curious question lies beyond. In 1912–13 the Great Western Company set up a committee to investigate the cost of working four selected branches: those to Aberayron, Cirencester, Faringdon, and Lambourn. A good deal of paper work was done, but unfortunately the inquiry was never completed, and no conclusions can be drawn from it.[44] What is clear is that the Company – by this time a very well-managed one – did not have this information, even in documents that have now perished. One is left wondering, more than ever, how it assessed the profitability of its business.

There will be more to be said at a later stage on this matter, bringing into account also the policies of the railway companies in developing road services. Here we must simply leave the problem as one plain enough to us but discerned at the time imperfectly or not at all. Even in these last

41. A pioneer study was H. W. Parris, 'Northallerton to Hawes': *JTH* 2 (1955–6) 235–48.
42. BTHR RAIL 491 4/1–4.
43. SRO GSW/4/28.
44. BTHR RAIL 253 4/458.

years the railway system continued to grow, almost as it were by its own momentum. It was only in one part of the country that the system was extended in those years to anything like a coherent and effective plan, designed to promote a broad public interest. That was in London.

5 Greater London

The railway system, as it developed in Victorian London, was peculiarly complex; perhaps of necessity, for London was then the largest city in the world. This complexity is baffling, and defeated almost every endeavour at accurate description. Even the meticulous Baedeker, in directing his readers, made occasional mistakes in referring to it;[1] and if he got things wrong, who could expect to be right? One must sympathise with him today, and with all the other people who tried to describe it; still more with those who had to use the complicated services it afforded. But the modern student of its history enjoys one great advantage. It has now been recounted by two writers who thoroughly know their business, in a book that makes a contribution to the history of towns that is as unique as London itself.[2] For this reason it will be possible to treat London, in the present context, more briefly than the rest of the country. Here alone the whole groundwork of the study attempted in this volume has already been laid.

It seems desirable to consider the London railways separately not only because they were so complex, but for other reasons as well. The London system differed from that of the rest of the country in that it was, to some extent, deliberately planned. At least certain negative controls were established by Parliament at a fairly early date; and though they were breached once, in their main principles they stood, influencing the shape, and here and there the intensity, of development.

Finally, London was the pioneer of underground railways; and since

1. For example, he is mistaken in stating that the Great Northern & City Railway ran to the Bank (K. Baedeker, *London and its Environs*, 1905 edn, 65); when he directs his visitors to Dulwich, he fails to distinguish between the North and West stations (421); he misplaces the Blackheath Tunnel on the North Kent line (452).
2. T. C. Barker and M. Robbins, *History of London Transport* (2 vols, 1963–74).

railways of that kind are different from others, it is convenient to treat them together, and at least in part in isolation.

So this chapter confines itself to Greater London. That expression came to be generally accepted in the years we are concerned with as denoting the City of London, together with the Metropolitan Police District, which comprised all parishes of which the whole was within 15 miles, or any part within 12 miles of Charing Cross. The City proper was immemorially ancient; the District was created in 1839, and its boundaries remained unaltered until 1947. When the London County Council was set up in 1888, it accepted this definition of Greater London. So did the Royal Commission of 1903. It will be convenient to do the same here. In 1841 its population was $2\frac{1}{4}$ million – that is, one seventh of the population of England and Wales; in 1911, $7\frac{1}{4}$ million, or one fifth.

Although plans were brought forward in 1824–5 for trunk railways leading out of London – to York, for example, to Birmingham and Dover – they were not carried far enough to require any careful examination of the special problems involved in entering or traversing the capital itself. When the business was taken up again in 1832–3, the promoters of the London & Birmingham and Great Western railways adopted a simple solution by stopping their lines on the very edge of the built-up area. Euston Square, intersected by the New Road, had been in course of development since about 1805; houses were still being erected there half a century later.[3] To the north of it lay open fields, and it was in them that the Birmingham Company's station was built; but (as Dickens shows us in *Dombey and Son*) the passage of the railway through Camden Town involved substantial demolition of houses. The Great Western originally intended to make a junction with the London & Birmingham line at Kensal Green and so run its trains into the same terminus at Euston Square; but that proving impracticable, it erected its station at Paddington, a suburban village just then beginning to grow into a part of the great city.

The first railway that can truly be said to have entered London was the London & Greenwich, authorised in 1833, opened as far as Deptford in 1836 and completed two years later. This had its terminus close to the south end of London Bridge, and its passage, on a continuous viaduct nearly 4 miles long, involved the demolition of a large number of close-packed and squalid houses.[4] It is the first example to be seen anywhere on

3. Sir J. Summerson, *Georgian London* (1945), 156, 176. The New Road is represented today by the Marylebone, Euston, and Pentonville Roads.
4. F. Sheppard, *London 1808–70* (1971), 124–5.

a large scale of a railway acting, in its construction, as a destroyer of slums. The London & Greenwich Railway, indeed, attempted something more. It laid down roads on either side of its viaduct. One of these was to serve as a promenade, the other to give access to the arches, which were intended to form dwellings and warehouses. Very few residents were found to occupy them, however, and they were let in the end for commercial purposes alone.[5] The Greenwich Company's viaduct was used also from 1839 onwards by the trains of the London & Croydon Railway, joined presently by others, of the London & Brighton and of the South Eastern, branching out of the Brighton line at Redhill for Dover. The viaduct had to be widened, and London Bridge station extended. This was the beginning of a process that led eventually to a set of 11 or 12 tracks, running into a station in three parts, side by side but distinct, having a total of 21 platforms.

The railway thus reached Southwark. But when it tried to penetrate into the City proper, north of the river, it met with a stiff resistance. The London & Blackwall Railway, incorporated in 1836 to build a line to the East and West India Docks, was refused permission to enter the City and compelled to establish its first terminus at the Minories, immediately outside the boundary. The ostensible reason for the Common Council's opposition was its dislike of the noise and dirt that the trains would occasion; the real reason the fear of benefiting the privately-owned docks at the expense of its Pool of London. This policy could not be maintained, however. At a second attempt the Company succeeded, gaining Parliament's sanction to taking its line on from the Minories to Fenchurch Street – an extension only a third of a mile long, built at the unexampled cost of £250,000.[6]

Here then an exception to the City's rule was made. But it remained for some time the only one. The Eastern Counties Railway ran into London no further than Shoreditch – though it soon tried to pretend something different by renaming its terminus Bishopsgate, and it made a limited use of Fenchurch Street by arrangement with the Blackwall Company. The London & Southampton stopped further out, at Nine Elms in Battersea, whence steamers took passengers down the river to two wharves, one at Hungerford Market, close to Charing Cross, the other not far from Cannon Street.[7] That arrangement proving unpopular, the Company purchased 10 acres of land near the south end of Waterloo Bridge in 1844 and carried its line into a station there in 1848. The 2-mile extension obliterated 700 houses. It was built from the outset with four

5. R. H. G. Thomas, *London's First Railway* (1972), 32–4.
6. Sheppard, *op. cit.*, 128; *JTH* 1 (1953–4) 163–4.
7. Williams LSWR, i. 36, 158–9.

tracks so that, as the Company's chairman said, 'we may not only have ample means of conducting our traffic, be it what it may, but all ability to let others come and hire.'[8] It was an intelligent prevision; but the four tracks have had to grow today into nine.

In terms of railway construction, the Mania of 1844–7 had curiously little effect on London. One new trunk railway arrived, the Great Northern, in 1850–2; the North London line was built, making its transverse sweep from the north-west to the Docks.[9] But those, and the Waterloo extension, are all the direct consequences that are assignable in London to the feverish activity of the 1840s in railway promotion.

This is largely to be accounted for by the deliberations of a Royal Commission, appointed in 1846, which advised Parliament to prevent the extension of railways into central London. The Commission was a small one of five members, well selected, comprising two very able young men, future viceroys of India (Canning and Dalhousie); an experienced politician, J. C. Herries; the current Lord Mayor of London; and Sir Frederic Smith of the Royal Engineers (cf. p. 31). No doubt in order to hasten and ease its deliberations, its brief was narrowly restricted, in its terms of reference and in the instructions it received from Peel's Government. It was to confine its attention to an area precisely determined: a rough rectangle formed by what we now call the Marylebone and Euston Roads, the City Road, Finsbury Square, Bishopsgate Street, London Bridge, Borough High Street, Vauxhall Bridge, Grosvenor Gardens, and Park Lane. What railways, if any, should be allowed to penetrate this area? It was a leading question, and the Commission came up with the expected answer: north of the river, none; on the south bank one – the Waterloo extension sanctioned in the previous year.[10]

The Commissioners had no doubt about making this sharp distinction between the northern and southern parts of the capital. Property on the south bank of the river was less valuable; no great street improvements had been effected there, which railways would damage, nor were there any in hand; the streets themselves were less busy, and could therefore accommodate the additional traffic arising from railway stations. These were negative arguments. There was one more that was positive: 'those

8. *Ibid.*, i. 161.
9. This company was incorporated in 1846 as the East & West India Docks & Birmingham Junction Railway, to run from the Birmingham line at Camden Town through Canonbury, Hackney, and Bow to the Docks; it changed its title to North London Railway in 1853.
10. Provision was also made for the possibility of extending this line to London Bridge, and for the construction of one from the South Eastern's 'West End Terminus' at Bricklayer's Arms (which had been opened in 1844) to join it: PP 1846 xvii. 23.

parts of Surrey and Kent which are within a short distance of London are generally more thickly inhabited by persons having occupations in London, and are more frequented for occasional relaxation than the corresponding parts of Essex, Middlesex, and Hertfordshire.'[11]

The Commission took evidence from a wide range of people concerned in railway promotion: among engineers Vignoles, Robert Stephenson, and Locke; George Hudson; William Tite, very experienced as a valuer of land and now known as the architect of the new Royal Exchange; Thomas Page, the engineer advocating a Thames Embankment; carriers, such as Chaplin, Horne, and Baxendale; Charles Pearson, Solicitor to the Corporation, who appeared for a particular purpose; military experts; and a number of less well-known people who had views to put forward of their own, or axes to grind. The Commission did not much consider the social consequences of railway building. But it did observe that the advantages of extending railways nearer to the centre of London had been exaggerated, that they did not produce an improvement in the value of residential property closely adjacent to them, and that the building of the Eastern Counties Railway and the extension of the London & Blackwall to Fenchurch Street had impeded street improvement.[12] One witness, the Rev. Timothy Gibson, Rector of Bethnal Green, said that two or three streets close to his church had been built 'for the accommodation of persons who have been removed by the railway', though he added that these people had enjoyed no priority in the allocation of houses there, and another witness virtually denied that there was any relationship between the two things, attributing the development to 'the general rage for speculation in building'.[13] Nobody else was seriously concerned on this occasion with the physical consequences of railway construction, except Pearson, who put forward a plan for erecting a central terminus, near Farringdon Street, to serve all the northern trunk lines and at the same time to relieve overcrowding by providing a quick suburban service to a housing estate to be built in conjunction with it.[14] The Commissioners rejected the arguments in favour of a central terminus put forward both by him and by Page. They thought the benefits it would bring were small, compared to the cost and upheaval it would entail. But if Pearson was defeated, he did not give up.

Such was the Commissioners' advice: no penetration to be allowed of central London north of the river; no new bridges; limited extension of railways in the south; and – a sensible supplement – support for a ring

11. *Ibid.*, 6.
12. *Ibid.*, 7, 11.
13. *Ibid.*, 99, 160.
14. *Ibid.*, 15, 165–74, 201–8.

railway, in some form, to provide links between the different systems, primarily for goods traffic but available also for other purposes in an emergency. This was a recommendation designed partly to please the soldiers, who thought in terms of internal security and defence against invasion.

So what may be called 'the London Quadrilateral' was established in 1846, by the Government fortified by the Commissioners' conclusions. No body of subscribers to any of the plans of 1846 felt sufficiently aggrieved to challenge this policy with persistence. It was examined again in the 1860s, and reaffirmed. It was not seriously questioned until two generations later, when the conditions had become quite different.

The indirect consequences of the Mania for London were profound. The skeleton of the national system that had appeared in 1830–41 was now clad in ample flesh. With few important exceptions, all the chief new lines that came into existence in 1847–52 served to bring traffic into or out of London: not exclusively, not even perhaps primarily, but still to important effect. In these years London began to be supplied with coal in substantial measure by railway conveyance, and with many of its other most necessary consumable goods. As for the influx of passengers that the developing system brought, that was evident, though no effort was ever made in the nineteenth century to compute it. The movement of passengers became, for a short time, spectacular: in the summer of 1851, when the Great Exhibition was open. It was then a commonplace to observe that the teeming horde who converged upon Hyde Park could not possibly have been seen but for the railways. To some people indeed, the success of the Exhibition appeared to be almost the railways' doing.

The extension of railways towards the centre of London, bridging streets and demolishing houses, was thus prohibited in 1846. There was, however, one other way in which that extension could be achieved: by putting the lines underground. The London & Birmingham Company had considered that idea in the 1830s when planning to carry its line on from Euston to the Thames. But nothing had yet been done in this way. The chief obstacle was not a technical one; it was legal. Anybody who proposed to tunnel under a building was obliged to purchase it outright, and that made a substantial length of railway of this sort prohibitively expensive unless it could run beneath streets, squares, or open spaces.

When in 1850 the arrival of the Great Northern Railway at King's Cross was imminent, two schemes for underground railways, converging at that point, were put forward: one running beneath the New Road from Bayswater, the other down the Fleet Valley to Holborn, to a large terminal station designed to accommodate both broad- and narrow-gauge trains. The character of the two plans was different. The first was a money-making venture, which incidentally provided the means of affording relief to the New Road, overcrowded with traffic. The second was in part a measure of civic improvement, designed to help towards the replanning of the festering district through which it passed, with the Fleet River as a sewer (partly open), many appalling slum dwellings, and Smithfield Market with its attendant slaughter-houses. Charles Pearson was a driving force behind this second project, together with William Malins, Chairman of the City Commission of Sewers. The first was backed by solicitors of another kind, William Burchell and John Parson, and by the great contracting partnership of Peto & Betts.

When the two projects came before Parliament in 1853, the first succeeded unopposed, to emerge under a new title as the North Metropolitan Railway. The second however failed, from financial weakness. The City Corporation declined to support its Bill because the three main-line railway companies that had been expected to favour it – the Great Western, London & North Western, and Great Northern – were not prepared to back it with capital, and the Government would give no assistance either.

The North Metropolitan was therefore left successful but high and dry, with an eastern terminus at King's Cross. Its promoters then adroitly enlarged their plans, in two ways: taking their line a little further west, and so linking it with the Great Western Railway; and continuing it eastwards along the route of the unsuccessful scheme to Farringdon Street and thence to St Martin's-le-Grand, to terminate in the very basement of the General Post Office. The central terminus for main-line trains was now dropped. In this form, after encountering still a strong opposition, the new plan was authorised by Parliament, running as far as Farringdon Street only, in 1854. It was then renamed the Metropolitan Railway.

The company encountered great difficulty in raising the £1 million of capital that was required. The Crimean War had begun, and soon after it was ended came the financial crisis of 1857. For a time it looked as if the plan would have to be abandoned, but with persistence and the financial aid at last of the Corporation (which subscribed for shares to the value of £200,000) it was possible to begin construction in the autumn of 1859. Many of the difficulties encountered were new to engineers, and the work took longer to finish than had been expected. It was opened for public traffic from Paddington to Farringdon Street on 10 January 1863.[15]

15. The promotion and building of the Metropolitan Railway are clearly described in Barker and Robbins, i. 99–118.

This was the first of all urban underground railways, and as such it has its place in world history. But it is important for other reasons too. The Corporation's large investment in it was highly unusual, disapproved of indeed by many of its own members: a resolution that it 'cannot with propriety embark in any railway scheme' had been defeated by a majority of one in 1852.[16] Few British municipalities were then willing – or indeed could then afford – to act in this way; though it may be added that the decision proved a shrewd one, for the Corporation presently sold its shares to advantage. The railway also offered a major contribution to suburban development. The Great Western Company was disadvantaged by the remoteness of its terminus at Paddington – nearly 3 miles from Charing Cross, more than 4 from the Bank. It was prohibited from any thoughts of extending its own line towards the centre of London by the decision of 1846. The Metropolitan offered it the chance to remedy this great defect, to run trains through from its own system to the City. The Great Western could almost regard the Metropolitan as an appanage, an eastward extension of its own. Looking at the matter in that light, it had subscribed £185,000 towards its capital, and agreed to work the new line.

In practice, things turned out differently. The two companies soon quarrelled, and the Metropolitan was obliged first to hire rolling stock and locomotives from the Great Northern and North Western Companies, and then to find them itself. Before long it was reconciled to the Great Western, but not brought to be subservient to it in any degree. Through trains did run across it from stations as far out as Windsor, and eventually from much further out still.[17] But nothing developed that could be called an intensive service, and the Great Western line generated suburban traffic slowly. That was due in part to the peculiar relationship of these two companies, as well as to the complication of the broad gauge. For the Great Western it was an opportunity missed. From 1858 onwards – the year in which the Metropolitan project really began to get off the ground – a new interest in the promotion of railways into London became apparent.

Another terminal station, Victoria, was authorised in that year, to which the East Kent (shortly to become the London Chatham & Dover) Company was granted access. In 1859 the South Eastern secured powers, through a subsidiary company, to extend its line from London Bridge over the Thames to Charing Cross – a clear invasion of the Quadrilateral of 1846. And then, with the session of 1860, there began a furious promotion of new railways, what may be called a 'London Mania'. Its

16. City of London Records Office: Common Council Minutes, 4, 11 March 1852, pp. 67, 71.
17. T. B. Peacock, *Great Western London Suburban Services* (1970), 39.

growth and decline can be indicated in terms of the railway Bills covering 'the Metropolis and Suburbs' that had to be considered by Parliament:[18]

TABLE 5. LONDON RAILWAY BILLS, 1860–9

Year	Number of Bills	Length of proposed lines
1860	22	72 miles
1861	23	67
1862	15	78
1863	28	123
1864	31	172
1865	25	91
1866	42	243
1867	10	12
1868	11	6
1869	12	18
	219	882

The startling fall in 1867 and 1868 was primarily due to the financial crisis of 1866, which cut back all railway promotion throughout the country. But there was another contributory cause. In 1867–9 a total of 109 miles of tramways were proposed. A potential competitor to the railways, for capital and for business, was beginning to appear.

In the 1860s, as in the 1840s, Parliament made some effort to control all this projection. The House of Lords appointed a Committee in 1863, which investigated the business laboriously;[19] the two Houses had a Joint Committee for the purpose in the following year.[20] They confirmed and reasserted their predecessors' doctrine that railways ought not to be allowed to penetrate central London, unless they ran underground; the Quadrilateral was still to be respected. But that reaffirmation represented, at least in part, a shutting of the stable door after the horse had been stolen; for in 1858–60 Parliament had sanctioned railways crossing the river, not only the lines to the new Victoria and Charing Cross stations, but also the London Chatham & Dover Company's extension right along the western edge of the City from Blackfriars and over Ludgate Hill to join the Metropolitan at Farringdon Street. This last plan was the most important breach of the Quadrilateral ever accepted. The chief argument in its favour was that it would provide a direct link

18. Source: *Reports of House of Commons General Committees on Railway and Canal Bills* (PP, annually).
19. PP 1863, viii. 1–203.
20. PP 1864, xi. 241–336.

between the northern and southern railway systems, which would be valuable for long-distance passenger and freight traffic and even more for suburban trains, taking travellers clear of the streets. On the other hand it involved a shocking disfigurement. A severe but not unjust critic remarked that its passage over Ludgate Hill 'has utterly spoiled one of the finest street views in the metropolis; and is one of the most unsightly objects ever constructed, in any such situation, anywhere in the world'.[21] There was indeed a furious outcry at all this railway promotion. 'St Paul's had best be converted into a terminus', said *Punch.* 'What else will it be fit for when every railway runs right into London?'[22] No other lines were allowed to offend like this, however; and at least those who wished to construct elevated railways in London – some of them came forward at this time[23] – never got their way.

A good deal of this projection was for railways to run underground: extensions of the Metropolitan, lines that were complementary to it, others that were intended to be its rivals. The Metropolitan was now permitted to extend eastwards to Moorgate Street, and in a southerly direction through Bayswater and Kensington to Brompton – or South Kensington, as it soon came to be more generally called. Two other allied companies built lines in conjunction with it, from Baker Street to Swiss Cottage, from Paddington to Hammersmith. A third, the Metropolitan District,[24] carried the line on from Brompton to Victoria and West-minster and thence alongside the river, underneath the new Embankment and Queen Victoria Street to Blackfriars and Mansion House. All this work was completed in 1865–70. The Paddington-Mansion House section was extravagantly dear (the 7 miles costing over £7 million), partly from the very nature of its construction and partly from the numerous special restrictions laid upon the work by Parliament.[25] Together, these lines made a kind of horseshoe; but already, under the influence of John Fowler, the engineer of them all, the notion of forming a circle by linking up the eastern ends had come to be accepted. The Lords' Committee approved it, liking this provision for an 'Inner Circuit' that would serve all the terminal stations then established north of the river. The Metropolitan Company moved in this direction by extending its line to Aldgate in 1875–6, taking in on the way the Great Eastern's new station at Liverpool Street; but the gap between Aldgate

21. J. R. Wilson, *Imperial Gazetteer* (?1869), 167.
22. *Punch* 44 (1863) 184; cf. also *ibid.* 45 (1863) 146.
23. PP 1863, viii. 88, 106, 154.
24. A railway always known colloquially as the District, and referred to by that title here.
25. For a sample of them cf. *Victorian City*, i. 283.

and Mansion House, burrowing under some of the most expensive property in Britain, took eight more years to complete. The Circle became a reality at last in October 1884.

The delay in finishing it was due largely to the cost of the work, but also to the quarrelling of the two companies involved, which was incessant, even though the final stretch was built by them both jointly. When the line was opened, there was at first chaos, and traffic from time to time came to a complete standstill.[26] A circular service presents from its nature certain special difficulties in operation; but they were much aggravated because, by this time, both the Metropolitan and the District companies were feeding on to the Circle traffic from extensions of their own system.[27] The Metropolitan's line to Swiss Cottage was being extended, by stages, to Harrow; the District and its connections reached out to Putney, Richmond, Hounslow, and Ealing. The Metropolitan had also to accommodate traffic from the Great Northern and the Midland systems, brought down to it at King's Cross and then going on eastwards. In this case there were four tracks available, for the 'widened lines' had been put in for this purpose in 1868. Everywhere else on the Circle, except in three or four stations and eventually between South Kensington and Gloucester Road, there were two tracks only. Nor was the service confined to passenger trains. Freight trains worked over the northern side of it too. These did not belong to the owning company, which had scarcely any, but to the main-line railways, running to the new Smithfield Market (the Great Western got its own station there, underneath the Market itself, in 1869) and between the northern railways and the southern, over the Chatham's line across Ludgate Hill.[28] Remembering that all this traffic – some 900 trains a day – was worked by steam locomotives and nearly all of it in tunnels, we can only marvel that the service was maintained, with general regularity. More wonderful still, it was maintained in safety, for not a single passenger was killed in an accident on the Circle through all the years when it was operated by steam.[29] That was a triumph.

The Metropolitan and the District systems of the Victorian age seem crude to us because of their steam traction. They did however effect a great improvement in urban transport. Why then did these lines not multiply? The plans of the 1860s had included a number for underground

26. Barker and Robbins, i. 232–5.
27. *Ibid.*, i. 118.
28. This was clean contrary to Fowler's original idea: 'You could not introduce suburban through trains upon the inner circuit without destroying its great value', he said to the Committee of 1864: PP 1864, xi. 296.
29. Barker and Robbins, i. 118.

railways. One from Euston to Charing Cross was sanctioned in 1864, and again seven years later, but it was not realised. Another, the Waterloo & Whitehall Railway for a line under the Thames, was not only sanctioned but in substantial measure built. A third, the Tower Subway, was carried through to completion; but it worked as a railway for only three months.[30] There was a common reason for the failure of all these undertakings. It was financial.

The Metropolitan had started life as a good investment, paying 7 per cent on its Ordinary shares in 1864–8. By 1870 that dividend had been halved. It recovered to 5 per cent in 1879–84. But that was a St Martin's summer; thereafter it did less well, and in the early years of the twentieth century very much worse. As for the District, it never paid a dividend on its Ordinary shares at all. A comparison with the London General Omnibus Company was not flattering, in financial terms, to the railways. Its dividends also fell, when it lost traffic to their competition in 1867–8; but it then lowered fares and, with increased efficiency of management, recovered, to pay an average of 8 per cent in 1868–75.[31] Although the underground railways might confer great benefits on London, they were not attractive to investors. This defect remained, and became glaringly obvious in the huge development that followed. In the end, the capital was found for that in some far-distant places.

The realisation of the 'Inner Circuit', after a 20-years' struggle, was by no means the only important long-term consequence of the London Mania. Let us now consider the railways that entered the capital above ground.

Some new lines of importance were promoted in the early 1860s and built forthwith. Besides those that have been mentioned we must note, for example, the South London line, from Bermondsey to Battersea, via Peckham and Brixton; the Brighton Company's new line from Croydon to Balham and its independent approach to Victoria from Clapham Junction; the extensions of the North London and the Great Eastern Companies into terminal stations on Broad Street and Liverpool Street, as well as the Great Eastern's new lines to Edmonton and Enfield; the Great Northern's branches, fanning out to Edgware, Barnet, and Hertford; the East London Railway, running to New Cross through the old Thames Tunnel. These lines were all open to traffic before 1875. By that time the railway system of inner London, as we know it today, was (except for the tubes) virtually complete.

30. C. E. Lee in *Transactions of the Newcomen Society* 43 (1970–1) 41–52.
31. Barker and Robbins, i. 166, 175–7.

With the opening of Holborn Viaduct and Liverpool Street stations in 1874–5, the capital had 14 terminals:[32] a provision quite unique. All the efforts of Charles Pearson and others to secure a great central station – a Grand Union, such as the Americans were beginning to build, a *Hauptbahnhof* on the German model – had failed.[33] They were not revived, except in passing discussion, again. Instead, London decided to live with this untidy system, the product of private enterprise, at once of Parliamentary control and of the resistance to it. Already in 1875 most of the terminal stations were linked by the underground railways, though the full benefit of that communication was not realised until the completion of the Inner Circle nine years later. By that time only two of the stations lying north of the river were not served in this way: Fenchurch Street (a confusing five-minutes' walk from the Underground station at Mark Lane) and Holborn Viaduct – but then all the trains into and out of that station stopped at St Paul's (now Blackfriars), which had a station of its own on the Circle. South of the river, however, it was different. Neither London Bridge nor Waterloo stood on the Circle line, or close to it; and that was a serious matter, for they were two of the busiest stations of all.

The river crossing for long-distance through traffic furnished by the Metropolitan line and the Chatham Company's bridge at Blackfriars was paralleled by another, higher up the river: the West London Extension Railway from Kensington, running over a bridge at Chelsea to Clapham Junction, opened in 1863. This was a southward continuation of the West London Railway, authorised in 1836 to link the London & Birmingham to the Kensington Canal. It had been opened, after much difficulty, in 1843, carried passengers for six months in the following year, and was then leased in 1845 to the Birmingham and Great Western Companies jointly. The railway was an object of endless fun to *Punch* in its early days.[34] With the building of the Extension it became a useful element in the railway system of London, providing a through route from the Great Western, the London & North Western (and subsequently the Midland) railways to all the lines in the south of England.

Another crossing of the river became available when the Thames Tunnel, running from Wapping to Rotherhithe, was adapted to take the trains of the East London Railway in 1865. This came to provide a

---

32. Fifteen if Baker Street is included, a development of the Metropolitan station, opened in 1863.
33. I have discussed this matter in *Victorian City*, i. 281–3.
34. The paper first noticed it satirically in 1844 (*Punch* 6: 105, 251); the last reference to it that I have noted there is in 1854 (*Punch* 27: 92).

through route from the Great Eastern at Shoreditch to the South Eastern and Brighton lines at New Cross. In 1884 a junction was put in at Whitechapel, which enabled through services to be operated from the Metropolitan and District systems.[35]

There came thus to be three railway routes crossing the Thames in London, at Battersea, Blackfriars, and Wapping. There was never a fourth. Higher up, in outer London, there were other bridges, at Putney, Barnes, Kew, and Richmond; lower down ferries, providing some railway connections, at Woolwich and Gravesend. The services afforded on the lines crossing the river varied in character, and changed with the years. The West London line was always most valuable as a carrier of freight. The Blackfriars line abounded in business of all kinds. Numerous freight trains ran over it, particularly at night; frequent passenger trains by day from the northern suburbs to the southern lines, though they were on their way out by 1914. This route also carried a number of long-distance trains, coming off the Midland and the Great Northern lines, to Dover and the Kent coastal resorts: either complete trains or through carriages, detached at Kentish Town or Finsbury Park. It seems strange, looking back, that none of these services attained any lasting popularity. One might have supposed that the traveller from the North to the Continent, or the holiday-maker, would have found them a boon, saving all the scurry and noise of battling across London by cab or bus, the expense of staying in an hotel. But the Victorians thought otherwise. Why?

Some answers can be given. A long journey from the Midlands or the North was, in the nineteenth century, fatiguing, especially for the elderly or for invalids and for children. It must have been better for family parties, if they could afford it, to break their journey in London. Where travellers to the Continent were concerned, most of the principal services departed too early to receive connections from northern towns, which had started out at any reasonable hour.[36] These through services could therefore only link up with the afternoon boats to Calais and Ostend. It was the same in the opposite direction. The main services arrived at the English ports too late in the day to allow convenient connections to be made for places far beyond London.

No doubt the railway companies would have preferred to carry passengers crossing London by means of their own trains. But seeing that so many of their customers did not take to that arrangement, they offered – or helped others to offer – alternatives. They ran horse-buses them-

35. Cf. C. E. Lee, *The East London Line and the Thames Tunnel* (1976).
36. This was explained by the South Eastern Manager, C. W. Eborall, to the Lords' Committee of 1863: PP 1863, viii. 96.

selves from the northern terminal stations to Charing Cross and Water-loo, free of charge to passengers who were booked through London.[37] And most of them maintained hotels, into which these travellers might be tempted.

When all this has been said, the failure to develop these services by Blackfriars remains something of a puzzle. The ultimate explanation must surely lie in the irresistible attractions that London afforded, even to travellers passing through it on their way somewhere else.

A survey of Greater London as a whole shows that by the mid-1870s not many houses were more than 20 minutes' walk from a railway station, except in southern Islington and in the district south of the Old Kent Road. Further out, you would not easily find any place within the Metropolitan Police District where a station was as much as three miles away. There was, however, one sector of the District – and one only – where railways were sparse: the north-western. Until 1867 that tract of country was served solely by two main lines, the Great Northern and the London & North Western, spaced very widely apart. Then the Great Northern thrust a branch across through Finchley to Edgware, and in 1868 the Midland opened another main line, crossing that at Mill Hill and running down through Hendon to St Pancras. Otherwise, however, this whole substantial tract of Middlesex remained unserved until 1880–7, when the Metropolitan opened its line, first to Harrow and then on to Pinner and Rickmansworth. Some villages here, like Harefield and Ruislip – or, even nearer to London, Northolt – remained totally secluded, scarcely touched one might say by the Victorian age.[38]

Everywhere else it was different. The development of the 1860s had produced not only the important lines that have been mentioned, but many others, small cross-lines and branches intended to act as har-bingers of suburban development: to Barnet and Chingford, to Addis-combe and Shepperton, from Tooting westwards by two routes to Wimbledon. In some of these places, though not in all, the expected happened. 'About the Barnet station has sprung up within the last few years', we are told in 1876, 'one of those new half-finished railway villages which we have come to look on as almost a necessary adjunct to every station within a moderate distance of London.'[39] Those are the words of a highly cultivated observer, James Thorne, who watched the whole process carefully, with a good deal of distaste. Again and again he

37. Barker and Robbins, i. 262.
38. M. Robbins, *Middlesex* (1953), 275, 314–15, 322–3.
39. J. Thorne, *The Environs of London* (1876), 31.

notes it: from Hendon to Buckhurst Hill, from Mottingham to Reigate[40] – all these places have been made 'the prey of the railway engineer, speculative builder, and "Conservative" and "Commonwealth" building societies'.[41]

But the last word should not rest with Thorne. There will be more to say about suburbs in the succeeding volume of this work. Even here, however, in passing it should be pointed out that their development often struck other people as commendable. We can still appreciate that, here and there, a century later. If Brixton no longer 'possesses all the appliances of an agreeable suburb', as it seemed to do in the Mid-Victorian age,[42] other places have been more fortunate in ways that remain evident still. Blackheath remains a study in development of this kind, a settlement slowly growing in the eighteenth century but jerked forward into something quite different in the generation following the opening of the North Kent Railway in 1849. Bedford Park is a special case, perhaps, a showpiece planned and laid out in 1875–8. But it would have made no sense at all without the prior arrival of the railway in 1869, running from Richmond to Hammersmith, and so conveniently into London.[43] Consider for a moment where some of the eminent Victorians lived, men and women who valued the purer air, out of the smoke of the city, yet who needed easy access to and from London on their business. Trollope established himself at Waltham Cross, Mill and Samuel Smiles at Blackheath, Blackmore at Teddington, Matthew Arnold and Gilbert at Harrow. In every instance, convenient access to a railway must have helped to determine their choice. It was the same too for more ordinary folk, living in small houses – those brick terraces and pairs, semidetached, so characteristic of the Victorian age. Their first establishment and multiplication, radiating out from focal points on the railway, can still, here and there, be observed quite clearly: at Bowes Park, for example, on the slope of the Northern Heights, at Walthamstow (with the aid of an excellent local museum), at Camberwell by anyone who will take a good map and Professor Dyos's book in his hand.[44]

The calculations of railway companies and speculative builders did not always prove right, however. The Midland Railway's line from Cricklewood to Acton, opened in 1868 to carry freight traffic down to the London & South Western system, received a passenger service in 1875, but though

40. *Ibid.*, 64, 336–7, 442, 481, 485.
41. *Ibid.*, 78.
42. Wilson, *op. cit.*, 281.
43. More conveniently still in 1877, when the District Railway began to run through trains from Richmond to Mansion House: Barker and Robbins, i. 209.
44. H. J. Dyos, *Victorian Suburb* (1961).

that was accompanied by the building of some houses near the station that was opened at Stonebridge Park, no other development took place at all, and the service, having been tried in various forms, was entirely withdrawn in 1902.[45]

Except in the north-western quarter that has been mentioned, the London railway system grew very dense in 1855–75. But not, in the same measure, convenient. 'It would be decidedly a triumph of ingenuity so to construct an equal number of railways as to give less practical accommodation than is given at present.'[46] That judgment on the London system was echoed by many of those who used it.

If we look closely at its working we shall find that it combined great merits – some of them lost now – with great deficiencies. It must, in the first place, be seen historically. It effected a vast, an overwhelming improvement on all that had gone before. Its trains provided communication at least twice as rapid as any that had been previously available. When we are caught in a traffic block today and halted for two or three minutes we curse the motor vehicle and the congestion it has brought. But traffic congestion was on the whole a good deal worse in the Mid-Victorian age, in a much smaller London with far fewer vehicles on the streets. Between 1850 and 1863 the number of carriages was thought to have increased from 13,000 to 20,000. Careful observation showed that cabs averaged 5–6 m.p.h. through the City, buses about 4 – only a little above walking pace.[47] The railway did not cure street congestion; at some points – outside its own main stations, for instance – it made things worse. But it offered many palliatives. If the underground lines are the most obvious, conventional railways made their contribution too. The business man who wished to get quickly from Charing Cross into the City, avoiding the evilly-congested Strand and Fleet Street, had at his disposal a service running every few minutes on the South Eastern Railway to Cannon Street. Here is the explanation, and the value, of those cross-London services that look so quaint and pointless now and have fallen almost entirely into disuse. Many of them were carried over Ludgate Hill, from the northern lines to the southern: from Enfield and Hendon to Victoria, for example, from Finsbury Park to Woolwich. Others went over the West London line, such as that from Willesden to Croydon. The Circle completed in 1884 was always called the Inner Circle. There was also a Middle Circle, from Moorgate Street via Hammer-

45. *Transactions of the London and Middlesex Archaeological Society* 26 (1975) 312–14.
46. *Dickens's Dictionary of London, 1879*, 214.
47. PP 1864, xi. 329–30.

smith to Mansion House; and an Outer Circle, from Broad Street to Mansion House by the North London line and Willesden.[48] Neither of these formed a true circle; both were discontinuous at the eastern end. They served a useful purpose, taking passengers at frequent intervals from one part of London to another, avoiding the streets. Again, here is one of the reasons why it seemed so great an advantage to pour traffic from outlying places on to the Metropolitan and District systems. At one time or another before 1914, through trains were run on to the underground lines from Oxford and Shoeburyness, over 100 miles apart. It was no mean attraction for the railways to be able to offer direct travel to a station in central London from which it was only a short walk to a place of business, so saving all the delays experienced in cabs and buses.

Thinking ourselves back into that world, we are apt to feel that the stench and murk of the underground railways must have made them almost intolerable. At times they did, and people complained of them loudly. There was a chemist who sold a special 'Metropolitan Mixture' to passengers who coughed and found themselves short of breath from travelling on the line.[49] *The Times* greeted the completion of the Inner Circle with a leader in which it remarked that 'a journey from King's Cross to Baker Street is a form of mild torture which no person would undergo if he could conveniently help it'.[50] By 1897 things had become so bad that the Board of Trade instituted an inquiry into these railways' ventilation. The Committee reported unhesitatingly that 'by far the most satisfactory mode of dealing with the ventilation of the Metropolitan tunnels would be the adoption of electric traction'.[51] Eight long years later, that remedy was at last applied.

Even here, however, we must avoid seeing things too simply. The choice for the Victorian Londoner was not between a foul-smelling underground train and pure air if he travelled through the streets. They stank too, especially in warm weather, of horse-dung;[52] and as for the atmosphere, even that in the Metropolitan tunnels was preferable to a pea-soup fog in the streets, the travelling there very much safer.

By the end of the Victorian age these railways were dirty, slow, many of them shabby, part of the ancient furniture as it seemed of the metropolis, an institution to be grumbled at incessantly, and with some reason. Yet they had been a great engine of improvement (with further

48. C. E. Lee, 'Railway circles round London', in *The Railway Enthusiast's Bedside Book*, ed. H. A. Vallance (1966), 193–203.
49. PP 1898, xlv. 181.
50. Quoted in Barker and Robbins, i. 235–6.
51. PP 1898, xlv. 143.
52. Cf. F. M. L. Thompson, *Victorian England: the Horse-drawn Society* (1970), 10.

capabilities in that direction still) and taken as a whole they offered a service superior in most respects to anything in the other capital cities of Europe.

For all that, radical change was on the way. It was signalled by the public opening of the first deep-level underground railway, electrically operated, the City & South London running from the Monument to Stockwell, on 18 December 1890.[53] Here, once more, London set an example to the world.

It was constructed like the Tower Subway (see p. 124) by the use of a shield devised by P. W. Barlow, and like the Tower Subway too with extraordinary speed. The first of its two tunnels was completed in less than four months. The railway was intended to be worked by cable haulage, but in 1888 electricity was decided upon instead: a bold resolution, for no railway at all like it, employing that form of traction, had yet been tried.

Like most pioneers – like the Stockton & Darlington and the Liverpool & Manchester railways 60 years earlier – it was not an unqualified success. It failed financially, never paying as much as a 2 per cent dividend. When it wished therefore to buy better equipment and to extend, investors fought shy of it. Both those improvements were needed: more powerful locomotives, superior signalling, and a line of a more viable length, envisaged when the Company secured Parliamentary powers to extend to the Angel and to Clapham in 1890–3. Its greatest technical weakness lay in the small bore decided on for its tunnels. That defect was observed and remembered when later tube railways were built.

As the City & South London approached completion, there was a fresh stirring of interest in the idea it represented. Another project, of a similar kind, was brought forward and sanctioned in 1891, for a Central London Railway, to run in a more or less straight line east and west, from Shepherd's Bush to the Bank. This was followed by a rush of other proposals – so great a rush that Parliament set up a Joint Committee of both Houses to consider them all, and the general problems they raised for London. A second similar inquiry was held in 1901. Both are important, for the evidence taken before them and for the decisions they arrived at. They did much to determine the shape of the tube railway system of London, as we know it today.[54] Indeed, if we except the Piccadilly line

---

53. The line had been opened formally by the Prince of Wales on the previous 4 November.
54. The reports are in PP 1892, xii and 1901 vi. On the first, cf. J. Simmons, 'The pattern of tube railways in London', *JTH* 7 (1965–6) 234–40; on the second, Barker and Robbins, ii. 65–7.

(a somewhat later addition) and one or two short extensions, the group of railways approved by the Committee of 1892 constituted the system of Inner London as it remained until the Victoria Line was built in the 1960s. The tubes sanctioned in 1892–3 were designed to serve five of the main terminal stations – Euston, King's Cross, St Pancras, Charing Cross, and Waterloo – and so to afford the cross-river railway connection that had been so much discouraged in the past. It was not intended to be a through connection, for the tunnels of the tube lines were to be (except in one case) of a small bore, and main-line rolling stock would not be able to pass through them. Some discussion of this matter took place in 1892 before the Committee. One of the engineers who gave evidence, John Wolfe Barry, argued that this policy was entirely mistaken, that it was tantamount to establishing a new break of gauge in the English railway system.[55] (The observation was topical, for he was speaking in the very month in which the old broad gauge of the Great Western was finally abandoned.) Such arguments were overborne by demonstrations of the enormous additional cost that would be incurred if the tube railways were made in tunnels of normal size, and no more was heard of them, save in one case: that of the Great Northern & City, which was designed to aid the Great Northern Company in its steadily-mounting struggle with suburban traffic by taking its trains southwards into the City from a junction at Finsbury Park. This line was built very slowly owing to financial difficulties and to the changing attitude of the main-line company, which turned from a friend into an enemy. It was completed in 1904. It was then, and remained, the sole London tube railway whose tunnels were large enough to take ordinary carriages, but it was never called on to do that, for the Great Northern ran no through trains on to it. Here was a notable opportunity missed.[56]

One other device was proposed to mitigate the effects of the 'break of gauge' that Barry condemned: the running of small-sized tube trains on to the main lines. That expedient was not tried before 1914, though preparations were then in hand for taking tube trains of the Baker Street & Waterloo line on to the London & North Western to Willesden and Watford, and they began to run in 1915–17.

The tube railways therefore remained physically a separate part of the London system. Their finance and management presented peculiar problems of their own. The financial interests behind the Central London project were international: largely American, though also German, and linked with Rothschilds. It went ahead very slowly, partly from the need

55. PP 1892, xii. 97.
56. It has been taken up again in 1976, as a part of the electrification of the suburban system out of King's Cross.

to observe and learn from the experience of the City & South London, and partly through difficulty in finding the right man to direct it. Henry Tennant, the retired General Manager of the North Eastern Railway, was the promoters' choice, but he had to be asked three times before he agreed to become chairman in 1895. The work then began to move. The team of engineers responsible for the City & South London line was employed again. The capital, of about £3¼ million, was raised, not easily but without undue difficulty. The work took longer than had been predicted, and the line was not opened to the public until July 1900.

It had a most promising franchise, as an underground railway moving straight across the heart of London, beneath two of its busiest arteries, Oxford Street and Holborn; yet it had taken nine years to build. Of the other lines authorised just after it, in the session of 1892, only one had yet been completed. This was the shortest, the Waterloo & City, opened in 1898. It was virtually a prolongation of the London & South Western Railway and was never intended to be anything bigger. To that simplicity it owed its comparative financial success, paying 3 per cent or a little more until the end of 1906, when the main-line company took it over. The others languished, or were built very slowly, because it proved so troublesome to raise the capital needed for them. The Baker Street & Waterloo Company[57] sought the capital it needed (originally £1¼ million in shares) from the London & Globe Finance Corporation and went ahead with construction in 1898. Two years later the London & Globe went into liquidation,[58] and the tube remained a little more than half finished. The Charing Cross Euston & Hampstead Railway also reached a contract for construction in 1897, but since the company entirely failed to raise the capital required it proved abortive.

In the summer of 1900, however, things suddenly changed. The American financier Charles Tyson Yerkes, who had very large interests in tramways and elevated railways in his own country, especially in Chicago, had for some little while past been investigating the London underground railways. He now determined to involve himself in this one and formed a syndicate for the purpose in the United States. Another contract was signed, and the work had at last a good prospect of being realised.

But the ambitions of Yerkes did not stop at financing a single tube railway. He had already begun to think in terms of developing an

57. Dubbed the Bakerloo by a bright journalist soon after it opened, and always known by that name since.
58. Its managing director, Whitaker Wright, was eventually convicted of misrepresentation and falsifying of accounts and committed suicide dramatically in the Law Courts in 1904.

electrified London underground system: something quite different from the small separate enterprises that had hitherto been launched, and embracing the old-established Metropolitan and District companies too. They had both accepted the need for electrifying their lines and had taken power to do so in 1897–8 – the District also contemplating a second line, in tube, underneath its existing one. The section between Kensington High Street and Earl's Court was electrified, and a train was put to work on it, experimentally and with success, in 1899. But where were the Metropolitan and the District companies – particularly the impecunious District – to find the money for conversion and equipment? Yerkes had the answer. Quietly he inserted himself and his associates into the affairs of the District, and in 1901 a Metropolitan District Electric Traction Company emerged, with him as chairman, to carry through the electrification of that railway and to build a further tube, the Brompton & Piccadilly Circus. This last project was combined with another shortly afterwards, to form what is called the Piccadilly line today. Before the year was out, the new company bought up the unfortunate Bakerloo concern, which had made no progress since the collapse of the London & Globe. The Traction Company now itself disappeared into a much bigger corporation, the Underground Electric Railways Company of London Ltd, with a capital of £5 million, found in many devious ways, through the agency of bankers; nearly 60 per cent of it came from America, only 35 per cent from Britain. Yerkes moved in to the chair of the new company.

Even this was not the limit of American concern with the business. The great banking house of J. P. Morgan & Co. had also become keenly interested in it, partly because it had a large stake in two manufacturing companies, British Thomson-Houston and Siemens Bros., which stood to gain profitable contracts for supplying equipment. Pierpont Morgan authorised his son to involve himself in a project for a tube out into the north-eastern suburbs, which became merged with another, for a line from Hammersmith and Piccadilly, running under the Strand and Fleet Street into the City. In this project Morgans' were allied with the London United Tramways Company, but that proved the weak link in the chain. Yerkes outsmarted them by buying up the tramways company, and Morgans' concern with London transport then ceased. More than 70 years later, Fleet Street awaits its tube railway still.

Yerkes had thus secured what was, immediately, a triumph. But it had an important consequence, less favourable to his ambitions in the long run. There was now an evident feeling that the control of London's transport system ought not to be a battleground for warring groups of financiers. The London County Council had declared its disapproval of the business. What it wanted to see was an independent authority, on the lines of the Rapid Transport Commission in New York, able to plan, and then control, a genuine system of underground railways. It did not get that. The criticism it voiced of the existing arrangements, and all the other disquiet that was making itself heard, led to the appointment of a Royal Commission on London Traffic in 1903, charged to investigate the traffic of the capital in all its forms, its inter-relationship and future development.

An inquiry of this kind was certainly very much needed: for the railways were only one element in a complicated and fast-changing situation. The electric tram, first seen in outer London in 1897, was now surging forward to conquer one district after another. By January 1904 it had arrived at Waterloo, Vauxhall Bridge, and the Elephant & Castle; it stretched across South London from Greenwich to Brixton and Streatham. Little systems were growing up in other districts further out – East Ham, Erith, Croydon. North of the river there were trams the whole way from Hampton Court and Hounslow to Hammersmith and Shepherd's Bush.[59] These were all run by private companies; but the London County Council secured powers to operate tramways in 1896, and by the end of the century it owned a system of about 100 miles, of which it worked half itself. It was authorised to electrify in 1900; its first electric trams ran in 1903. Nor was that all. Vigorous efforts were being made to develop the mechanised bus, and although they did not yet succeed, here was one more potential competitor for the passenger traffic of London.[60]

The Royal Commission's survey lasted two years. It was thorough and comprehensive. Its report, completed in June 1905, did not recommend a Rapid Transit Commission on the American model but an independent Traffic Board, charged with the tasks of examining all Bills in its field and of producing an annual survey of traffic in Greater London. The Commission's advice was not taken. All that emerged in this way, in 1907, was a London Traffic Branch of the Board of Trade, entrusted with similar duties but part of the civil service and not independent. As one contemplates the eight volumes that embody the Commission's work,[61] the 26,000 questions asked of the witnesses before it, the copious set of maps with which it is illustrated, one is bound to feel a sense of disappointment. Here is the most comprehensive survey of the transport

59. For a map of tramway development see Barker and Robbins, ii. 100–1.
60. Professor Barker and Mr Robbins argue cogently that if the motor bus had been able to prove itself satisfactorily in its experimental development in 1901–2, the tube railways then struggling to find capital would probably have been abandoned: *ibid.*, ii. 118–9.
61. PP 1905, xxx; 1906, xl–xlvi.

system of Greater London that has ever been made, and judged by its practical results it seems to have been quite fruitless. All that can be said is that it is a gold mine – as yet very much under-worked – for the student of history.

As it looked at the railways of London, the Royal Commission concluded that the whole development of the system had been wrong. The Quadrilateral ought never to have been established in 1846.[62] Competition had been thoroughly injurious: 'We have no doubt that the public interests have suffered from antagonisms between the various railway companies, and that a much better result would have been obtained if there had been some unity of ownership and management'.[63] The development of tube railways had been a mistake. They were no cheaper than shallow underground lines; the lifts required had added 8 per cent to the cost of the Central London Railway, for example, and had largely nullified the economies that tube construction offered in other directions.[64] The Commission supported the main-line companies' ideas of electrification and displayed impatience with the slow progress they were making.[65] It is fair to those companies to point out that the Commission made almost no attempt to face up to the crucial difficulty of raising the large capital that development demanded. In this matter it went no further than giving support to a proposal made by one of the witnesses that railway companies should be empowered to buy land in districts they served, to be sold off profitably for development.[66]

The only signs of enthusiasm that can be detected in the Commission's report appear when it speaks of electric tramways. It wished to see them rapidly extended – right into the centre of London, from which they had been barred very much as the railways had been 60 years earlier, and freely in the outer districts and the suburbs. This was the short golden time for those trams, and much of their success was achieved at the expense of the railways. There was nothing mysterious about it. Why should people go to Gunnersbury station on the London & South Western Railway, served by one train an hour, when trams ran past it along Chiswick High Road every few minutes, at much lower fares?[67] That railway calculated that tramway competition, still on a small scale, was

62. PP 1905, xxx. 609.
63. *Ibid.*, 613.
64. *Ibid.*, 621–2.
65. *Ibid.*, 630.
66. *Ibid.*, 621. The only British railway company that had done this on a substantial scale, and legally, was the Metropolitan. It had had a Surplus Lands Committee since 1887; its history is informatively set out in the evidence of (Sir) Robert Perks to the Commission: PP 1906, xl. 712.
67. G. Wilson, *London United Tramways* (1971), 65.

already costing it £10,000 in 1901 alone.[68] Presently things grew much worse. All the main-line companies were losing suburban traffic very fast. One, the London Brighton & South Coast, responded ahead of the rest by electrifying its South London line.[69] The work was completed in 1909, at the low cost of £250,000, and the whole of the traffic that had been lost was regained. The Company then went on to electrify its lines to the Crystal Palace in 1911–12. The other railways reacted more slowly. The London & North Western and London & South Western drew up plans for electrification in 1911–12, which were realised in 1915–22. The South Eastern & Chatham and the Great Eastern, deterred by their poverty, took no steps in this direction before the War. The Midland, which was not poor, showed no serious intention of redeeming its pledge to electrify the Tilbury line (cf. p. 187), given in 1912.

The competition of the electric tram in London was thus met mainly by an intensification of existing services, whether by adopting electric traction or through more limited improvement in detail. Very little new construction was attempted within Greater London: between 1900 and 1914 three lines only perhaps that deserve notice. Two of them were very short: the Fairlop loop from Ilford to Woodford on the Great Eastern (opened in 1903); the extension of the Great Northern from Grange Park to Cuffley (1910), an instalment of a long-planned line through to Hertford and Stevenage, seen chiefly as an alternative route to the hard-pressed main line. The third was the joint operation undertaken by the Great Western and Great Central companies, opened in 1903–4 (see p. 97), which provided two lines, from Old Oak Common and Neasden, joining at Northolt, and a continuation across what was then largely empty country to High Wycombe, together with a branch from Park Royal to Hanwell on the main Great Western line out of Paddington. No part of this line should be seen as competing with electric tram routes, existing or yet projected. The aggregate length of all these railways within Greater London was about 25 miles.

If extension and improvement took place on some lines in face of the new competition, elsewhere the railway companies retreated. The Great Eastern conceded that one line, opened as recently as 1891, was a hopeless failure: the Southbury loop, from Edmonton to Cheshunt. This ran parallel to the Hertford Road, which came to be served by electric trams out to Waltham Cross in 1904. Five years later the passenger service was

68. *Ibid.*, 83.
69. The fall in its traffic at some individual stations in 1905–7 appears very plainly in BTHR RAIL 414/537, pp. 99–102.

withdrawn. That was an exceptional case. But a good many suburban services were discontinued, over lines that remained open and busy with other traffic. All the local services from the Great Northern to the South Eastern & Chatham system were taken off in 1907. It is easy to see why. Finsbury Park and King's Cross got tube railways in 1904–7, providing a quick service, direct or with only one change, to the South Eastern & Chatham stations at London Bridge and Charing Cross, as well as to Waterloo. Victoria could be reached from King's Cross by the Inner Circle, circuitously indeed but after 1905 in the comfort of a new electric train. Rather oddly, as it may seem to us, the effort to provide main-line connecting services across the river continued and was developed in these years: a new service from Deal and Ramsgate to King's Cross appeared in 1911–13. Other services of the kind came and went: one from Weymouth and Bournemouth to King's Cross, instituted in 1905, lasted for six summer seasons; another from Birmingham by the new Great Western line to Victoria, with through carriages to Queenborough and Folkestone for Continental passengers, was a failure, which disappeared after 15 months, at the end of January 1912.

By 1914 there were about 550 railway stations open to passengers in Greater London, as well as a large number more used for freight traffic only. Fourteen of these were terminal stations of main lines, and 40 more stood on main lines in Inner London. There were over 150 on the underground system. The rest, some 350 in all, lay beyond in the outer districts, some of them serving communities that were still entirely rural. Nearly all these stations played their part in the growth of Victorian London, in lubricating movement into it and out again, and across the city itself. If some were now declining in usefulness, a great many others had not yet come near their potential. An unimaginable fate awaited those on the Bexleyheath and Dartford Loop lines in Kent; some of these stations, like Kidbrooke and Barnehurst, 'carried more grass than passengers' until the late 1920s and the 1930s.[70] Then, with the coming of the electric train, their business was transformed.

Looking at the surface railway system of Greater London as a whole, as it was when the First World War broke out, two things strike one, of opposite tendencies. Much of it was still conducted in the leisurely Victorian style. Some important towns in the outer belt enjoyed what seems to us a quite inadequate service. There was one interval as long as 50 minutes between trains from Euston to Watford; a passenger could wait more than $1\frac{1}{4}$hr for a train up from St Albans on the Midland line.

70. E. Course, *London Railways* (1962), 214.

On the other hand the service rendered by these railways in carrying commuters from a distance was one that they performed excellently. The Royal Commission reckoned that they were still bringing in four out of five of those who arrived in Central London before 10.30 a.m.[71] In the next ten years the tubes must have taken some of this traffic away from them. But in 1914 it still stood as their great contribution to the internal movement of passengers in London. Here they were, beyond question, indispensable.

The Underground Electric Railways Company established by Yerkes and his international associates pushed forward the completion of its tubes with energy. By 1905 all three, the Bakerloo, Hampstead, and Piccadilly lines, were nearing completion. Late in that year electric traction began on the Inner Circle. And then, in its last week, Yerkes died in New York, at the age of 68.

He bequeathed a difficult succession. His own fortunes were in disorder, and the Underground Company faced bankruptcy. In 1906–7 things moved from bad to worse. The high hopes that had been set on the electrification of the District lines proved illusory. The number of passengers the Company carried rose the year after the conversion, by about 10 per cent. Then in 1907 it actually fell. Even in 1910, when things were going on a good deal better, the increase over the traffic carried by steam traction was no more than 45 per cent. Before the three tubes were opened, an expert prediction had been that they would carry 145 million passengers a year. In fact in their first full year of working the number was less than half that, 71 million. By 1910 that figure was up by 35 per cent to 96 million. The independent tubes were unhappier still. The Central London and the Great Northern & City both carried fewer passengers in 1910 than they had done four years earlier; the City & South London 29 per cent more. The Metropolitan, which was never swept into the empire of Yerkes or his successors, did almost the same amount of business throughout these years.[72]

Why were these results so disappointing? The competition of the tramways continued formidable. But now, in addition to that, the motor bus began to overcome its teething troubles, to become a reliable means of transport; and it was permitted – unlike the trams – to travel all over London, even in the centre, which had been served hitherto only by horse buses and underground trains. In 1907, 1,200 million passenger journeys were taken in London, made up thus:

71. PP 1906, xli. 168–9, 179.
72. Figures in Barker and Robbins, ii. 116–17, 144.

TABLE 6. PASSENGER JOURNEYS IN LONDON, 1907

By tram	590 million	49.2%
By bus	330 ,,	27.5%
By underground	280 ,,	23.3%

Although no precise figures are available, it looks as if about 150 million of the bus journeys were made in motor vehicles – already perhaps half as many as by underground train. By 1914 that figure of 330 million bus passengers had rocketed up to 757 million.[73]

In financial terms the result pleased nobody. If the underground railways were doing badly, so were the bus undertakings. The shares in the General Company had stood at 218 in 1900; by 1907 they were down to 18. Its smaller rival, the London Road Car Company, made a loss in 1907 and could pay no dividend. The truth was plain: 'the new technologies which had produced the electric railway and the petrol bus had between them led to so much extra capacity that very little profit remained anywhere in the business'.[74] For the moment at least, London seemed to be over-supplied with transport; or perhaps, as some social reformers would have argued, it was wrongly distributed.

Clearly there would have to be some rationalisation. That might come through an extension of municipal control; but the London County Council, though it had become a large tramway operator, had no powers to run buses. Its municipal socialism was widely disliked and suspected, and there was no great enthusiasm for extending its activities in that field. The solution was found instead, as it had so often been when railways had competed in the past, by combination. The chief bus companies came together into an enlarged London General Omnibus Company in 1908–11. All of them were troubled still by the continued unreliability of their machines, until in October 1910 the General made the critical breakthrough with its B type, which proved a thorough and lasting success. Within a year, almost to the day, the General's bus fleet was entirely mechanised.[75]

The enlarged General Company now moved towards an understanding with the Underground Electric Railways Company. The upshot was a total merger, which brought the buses into the railway combine early in

73. *Ibid.*, ii. 134, 149, 215. No comparable figures are available for the surface railways. By 1914 it was thought that they were carrying about 250 million passengers a year, as against 400 million on the underground system: *ibid.*, ii. 163.
74. *Ibid.*, ii. 134–5.
75. The last horse bus in London ran on the day war broke out, 4 August 1914: *ibid.*, ii. 170.

1912. Then, on top of that, the two chief tubes that were still independent were added to it, on 1 January 1913.[76]

So, in terms both of management and of operation, the London transport system was set by 1914 on the path to rapid change. Electric traction had come to be accepted as a necessity – expensive but inescapable. If it had as yet been applied very little to the surface railways, there was no doubt that it would reach them in the future. The great majority of the underground railways had been brought under a single management, and since that management also controlled most of the buses, it had before it the chance to produce an integrated transport system – a true *system* indeed – such as had never arisen in Britain before. That took some time to realise, but as the historians of London Transport observe, with an elegant brevity, the creation of the London Passenger Transport Board in 1933 was 'the ultimate political result of decisive economic events which had occurred 20 years earlier'.[77]

76. The Great Northern & City was bought up by the Metropolitan later in the same year.
77. Barker and Robbins, ii. 191.

6

Way and Works

The essence of a railway is its track: the rail way – in contrast to the road way – from which it takes its name. By 1830 the track had already developed far from its rude wooden originals, which had been no more than a pair of timber baulks, through several successively improved stages of iron construction.[1] Its weakness in the past had materially hampered the use of the locomotive. That was what had put an end to Trevithick's promising experiments: the weight of his locomotives broke the track. When the plan of the Liverpool & Manchester Railway was being worked out, and the debate came to a head on the issue of motive power, the protagonists of the stationary steam engine pointed out that its use avoided imposing the great weight of locomotives upon the rails. One of the conditions laid down by the Company for the Rainhill competition, held in October 1829 to determine the best sort of locomotives to be adopted, was that the competing machines must not weigh more than 6 tons in working order, and that if they weighed more than $4\frac{1}{2}$ they must run on six wheels (a condition not fulfilled by one of the entrants, *Sans Pareil*). The victorious *Rocket* weighed $4\frac{1}{4}$ tons, of which just over $2\frac{1}{2}$ rested on the axle of the driving wheels.

The history of locomotives is too often thought of solely in terms of mechanical engineering. Their relationship to the track on which they ran is a fundamental element in their design. The strength of the rails was not the only factor involved. Smooth riding was almost as important – to the passengers, of course, but also to the locomotives, which soon rattled to pieces on a rough road.

There were four ways in which the track was open to improvement: by close attention to the bed on which it rested; by changing the shape of the

1. See M. J. T. Lewis, *Early Wooden Railways* (1970), and C. E. Lee, *The Evolution of Railways* (1943).

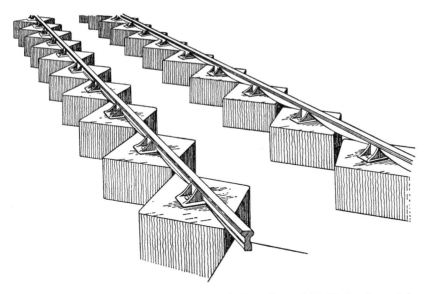

Fig 1. *Liverpool & Manchester Railway track: the rails are fish-bellied and mounted on stone blocks, set diagonally*

rails, their support and their jointing one to another; by increasing their weight, and so it might be expected strengthening them; and by altering the composition of the metal of which they were made.

On the Liverpool & Manchester Railway at its opening the standard rail used was of wrought-iron, 15ft long and weighing 35lb to the yard. The rails were 'fish-bellied' in shape, curving out underneath to give greater thickness at the mid-point between each of the pairs of 'chairs' in which the rails were supported. These chairs rested generally on stone blocks. But on certain sections of the line – as in crossing Chat Moss, for example, where such blocks would have sunk into the spongy ground – timber cross-ties or 'sleepers' were laid instead; an expedient that would hardly have been practicable when horses had been in use, for fear of causing them to stumble.

These rails soon proved too weak to carry the loads imposed on them by steady and continuous traffic. They were constantly breaking. A series of experiments was made in 1832, to improve them in a number of ways. The new rails used were heavier – none weighing less than 50lb to the yard, some perhaps as much as 75. Parallel rails were tried, on test against the fish-bellied pattern. The use of timber sleepers increased; the oak that had been selected at first gave place to larch, 'kyanised' – i.e. saturated in a solution of bicarbonate of mercury. The Company raised additional capital for these purposes in 1837. By the end of that year the whole line had been relaid.[2]

A steady improvement was thus wrought, by trial and error and observation. But that was not enough; progress in design could be nullified if the track was poorly maintained. The Company's directors – conscious always that theirs was 'the Grand British Experimental Railway'[3] – kept a meticulous eye on all these matters themselves. For a time, in 1833–7, they let out the maintenance of the track by contract, under the close supervision of John Dixon, their Engineer. This was a common practice, followed by many of the early railway companies, and it offered a fairly even balance of advantages and drawbacks. Dixon himself analysed them lucidly, in a paper he wrote for the Stockton & Darlington directors in 1843.[4] The gist of the advice he gave them was that maintenance by contract could be made to work satisfactorily if the agreement with the contractor was drawn up in the greatest detail, and if the contractor himself was closely supervised by the Company's officers. The Liverpool & Manchester directors decided in 1837 to abandon the practice in favour of doing the work through their own servants, in the interests of economy. They reconsidered it five years later but again rejected it.[5]

The experiences of other railways were similar. By the early 1840s it was becoming usual to lay down rails weighing 70lb and more to the yard, which meant heavier chairs to support them. The total weight of metal in the track had trebled on the Stockton & Darlington Railway by this time since 1825.[6] Costs naturally increased accordingly, though they were subject to great fluctuation owing to the volatile prices of iron. When the London & Southampton Railway was being built early in 1837 the directors flatly declined to order rails for a time, considering the prices extortionate. They were proved right: in July of that year the price had dropped by nearly 40 per cent.[7]

The standard rail that emerged on most British railways in these years was parallel, not fish-bellied, and double-headed: a form that gave great vertical strength and was attractive from its apparent economy in allowing the rails to be turned over and used twice. In practice, however, this second advantage proved illusory, for the under side inevitably became corroded and worn where it rested on the chairs, and it was not therefore

2. The problems presented by the track are clearly explained in Donaghy, 32–6.
3. The phrase is Whishaw's: *Railways of Great Britain and Ireland* (1840), 186.
4. MS. report, 24 Oct. 1843, Darlington Public Library.
5. Donaghy, 24–6.
6. Tomlinson, 405–6.
7. Williams LSWR, i. 135.

totally smooth when reversed.[8] Still, rails re-used in this way could be laid down on sidings and on minor branch lines. For main-line track the

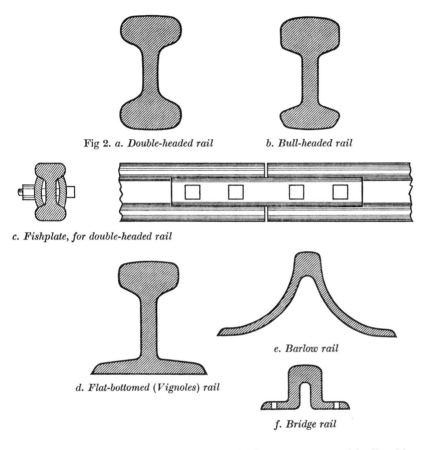

Fig 2. *a. Double-headed rail*   *b. Bull-headed rail*

c. Fishplate, for double-headed rail

e. Barlow rail

d. Flat-bottomed (Vignoles) rail

f. Bridge rail

'bull-headed' rail came to be preferred, which was not reversible. Double-headed track was greatly improved by the invention of the fishplate for joining one rail to another, which was patented by W. B. Adams and Robert Richardson in 1847.[9]

The alternative to this type of rail was the flat-bottomed pattern invented by C. B. Vignoles in 1837 and often called by his name. Its great merit was that its broad base allowed it to be laid without chairs, or with chairs very much smaller than those required to give stability to double-

8. Cf. the Inspecting Officer's remarks on an accident that arose from this cause near Woking in 1860: PP 1861, lvii. 79.
9. On this see *Engineering* 14 (1872) 64.

headed rails. Although it did not in the end find much favour in Victorian England, it was widely used elsewhere; and since the Second World War it has prevailed in this country too.

Many other experiments were made with rails of different shape, fastened down to the track bed in different ways. The Barlow rail, patented by W. H. Barlow in 1849, was designed to avoid the use of sleepers and chairs altogether: it was saddle-backed, and held in place by the ballast, packed tightly underneath and around it. Although it was widely used for a time, it proved unequal to the demands of heavy traffic. Brunel, original in so many directions, had his own peculiar ideas in the design of permanent way. He used bridge rails (at 43lb to the yard) laid on continuous longitudinal timber bearings, with cross-sleepers supported on piles. The original cost of construction was higher, but he believed that would be offset by lower maintenance costs and a continuously even surface, which would produce smoother riding. The piles proved unsatisfactory and were quickly abandoned; but the bridge rails, increased in weight to 62lb to the yard in 1839, and longitudinal sleepers continued in use as long as the broad gauge itself.[10] That was not due solely to the Great Western Company's well-known conservatism. The 62lb bridge rail, supported in this elaborate fashion, continued to be satisfactory in service when it had become necessary to make bull-headed rails much heavier – up to 75–85lb in the 1870s.[11] Brunel was not unique in supporting his rails longitudinally. Hawkshaw (a scathing critic of Brunel's piling) used longitudinal sleepers on railways in the Bolton district in 1837; they were still in service – carrying a second set of rails, to replace the first, which were worn out – in 1850.[12]

The stone blocks that had originally been favoured for supporting the rails yielded place almost everywhere to wooden sleepers, which were found to give a much smoother ride. Early engineers – here the Stephensons and Brunel were at one – thought that the track ought to be made as rigid as possible. Gradually it came to be appreciated that some degree of elasticity was required.[13] The timber considered to be ideally the best

10. Even Brunel did not use this form everywhere. He tried Barlow rails on the South Wales line from Landore to Carmarthen, and between Hayle and Penzance in 1851–2, and cross-sleepers and chairs on most of the line from Trowbridge to Bradford-on-Avon five years later. MacDermot, i. 415, 569; ii. 305.

11. J. W. Barry, *Railway Appliances* (4th edn, 1884), 63. The account given in chap. ii of this book of the various forms of track is a simple and compendious summary, by a thoroughly competent engineer.

12. *Lancashire & Yorkshire Railway: Mr Hawkshaw's Report on the Rolling Stock and Permanent Way* (1850), 8. (Lancashire Record Office DDX 87/4.)

13. W. B. Adams was one of the first to insist, in 1837, that the track needed 'the quality of vibration': *English Pleasure Carriages* (1971 edn), ix, 303.

for sleepers was oak or pitch-pine; but those woods were costly, and fir from the Baltic was generally used instead.[14]

The making of the bed on which the track rested came to be recognised as an art, scarcely inferior to that developed by Telford and McAdam for turnpike roads. Although gravel and broken stone were the materials most favoured, the choice varied according to locality. Some railway companies owned and worked quarries, almost entirely to supply ballast for their rails: the London & North Western at Shap, the London & South Western at Meldon, on the western fringe of Dartmoor. Railways serving ironworks often used slag from their furnaces – an arrangement that suited both them and the ironmasters, who were anxious to dispose of the waste product, equally well. Those that ran to the sea, such as the London Brighton & South Coast, frequently used shingle from the beach, which answered satisfactorily if it did not include many soft shells. For ballast was required to serve two purposes, not always compatible: it had to provide a firm basis for the heavy track, and it had also to be such that water could drain down through it, percolating easily. The art of laying a railway consisted largely in reconciling these demands; and it was the business of the army of platelayers that came to be employed on the Victorian railways to keep the state of the road – the bed as well as the sleepers and rails – under vigilant and unceasing surveillance.

So far we have been considering only the straight rails. What happened when they needed to diverge or cross? The mechanism of points, requiring movable pieces of rail, had been devised in a rudimentary form before even the Stockton & Darlington Railway was opened.[15] Their movement and control raised many difficulties, especially when they occurred on lines travelled on by heavy and fast trains, which might dislodge them unless they were securely fastened, or might take the wrong road. Five accidents occurred from this cause, for example, in 1842.[16] In one of them the danger was aggravated because the points were 'facing' – laid out, that is, to allow a divergence, rather than 'trailing', when the joining line was brought in from the rear. Facing points could not be avoided, of course, at junctions; but everywhere else good managements, exhorted by the Board of Trade's Inspecting Officers, tried not to use them.

Level crossings, of one railway by another, occurred here and there, and when they did they were an evident cause of danger. They were avoided, or later eliminated, on almost all main lines – though three

14. Barry, *op. cit.*, 38–9. For an interesting analysis of the timbers used by 14 British railway companies in 1867 see Dow GC, ii. 46.
15. Cf. the 'movable iron tongues' on the Middleton Colliery Railway at Leeds shown on the plan reproduced in Lee, *op. cit.*, 79.
16. PP 1843, xlvii. 25, 64, 71, 77, 78. One of the five was in Scotland.

survived in 1914 between London and Newcastle, at Newark, Retford, and Darlington. Level crossings over roads were very much more numerous. At first they were held to be unobjectionable even within towns, as at Canterbury and Lincoln.[17] But they were forbidden over any 'public carriage road' by the Railways Clauses Act of 1845.[18] Some important early railways, like the North Midland and the London & Brighton, had few or none. All the same, they were widespread up and down the country, a constant cause of danger, and at times of acrimonious dispute – as in the classic case at Atherstone in 1898, where the Warwickshire County Council secured an injunction to prevent the London & North Western Company from running the trains on its main line over the crossing at any speed greater than 4 m.p.h., so forcing it to build a bridge.

In the 1860s a very important change in the track began to get under way: the substitution of steel for iron. Experiments had been in progress with incorporating an element of steel into iron rails for some time – Gooch took out a patent for this purpose in 1840; but they had not succeeded.[19] Until the 1850s the notion of making rails wholly of steel would have been unthinkable because steel was a costly material, used only in small quantities, as for cutlery. But in 1855–6 Bessemer's process became known, offering the possibility of making steel on a large scale at a low price. In 1857 the first steel rail was laid down experimentally, on the Midland line at Derby.[20] The rail proved itself admirably in service. Further experiments were made in 1861–4, by the London & North Western Company at Crewe and Chalk Farm, by the North Eastern, the Manchester Sheffield & Lincolnshire, and the Great Northern.[21]

These steel rails were all adopted at points where there was particularly heavy traffic, and they showed themselves much more durable than the older ones of iron. The first cost was still a good deal higher, but they promised a long-term economy. The Great Western laid them down cautiously in Paddington goods yard in 1867. Within three years the directors accepted their Chief Engineer's recommendation that they should be used extensively on the Company's main lines. It was steadily implemented, and by 1878 four-fifths of them were laid with the new rails. This was a far-sighted policy, and in an engineering sense unquestionably correct. But engineering considerations were in conflict here

17. Sir F. Hill, *Victorian Lincoln* (1974), 114.
18. 8 Vict. cap. 20, sect. 46.
19. Sir D. Gooch, *Memoirs and Diary* (ed. R. B. Wilson, 1972), 40.
20. See J. Dearden, 'The centenary of the steel rail': *Railway Steel Topics* (1957), 11–24.
21. W. H. Chaloner, *Social and Economic Development of Crewe* (1950), 71; Tomlinson, 648; Dow GC, ii. 48; G. R. Hawke, *Railways and Economic Growth in England and Wales 1840–1870* (1970), 242–3.

with other economic interests. As recently as 1861 the Company had completed a rolling mill for iron rails at Swindon, at a cost of some £20,000. Its profitability had been called into question on the board. Hardly had it begun to justify itself when the demand for steel rails (which could not be made on this plant on any large scale) began to be heard insistently. When it adopted them widely in the 1870s the Company had to revert to its former policy of purchasing its rails from outside manufacturers. The rolling mill ceased to turn out rails altogether in 1878, though it continued in use for plates and other iron work.[22]

The London & North Western Company's policy in this matter was different. It had established its own plant for rolling iron rails at Crewe in 1853, and this was kept abreast of the latest improvements in technique, some of which indeed it introduced.[23] When Bessemer proposed that steel rails should be tried, John Ramsbottom, the Company's Locomotive Engineer, was appalled: 'Mr Bessemer,' he asked, 'do you wish to see me tried for manslaughter?' But he overcame his fears, and the experiment was made. It succeeded: with the result that in 1864 the Company established its own Bessemer steelmaking plant at Crewe. The steel it produced was not used for rails alone. Steel tyres, first made in Germany by Krupp in the early 1850s, were now coming to be used widely in Britain. The London & North Western had purchased some in Sheffield in 1859. By the mid-1860s it was beginning to incorporate steel extensively into its locomotives. All these developments were a natural, a necessary consequence of the establishment of the Bessemer plant at Crewe, which had to be kept as fully occupied as possible in order to justify its capital cost. They were due also to the advocacy of Ramsbottom, and of F. W. Webb, who succeeded him in 1873 after four years as manager of an iron and steel works at Bolton.[24]

Steel thus came gradually into general use in the 1860s and 1870s. But the process was not rapid: the North Eastern Company relaid only 18 miles of its system with steel rails in 1873, 62 miles in 1874.[25] The work was far from completed, even on the main lines, by the end of the century. Although, for example, the North Staffordshire Railway had begun to replace iron rails with steel in the 1870s, the process was still continuing on its line through the Potteries, which carried some of the chief expresses between London and Manchester, as late as 1904.[26]

22. MacDermot, ii. 502; *VCH Wilts.*, iv. 212–14; Gooch, *op. cit.*, 85.
23. Chaloner, 69–70.
24. *Ibid.*, 71; Ahrons BSRL, 163–5, 206–7. The Manchester Sheffield & Lincolnshire Railway also made its own steel in its works at Gorton from 1871 to 1886: Dow GC, ii. 48–9.
25. Tomlinson, 671.
26. Christiansen and Miller NSR, 99, 124.

The rails were made stronger not only by the use of steel in place of iron. The increase in weight that was so marked at the beginning was maintained, rising from about 75lb a yard in the 1870s to 95lb as a standard for most first-class main lines in the early years of the twentieth century.[27] The rails were also lengthened. On the London & South Western system, for instance, the ordinary length of rail in the 1860s had been 21–24ft. By the 1880s it was 30ft; in 1903 it became 45ft.[28] The London & North Western adopted a standard length of 60ft.

The same company had also taken the use of steel in its permanent way one stage further by making sleepers of steel, to a design patented by Webb himself. This, however, did not in the end prove satisfactory in service, and the practice was abandoned.[29] Timber cross-sleepers prevailed universally on the British railways in 1914.

The further strengthening of the rails and the simultaneous adoption of steel for the tyres of locomotives and carriage wheels allowed heavier locomotives to be used, without risk. Whereas it had been rare in the 1860s to place a weight above 14 tons on the driving axle of an express engine, the average weight was over 17 tons 30 years later.[30] The new practice was accepted chiefly because it offered a long-term economy. It turned out to have another advantage. The harder metal and firmer track made running easier and helped to facilitate the great increase of speed that took place from about 1880 onwards (cf. p. 178). Observers of the performance of locomotives in daily service noted that in these years some seemed capable of running faster as they grew older. The explanation was that the locomotives' adhesion had increased by the contact of hard steel on hard steel.[31] Express trains grew at once heavier and faster in these years. That was not brought about solely by a decree of railway managements, nor even by progress in the design of locomotives. If the track had not been made stronger, in the ways that have been described, the achievement would have been impossible.

Another development connected with the track, which also helped to reduce journey times, was the installation of water-troughs: shallow metal containers placed between the rails from which locomotives could pick up water by means of a scoop lowered from the tender. This could be done while the train was travelling at full speed, so reducing the number of

27. Cf. Dow GC, ii. 49.
28. Williams LSWR, ii. 43, 89, 100, 214, 258, 310; Marshall SR, 454. Oddly, the Great Central Railway used a rail no more than 30ft long on its London Extension in 1894–9: Dow GC, ii. 330.
29. Findlay, 381–2.
30. Calculated from the table in Ahrons BSRL, 302.
31. For discussion of this matter see Ahrons LTW, ii. 134–5 and BSRL, 232, 312.

stops required on a long run. The idea was John Ramsbottom's, and he installed the first set at Mochdre in North Wales in 1860, to enable the Irish Mail to run from Chester to Holyhead without stopping. They gave satisfaction, and the London & North Western Company gradually multiplied them.[32] With the quickening of service after 1885 they passed into general service. All the big English companies laid them down except the London & South Western. The Lancashire & Yorkshire Company adopted them as a contribution towards the intensive use of locomotives on its intricate system.[33]

Laid, manufactured, and equipped in this way, expensive and superbly maintained, the permanent way in Britain could stand comparison with any to be found elsewhere. It was sometimes asserted – and probably with justice – that the track on the London & North Western main lines was the most excellent in the world. And the British track passed its final test. Not a single accident of consequence occurred in the country in 1913 that could be attributed to any failure in the permanent way.

'Why are our architects so inferior to our engineers?' 'The civil engineering of railways had aesthetic merit so considerable that the architecture

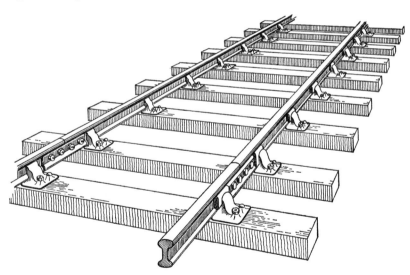

Fig 3. *London & North Western Railway track, 1894*

32. P. E. Baughan, *The Chester & Holyhead Railway*, i (1972), 192–4.
33. Marshall LYR, iii. 97, 135, 281. Water-troughs were also laid down in France and in the eastern United States; but nowhere else.

of the first railway stations seems somewhat tame and inappropriate in comparison with it.' The first of those two remarks came from a publicist in 1851,[34] the second from an architectural historian in 1934.[35] Writing from very different points of view, 80 years apart, the substance of their comment is the same. For both of them the railways' civil engineering ranks among the triumphs of the age, hardly if at all below their more spectacular achievements in the mechanical department, and above any other physical manifestation of their power. We still need to remember such verdicts today: for when disputes arise about the preservation of major railway monuments, they nearly always concern stations and buildings. We patch and sometimes maul bridges and viaducts, to allow them to carry the unsightly equipment demanded for electric traction, with scarcely a murmur of protest. But they, with the embankments and cuttings and tunnels that go with them, were, and are, the most powerful and far-seen demonstration of the might of the new means of transport. They had been foreshadowed by some of the similar works called forth by the roads and canals, but these were much fewer in number, and they seldom equalled the railways' in scale.

Still, that said, one must begin any consideration of the railways' civil engineering, in common parlance their 'works', by looking at what their predecessors had done, and at the way in which that had been organised: for the railways necessarily looked to them for example. Every element in the railways' engineering in the 1830s and 1840s had been seen before. As far as tunnels were concerned, a few of the canal companies had undertaken stupendous works: the one at Harecastle on the Trent & Mersey was nearly 3,000 yards in length; that at Sapperton, on the Thames & Severn, some 4,000. The biggest of all was the Standedge Tunnel under the Pennines, nearly 5,500 yards long and running at its deepest 700ft beneath the surface. In constructing them, the canal companies could call in aid the skill of miners; but nothing so large as these had ever been seen in Britain before, and they went ahead very slowly. Eleven years were required to complete the Harecastle Tunnel.

These were great enterprises. So, in a much more evidently spectacular way, were the aqueducts that carried the canals across river valleys, beginning with the one at Barton on the Duke of Bridgewater's Canal near Manchester and reaching a climax in the magnificent works on Telford's canals close to the Welsh border at Chirk and at Pontcysyllte, where iron was used on a much larger scale than ever before. Here already we are half-way towards the iron railway bridge. The flights of locks,

34. S. Sidney, *Rides on Railways* [1851], 14.
35. H. S. Goodhart-Rendel, *English Architecture since the Regency* (1953), 77.

necessary to canals in hilly country – at Bingley or Hatton or Devizes – had no counterpart on the railways; but they were most impressive achievements and helped to mould the landscape to the purpose of the new means of transport.

Road engineering works, though less obviously imposing, were noticed more widely: for they made possible the fast travelling that became a matter of national pride in the 1820s and 1830s. They too were in some senses the forerunners of the railways. They might cleave their way through hills: on the Holyhead road, for instance, by Dunstable; north of Market Harborough on the road from London to Leicester. On the other hand they differed essentially from the railways in that their acceptable gradients were much steeper, so that they could mount a hill or wind round it where a railway was obliged to slice through it in a cutting or bore its way underground in a tunnel.

What the canals and roads contributed to the railways that to a large extent displaced them was their experience of construction, and the skill and habits of work of the men who had laboured on them. Not that there was any smooth transfer of the engineers' allegiance from the old means of transport to the new. Telford laid down one or two small railways, but he never had anything to do with the locomotive; George and John Rennie (a generation younger) did accommodate themselves to the new business, but they did not make the same mark upon it as their father had done with his canals, or with his bridges in London. I. K. Brunel worked on his father's Thames Tunnel and learnt much from that experience; and he had designed his suspension bridge at Clifton before any of his railway work began. Still, the Great Western Railway – and the *Great Western* steamship, associated with it – were the first large-scale works he carried through to completion. Of the other principal railway engineers only Vignoles and William Cubitt could be said to have learnt their business in other branches of engineering, military and civil. The railway indeed did much to erect that barrier between the branches of the engineering profession which became characteristic of Britain. When other civil engineers turned to railway work, they were seldom happy in it. James Walker, for example, laid out only one important railway, the Leeds & Selby. As President of the Institution of Civil Engineers from 1834 to 1845 he was frequently called in to adjudicate and give advice in difficult railway questions; but his touch in dealing with them was often unsure, and his counsel was apt to be set aside.[36]

36. Most notably when he advocated the use of stationary engines to the directors of the Liverpool & Manchester Railway; but also later, in relation to the Chester & Holyhead (Baughan, *op. cit.*, i. 42–3).

On the other hand it must be recognised that nearly all the great railway contractors, the men responsible for the actual work of building the lines, had undertaken road, canal, and harbour works, and often house-building operations too, before they came to railways. Brassey began his career as an articled pupil to a land surveyor; he was first employed to assist in making surveys for the Holyhead road and then applied himself for eight years to the development of Birkenhead, before getting his first railway contract, on the Grand Junction Railway, in 1834. The partnership of Grissell & Peto was established in 1830, but it did not turn to railway business for ten years, having in the meantime constructed a number of major works in London, like the Hungerford Market, the Lyceum Theatre, and the Reform Club.

The railways did not, then, establish a wholly new school of engineering. They built on what their predecessors had done. But their operations were bigger in scale, and far more complex, because they were designed for mechanical equipment, as neither the canals nor the roads had been; they faced new problems, which had never had to be tackled in a similar way before. George Stephenson's tunnel down into Liverpool and his Sankey viaduct were things of wonder, but they were constructed by means that had been familiar to those who had built the canals in the two preceding generations; the Olive Mount cutting was only a little more impressive than Telford's work at Smethwick, which was going on at the same time for the Birmingham Canal.[37] On the other hand, nothing at all like the crossing of Chat Moss had ever been seen in the past. Embanked roads had been built across marshes; but the problem here was quite new – how to support the weight of the iron track, with its ballast, constantly pounded by passing trains, weighing up to 50 tons each in 1830 and soon a great deal more. George Stephenson expressed his confidence that he could produce a solution. He was ridiculed, but still proved himself right. Those who visited the line, and knew what they were talking about, pointed to this as his outstanding achievement.[38]

The early railways were built by the same methods and with the same equipment as had been used on the canals: by the power of man, wielding the spade and assisted by the horse.[39] The earliest trial of mechanical

37. The word 'cutting' itself appears to come in with the railway. The first example of it adduced by the *Oxford English Dictionary* is from the Hull & Selby Railway Act of 1836; but it was used in contemporary accounts of the Liverpool & Manchester line when it was new – e.g. J. S. Walker, *Accurate Description of the Liverpool & Manchester Railway* [1830], 33.
38. It is worth noting that when the M62 was being built to cross Barton Moss near Patricroft in 1972, Stephenson's plans for the passage of Chat Moss were carefully examined by the engineers: BTHR AN 37/3.
39. Cf. B. Morgan, *Civil Engineering: Railways* (1971), 40–1.

excavation in England seems to have been made by John Braithwaite on the Eastern Counties line, in the cutting at Brentwood, in 1843. The machine he employed was American, invented by Elisha Otis, who later became famous for his lifts. Though it seemed to the Government Inspector, when he watched it, to succeed,[40] the use of such equipment did not become general in Britain for another 40 years. In the great age of railway construction labour was cheap and abundant in Europe; but it was dear and scarce in the United States, and such machines were at a premium there. In the Mid-Victorian age things became different. Ruston's Steam Navvy was first put to work on the Midland line between Melton Mowbray and Nottingham in 1880; eight such machines were used in the building of the Hull & Barnsley Railway in 1881–5;[41] the last main lines – the London extension of the Great Central and the Great Western 'cut-offs' (see pp. 96–7) – were built very largely with their aid. Back in the 1830s, however, human power alone had to suffice: the power of the railway navvies.

Their conditions of employment, and their character, will fall to be considered later in this work.[42] We are concerned here only with the methods of construction, and with the results that were achieved. The number of these men can never be computed exactly. The total of those engaged in railway construction in England and Wales on 1 May 1847 was given as 169,838, of whom 152,172 were 'labourers and artificers',[43] but that can be taken as only a very rough indication. It is the aggregate of stated totals for each railway; but at that frenzied time nobody had the means or the leisure to make any exact reckoning. Men constantly drifted from one job to another; one of the contractors' chief difficulties lay in keeping their labour forces intact.[44]

40. PP 1841, xli. 171. Cf. also J. Weale, *Ensamples of Railway Making* (1843), xxi–xxvi.
41. K. Hoole (ed.), *The Hull & Barnsley Railway*, i (1972), 239.
42. A vivid and lively account of them is given in T. Coleman, *The Railway Navvies* (1965).
43. Calculated from PP 1847, lxiii. 162–75. Another 19,839 labourers and artificers were said then to be employed on railways in operation, making a total of 172,011. The total for the whole United Kingdom was 263,594, 240,301 of whom were employed on railways under construction. Although the navvies were mainly 'labourers', the 'artificers' must be included too, since in some of the returns the two categories are shown as one.
44. It is difficult to use the census returns for any such calculations, since their definitions are either too narrow or too broad to enable us to isolate the men specifically employed on railway work. But the notes attached to the returns for individual places sometimes indicate the numbers of men engaged there at the moment when the census was taken: e.g. a total of well over 3,000 working on the Great Western Railway in North Wiltshire in 1841 (returns summarised in *VCH Wilts.*, iv. 319–20).

We have some figures that are perhaps more useful in relation to individual railway lines. Peter Lecount tells us that on the London & Birmingham the number of labourers employed was between 15,000 and 20,000. On the line from Basingstoke to Winchester, 17 miles long, $3\frac{1}{4}$ million cubic yards of excavation had to be undertaken in 1838–9. Brassey was the main contractor, and he employed 1,100 men. They took day and night shifts, were highly paid, and finished the task punctually. The great work stands, unchanged, 140 years later. From the moment when it veers to the south at Worting, to slice its way through the chalk, riding high on its embankments, the railway displays a Roman grandeur. It must surely be judged one of the masterpieces of English civil engineering: a monument to Francis Giles and Joseph Locke, who laid it out, to Brassey, and to the men who worked under them.

The physical labour involved staggers us now. One of Brassey's assistants analysed the navvy's work carefully, observing that, in a full day, each man shifted nearly 20 tons of earth, on a shovel, 6ft above his head into a wagon. Even so, there were some men who could do more, or could complete that stint by 4 o'clock in the afternoon.[45] When English contractors moved into work on the Continent, and some of their men followed them across the Channel, it was found that no others equalled them. The Frenchmen employed on Brassey's railway contracts in the early 1840s – from Paris to Le Havre and from Orleans to Bordeaux – proved able to shift just half as much earth as British labourers; the Germans (mostly Bavarians) who worked for him side by side with them were inferior in strength to the French.[46]

The methods used in early railway construction, then, were not new. Neither were the materials. With few exceptions, they were local. When good building stone was at hand, it was used for preference, as it had been in the past. So, for example, the noble Victoria Bridge over the Wear, on the Durham Junction Railway, was constructed in 1836–8 mainly of stone from Penshaw quarry, $1\frac{1}{2}$ miles away.[47] A passenger by the Newcastle & Carlisle line, built at the same period, can follow the changing geology of the local building stones by observing its works as they are still. This practice continued to be common far into the Victorian age. Travelling up the valley of the Medway from Strood to Maidstone, one notices the Kentish rag in the over-bridges; that line was completed in 1856. The famous Talerddig cutting, on the line from Newtown to

45. Helps, *Brassey*, 77–8.
46. *Ibid.*, 81, 89.
47. Whishaw, *op. cit.*, 73.

Machynlleth, was made a cutting and not a tunnel largely because the stone taken from it was needed for building the stations and bridges on the railway.[48] The high Pontsarn viaduct on the Brecon & Merthyr Railway was built almost entirely out of limestone taken from a quarry immediately above it.[49] The constructors of these works were all fortunate in having good building stone to hand. Where nothing of the kind was available, other local materials were commonly employed: Sittingbourne bricks, for instance, were dispatched in barges up the Thames and the Surrey Canal for the London & Greenwich Railway's viaduct in the 1830s;[50] 60 years later the Great Central drew the bricks for its station in Leicester from Heather and Hathern, less than 20 miles away.[51]

As the railway system grew, however, such expedients became a matter of choice, not of necessity. For it was one of the consequences of that growth that the railways were able to distribute building materials of all kinds, cheaply and fast, throughout the country. The process is plainly to be seen on their own works. It was they who conveyed, for example, the blue engineering bricks made in Staffordshire and elsewhere on the Coal Measures: exceptionally hard, and resistant to water, they came to be adopted everywhere. The railways did much to pioneer their use, and made them generally available – not only for engineering works but also in domestic building, for damp courses. The white bricks of Bedfordshire, made beside the Great Northern Railway at Arlesey and Three Counties, are to be seen all along that main line from Finsbury Park to Retford.

One other material, which had been used by engineers from time immemorial, was taken up by the railways and turned to quite new account: namely, timber. Though always valuable for small works, like footbridges, it had fallen out of favour with the builders of roads, who steadily preferred stone for their major bridges and viaducts; and it was obviously unsuitable for the under-bridges on canals, from its susceptibility to damp. The railways, however, used it extensively: in early days on the Whitby & Pickering line, where the trains were drawn by horses, but soon for much larger works, which had to sustain the weight of locomotives. Although the Stephensons never favoured it,[52] substantial works were constructed in timber in the 1830s, such as the long skew bridge at Scotswood west of Newcastle. On the other side of that city a striking variant appeared: the famous Willington and Ouseburn viaducts,

48. I. Thomas, *Top Sawyer* (1938), 62.
49. T. Jones, *History of the County of Brecknock*, iv (1930), 59.
50. R. H. G. Thomas, *London's First Railway* (1972), 29.
51. Dow GC, ii. 317.
52. Timber bridges occurred, however, on the Northern & Eastern Railway, for which Robert Stephenson was consulting engineer: PP 1843, xlvii. 206.

built entirely of laminated timber on masonry piers. Whole sequences of timber bridges became common, like those provided by Cubitt for the South Eastern Railway on its level course from Redhill to Ashford[53] and the much bigger ones he used on the Great Northern line in Lincolnshire.[54]

The longest and most celebrated series of these bridges was designed by Brunel for the Great Western and the other railways associated with it.[55] The first of them appeared in 1840 as an over-bridge, to carry a road across the Sonning cutting, followed later that year by another at Bristol. There were not many more on the main line, but they were numerous on its extensions to the north and west. All the under-bridges on the Oxford branch were of this type; there were nine in the Golden Valley through Stroud, six between Taunton and Exeter. They abounded in South Devon and Cornwall, and throughout South Wales. Some of them were very large works indeed: the Landore viaduct outside Swansea was a third of a mile long, the St Pinnock viaduct, in the Glynn valley in Cornwall, 151ft high.

Brunel had excellent reasons – chiefly economic – for using this form of construction, and it justified itself. It is true that the timbers had often to be replaced and that maintenance costs in the end became so heavy that slowly, over the years, all these bridges were reconstructed in other materials. But the first cost was low, and that was a vital matter for many of the companies concerned, especially for the Cornwall Railway. The bridges were marvels of construction, and though they looked fragile (which was apt to alarm intending passengers in early days) they in fact proved strong and gave little trouble for 20 years and more. Some of them continued in their original form far longer. The last of the Cornish series, at College Wood on the Falmouth branch, was rebuilt only in 1934. The last of them all survived nearly into nationalisation: the Dare and Gamlyn viaducts, near Aberdare, removed in 1947.

These timber bridges have too often been thought of as another of the vagaries of the great engineer who designed them. They were much more than that: an elegant and imaginative solution to a difficult problem. When the need or the opportunity arose, Brunel could stand in the *avant garde* of the engineers of his time who were pioneering the introduction of iron. At Chepstow and Saltash, where the use of timber would have been impracticable, he produced two of the boldest, most advanced, and most successful structures of the kind that were to be seen anywhere in his age.

53. PP 1843, xlvii. 207–9.
54. A fine water-colour drawing of one of the biggest of these, at Bardney, is reproduced in J. Simmons (ed.), *Rail 150*, facing p. 80.
55. Cf. H. S. B. Whitley, *Railway Engineer* 52 (1931) 384–92.

The first railway bridge constructed wholly of iron seems to be one erected in 1811 at Robertstown, near Aberdare, in South Wales. That carried horse-drawn traffic only. In 1822 George Stephenson designed one, to span the River Gaunless on the Stockton & Darlington Railway and perhaps to bear the weight of locomotives. It was completed in 1823, damaged by flood-water in the following year, and then extended by the addition of a fourth span to the three with which it started. In this form it continued in service for more than 75 years. When at length it came to be replaced in 1900 the North Eastern Company, with admirable piety, determined to preserve it; and it stands today as a distinguished possession of the National Railway Museum at York.[56]

Nevertheless it was Robert Stephenson, rather than George, who did most to develop the use of iron in railway structures, first on the London & Birmingham line and eventually on the largest scale, in the High Level Bridge at Newcastle and the Britannia Bridge crossing the Menai Strait. It was not a smoothly successful process. Stephenson met with a severe setback by the collapse of his Dee Bridge outside Chester in 1847, which even for a time tarnished his reputation.[57] There he had used cast and wrought iron together in a system of 'compound girders', which he thought had proved itself satisfactorily elsewhere. That was in itself a mistake; but the whole design was faulty. The accident could not have occurred at a worse time for Robert Stephenson himself, for work on his High Level Bridge at Newcastle (built wholly of cast iron, on tall masonry piers) was actually in progress, and he was wrestling with the plans for the far bigger bridge over the Menai Strait. But he did not lose his nerve; neither did the directors of the Chester & Holyhead Railway. He evolved an original solution to the problem that confronted him in North Wales: that of producing spans as wide as 460ft, raised nearly 100ft above the water. The work could not be done in masonry. The suspension principle, which Telford had employed close by on his graceful bridge for the Holyhead road, had proved unsuitable for railways.[58] Something quite new was needed. Stephenson provided it in the form of rectangular tubes, constructed of wrought iron – though provision was made for adding chains if the suspension principle proved necessary as a supplementary precaution. The Britannia Bridge stood, very little modified for 120 years, until it was severely damaged in a fire started by trespassing vandals in

56. That museum also contains good models, well explained, of some of the other bridges mentioned here: e.g. the timber bridges of Cubitt and Brunel.
57. The matter is clearly and well discussed by L. T. C. Rolt in his *George and Robert Stephenson* (1960), 300–4.
58. Samuel Brown's suspension bridge over the Tees by Stockton, completed in 1830, had been an unhappy failure; Robert Stephenson had been called in to replace it in 1842.

1970. It has now been totally reconstructed. The tubes have been replaced by steel arches, though the original piers and towers have been retained. The bridge was a noble achievement, and rightly acclaimed as such. But it was also very expensive. Already, while it was being built, Brunel was evolving a different kind of structure, to serve the same purpose of carrying a railway high above water on very long spans, first at Chepstow and then, on a scale even larger than that of the Britannia Bridge, at Saltash in Cornwall. Here he used a design that incorporated, in part, the idea of suspension. It was far lighter and less costly than Robert Stephenson's tubes. The main spans of the Britannia and Saltash bridges were almost exactly the same in width and height. Brunel's whole bridge was more than a third as long again as Stephenson's; and yet the structure was completed in 1859 for £225,000, a good deal less than the cost of the ironwork alone that had gone into the Britannia Bridge only nine years before.[59]

Great progress, then, was being made in the design of these unprecedented structures; progress based on research, on trial and error, as well as on experience, sometimes harsh. The methods of construction, too, became more sophisticated. Nasmyth's steam hammer was available for use on the bridge at Newcastle. That was the first bridge of importance to be built on piles driven in by mechanical power. Bessemer soon began to open up the possibility of using steel in large-scale engineering work. Not yet in bridges; but as it made its way into one department of the railway after another, in the 1860s and 1870s, its possibilities for that purpose began to be considered.[60]

Other very large iron bridges continued to be built. Thomas Bouch designed a remarkable pair, wholly of metal, for the South Durham & Lancashire Union Railway, which crossed the Pennines at Stainmore and was opened in 1861. The loftier of the two reached a maximum height of almost 200ft. Three big estuaries were bridged in this way: Solway, Tay, and Severn. The Solway Viaduct was seriously damaged by ice-floes in 1881. Like the two on the Stainmore line, it was constructed entirely of cast iron, and the Board of Trade's Inspecting Officer criticised the use of that material. The engineer, James Brunlees, however, attributed the failure solely to the exceptional weather conditions.[61] The Severn Bridge stood securely for 80 years from its opening in 1879 till it was breached by the crash of a ship into it in 1960. The Tay Bridge encountered a different and more famous fate. After carrying traffic for less than 18

59. Rolt, *op. cit.*, 313; P. S. A. Berridge, *The Girder Bridge* (1969), 61.
60. PP 1881, lxxx. 473–4.
61. Thomas Bouch intended to use it in a bridge he designed for a railway proposed in 1864, crossing the Thames close to the Tower of London: PP 1864, xi. 302–3.

months, it was destroyed in a gale in December 1879. The searching inquiry that followed put the responsibility on its designer, Bouch, and on the manufacturers of the iron used in the bridge, Gilkes Hopkins of Middlesbrough. It revealed with alarming clarity the engineer's neglect in supervising the contractors' work and his failure to appreciate the force of the wind that blew on occasion with great violence up the estuary of the Tay. When the bridge was rebuilt, it was a conservatively-designed structure – the last big wrought-iron bridge in the world; showing a massive solidity altogether lacking in the carelessly-constructed original.

The Severn and the Tay bridges were dodos. Bouch had also been engaged in designing a bridge to span the Forth. After the accident the work was taken away from him and entrusted to John Fowler and Benjamin Baker, who produced a design of an entirely different description: a cantilever bridge in steel, completed in 1890 and totally successful. It was followed by another steel structure in Scotland, much smaller but lighter and more prophetic of what was coming: the Connel Ferry Bridge of 1903.

Steel now came to replace iron in most large railway structures: in the bridges on the Great Central Railway's London extension, for example, built in 1894–9, and in the King Edward VII Bridge at Newcastle, opened in 1906, the last major enterprise of the kind undertaken in England before 1914.

Concrete began to be thought of for the building of bridges as early as the 1860s.[62] The Metropolitan District Railway, at the instance of its engineer John Fowler, played a modest part in pioneering its application to railway construction, when in 1867 it built a bridge of that material near Gloucester Road. Four years later, in its works at Lillie Bridge (West Brompton), it used the material on a larger scale than had ever been seen before.

But that promising development then stopped. Here and there concrete was used on a very small scale in railway work: for a station platform at Leeds, for instance, in 1881.[63] It did not appear again in Britain until the construction of the West Highland Extension Railway in 1897–1901, when it was used chiefly in arches of a standard 50ft span; Borrodale Bridge, with a central span of 127½ft, attracted attention even in America.[64] Again an advance had been made in Britain, and again it went no further. One or two other concrete bridges were built in England, such as the Cannington viaduct on the Lyme Regis branch in 1903. The bridges on the Great Western & Great Central Joint line through High

62. Cf. W. B. Adams, *Roads and Rails* (1862), 127.
63. *Builder* 41 (1881) 94.
64. J. Thomas, *The West Highland Railway* (paperback edn, 1970), 95–6, 100–1.

Wycombe (completed two years later) were of concrete faced with brick; the handsome Calstock viaduct over the Tamar, brought into use in 1908, was constructed of concrete blocks.[65] For the rest, cautious trials were made of the material for lineside equipment. On the Midland & Great Northern Joint Railway William Marriott adopted concrete for fencing posts in 1909 and then for other things too.[66] But, in general, British railway engineers were slow to accept concrete. In that they were in line with the civil engineers of their country as a whole.

The most extensive engineering works of the late Victorian age were in tunnelling. The Severn Tunnel, 4 miles 624 yards in length, took 14 years to construct (1872–86), in the face of unexpected and baffling difficulties. Its completion was a work of dogged and honourable tenacity, alike on the part of the railway, the engineers responsible (Charles Richardson and Sir John Hawkshaw) and the remarkable contractor, Thomas Walker. Tenacity was intensified into heroism in Diver Lambert, who twice undertook to close doors beneath the water at the instant danger of his life. Together with the short piece of railway giving access to it on the two sides of the river, the tunnel cost £1,806,248.[67] 'One sub-aqueous tunnel is quite enough for a life-time' observed Walker quietly. He then worked on docks at Barry, Preston and Buenos Aires, and started on another undertaking he did not live to carry through, the Manchester Ship Canal. But he also found time to publish a full and plain account of the building of the Severn Tunnel, which is one of the most valuable works about the construction of a railway ever produced by a man who was himself engaged in it.[68]

Meanwhile, a much greater length of railway in tunnel was being steadily constructed in London (see pp. 131–4). The first section of the Metropolitan line, $3\frac{1}{2}$ miles long, was opened in 1863. The Inner Circle, finished in 1884, extended for 13 miles, continuously below ground level; it never rose above the surface of the streets, as some of the underground lines were to do later in Paris. The 'cut-and-cover' method used on the railway was relatively simple, involving the construction of a cutting, which was then roofed in and the ground restored to the natural level above.[69]

Electric traction was used from the outset on the deep-level tube railways of London, which came into use from 1890 onwards (cf. p. 131),

65. Williams LSWR, ii. 211; *Railway Magazine* 22 (1908) 106.
66. A. J. Wrottesley, *The Midland & Great Northern Joint Railway* (1970), 123.
67. MacDermot, ii. 191.
68. T. A. Walker, *The Severn Tunnel: its Construction and Difficulties* (1888). For a good summary see L. T. C. Rolt, *Victorian Engineering* (1970), 251–64.
69. B. Baker, 'The Metropolitan and Metropolitan District Railways': *Minutes of the Proceedings of the Institution of Civil Engineers* 81 (1885) 1–74.

producing a system of deep-level tunnels nearly 40 miles in length. That system was made possible by three advances, in equal measure: the civil engineers' tunnelling and the electrical engineers' lifts and motive power.

After 1880 the English railways seemed, to many observers, to have lost the leadership they had hitherto enjoyed. But that view was by no means wholly right. They continued to provide a service for passengers that was in some important respects superior to that afforded by any other system in Europe (see p. 271–2); and here in the development of the deep-level tube railway they not only ran far ahead of anybody else, on either side of the Atlantic, but they also kept their lead for a whole generation. Underground railways did not become general in other great cities until after 1945. When they did, the experience gained in London was sought out by those who wished to establish railways of this pattern, to be placed at the disposal of the rest of the world.

The railways were also builders in another sense: they erected buildings of their own, stations, hotels, warehouses, depots, factories, as ancillaries to the development of their system. Some of these – particularly stations and hotels – will fall to be treated in later volumes. A word must be said here, however, to show all these buildings beside the 'works' proper that have been considered in this chapter: for they form part of one whole.

As soon as the railways' business was well under way, they could no more exist without engine sheds and signal boxes and warehouses than they could without locomotives or track. Excepting their passenger stations, some of which soon came to display a certain degree of architectural pretension, most of these buildings were plain and utilitarian. The signal box, for example, did not exist at all until the control of junctions began to become complicated, and it was at first an erection of the very simplest kind, of wood.[70] An important one at Victoria station in London, famous in the history of signalling, was accurately characterised by its nickname 'The Hole in the Wall'. But as the apparatus grew more elaborate, and the junctions too, these shelters developed into imposing structures: some very tall, to give the signalmen an adequate view, like those on the Brighton side at London Bridge and the long boxes, containing 200 levers and more, at strategic points on the London & North Western Railway; some straddling many tracks, as at Waterloo, Cannon Street, and Charing Cross.

Locomotive and carriage sheds grew similarly. The roundhouse

70. One of the earliest illustrations of a signal box is given in a print of the flying junction at Norwood, on the London & Croydon Railway, erected in 1845, reproduced in C. Hadfield, *Atmospheric Railways* (1967), facing p. 49.

appeared on the London & Birmingham line at Camden Town about 1840: a prototype that was to have a large progeny, designed so it seems in collaboration between Robert Stephenson and R. B. Dockray, the Company's resident engineer. It was 160ft in diameter, and top-lighted by sheets of glass 9ft long; it accommodated 24 engines.[71] The building had brick walls, 14ins thick. The danger of fire made it usual to construct these engine sheds of brick or stone, though timber was sometimes risked.

The example set by the roundhouse at Camden was followed widely thereafter – though the rectangular pattern, with a turntable outside, was also used. There were variations in the roundhouse. Richard Peacock, for example, designed one for the Manchester Sheffield & Lincolnshire Railway at Gorton, whose central turntable carried a double track, allowing either one or two locomotives to be turned at once. This depot, which housed 17 engines, remained in use until 1879, when it was converted into a smith's shop; a new engine shed then took its place, to accommodate 90.[72]

The largest of these depots became very big indeed. In the 1850s the shed at Crewe provided for 16 engines. It was then extended by successive stages until 1878, when it could take 140. Finally, in 1896 an entirely new depot was built in addition to the old one. These two, Crewe North and Crewe South sheds, between them, had a staff of more than 700 men The sheds were equipped with mechanical coaling plant in 1913.[73]

The London & North Western Company also set another precedent in the provision it made for handling freight traffic, in London and Liverpool. For some time it did not distribute the goods it conveyed, making agreements for the purpose instead with the two great established firms of carriers, Pickford's and Chaplin & Horne. The accommodation required was provided at Camden Town in very large 'General Receiving Sheds' (Pickford's had an area of 65,000 sq. ft), equipped with much plant that was mechanically operated – steam cranes and hay-cutters, a steam capstan, even a 'steam doller or lift'.[74]

Some ten years later a more sophisticated goods depot of this kind appeared, built by the Great Northern Railway at King's Cross (and still

71. Head, *Stokers and Pokers* (1849), 66–7, 76.

72. Dow GC, i. 212–13, ii. 96.

73. Chaloner, 81, 83.

74. Head, *op. cit.*, 71–2. What was a 'doller'? The word is not known to the *Oxford English Dictionary*. Can it be a variant of 'dolly', a term used in pile-driving and metal-working? And was this the first power-operated lift? Lifts had been used on canals (cf. C. Hadfield, *British Canals*, 1950, 60–1), but they had been worked simply by counterbalances. The hydraulic 'elevator' was developed in the United States by Elisha Otis from 1854 onwards: C. Singer *et al.*, *History of Technology*, v (1958), 478.

in use today). This was a massive rectangular building, six stories high, erected immediately above an arm of the Regent's Canal. The main shed, therefore, was able to cater for three types of transport side by side: by railway, water, and road. The top-lit roof of the building was constructed of timber; otherwise the whole of the great shell was of yellow brick. Here was a completely-realised plan of transport co-ordination.[75] From such pioneers there sprang the immense railway warehouses and goods depots that became an impressive element in many large manufacturing towns.

The equipment with which these buildings were furnished grew more elaborate until it reached a climax in the depot erected by the Great Central Railway for its London traffic at Marylebone in 1899. This afforded 510,000 sq ft of space, on five stories. It was steel-framed, fitted up with the whole battery of mechanical apparatus then in use, and centrally heated throughout. The whole installation cost not much less than £300,000.[76]

Such elaborate buildings as these were serviced by very large goods yards, for the sorting of wagons, their loading and unloading. These might be on the spot, but often in large towns they stood some distance away. The warehouse needed to be central, for the convenience of the railway's customers, and that meant building it on very expensive land; the goods yard might well be allowed to develop further out, where land was cheaper. So, once again at Liverpool, the London & North Western Company came to develop its huge marshalling yard at Edge Hill, $1\frac{1}{2}$ miles from the centre of the city, servicing from there the warehouses and depots in the commercial quarters and the docks below. It cost the Company altogether some £2 million.[77]

Most of the buildings just considered here have been large. But the railways proliferated small buildings of many kinds all over the system. They became as familiar a part of the rural landscape as the tracks and bridges, the locomotives' white steam in the sky. The small goods shed, for example, was an adjunct to most passenger stations: with a platform for loading and unloading two or three wagons and a space for sorting, all under one overall roof. Some were mass-produced to a standard pattern, prefabricated of timber. Others were of brick, sometimes conforming to a general pattern of design applied to all the railway's buildings as a group. Such depots formed the centre-piece in tiny goods yards with which almost all stations handling freight traffic came to be equipped: with a hand-operated crane and perhaps a cattle dock as well.

75. *Illustrated London News* 22 (1853) 427–8.
76. Dow GC, ii. 328; Rolt, *Making of a Railway*, 115.
77. Findlay, 229–38; Acworth RE, 125.

These yards often became the commercial centres of the villages they served. Unless there was navigable water close by, all the coal needed for their fires was delivered here; much of the bulk provisioning of the shops went on in the same way; the produce of the neighbourhood, in corn or vegetables, horses or cattle, was distributed from here. The goods station had to be equipped, however simply and crudely, to handle all this traffic. It complemented – it might even overshadow – the more imposing passenger station.

This chapter has been concerned with a diversity of things. It began with the laying of the track; it ends with village stations. It has dealt throughout with the fixed equipment, on and beside the railway line, needed for the working of its trains – except for safety devices, which will be considered in Chapter 9. In the general study of railways such things as these are apt to be taken for granted, little examined or illustrated. But they must never be overlooked: for they were, both in a literal and in a figurative sense, the foundation of the railways' business.

7

Motive Power

The Liverpool & Manchester Railway opened with a stock of eight locomotives, to which two more were added before the end of 1830. These
ten machines had to suffice for the whole work of the line, in the conveyance of passengers and goods, except for the short final stage at the
Liverpool end, where trains were worked up and down through a tunnel
on a steep incline by stationary steam engines.

The ten had all been built by Robert Stephenson & Co. at Newcastle.
With one exception, they may be said to have been based on a common
design – the design of *Rocket*, which had shown its capabilities in the trial
at Rainhill in the previous year; but they incorporated improvements
derived from the experience that *Rocket* had afforded under observation
and test. They had somewhat larger boilers, and cylinders with a diameter of 10ins or 11ins, as against *Rocket*'s 8ins. In the eighth of them,
Northumbrian, the firebox was made an integral part of the boiler, an
important change. The ninth, *Planet*, represented a more obvious innovation. In its predecessors on the Liverpool & Manchester Railway the
cylinders had been fixed at the rear of the engine, inclined upwards,
immediately in front of the footplate. *Planet* had them at the front end,
under the chimney; and they were placed horizontally, inside the frames.
Here, in this engine, we have in its main features the ancestor of most of
the locomotives of Victorian England, where engineers usually showed a
marked preference for inside cylinders.

The design of *Planet* had been well worked out. It was the first of a
series of 16 engines, on similar lines, built down to 1833. And *Planet*
proved itself satisfactorily in service: of the original ten machines, it was
the longest lived, still at work in 1840.[1] Stephenson's *Patentee* of 1834 was
in essence an enlargement of *Planet*, with the addition of a third pair of

1. A list of the Liverpool & Manchester Company's locomotives is given in Marshall
CH, 75–7. For the significance of *Planet* see Ahrons, BSRL, 19.

wheels, placed behind the firebox, to allow a greater weight to be supported without overloading the light and brittle track. *Patentee* was bought by the Liverpool & Manchester Company for £1,000.[2] The 2–2–2 type[3] that thus emerged had a long progeny during the Victorian age: the last with this arrangement of wheels was built, for express work on the Great Northern Railway, in 1894.[4]

These engines stand at the head of the main line of descent of British locomotives; but there were other patterns, by other manufacturers, that were successful too. Timothy Hackworth never cordially accepted the multi-tubular boiler, generally thought to have been one of the chief elements in the success won by *Rocket*. And he continued to design locomotives with cylinders placed vertically, or steeply inclined; his brother Thomas, in his works at Stockton, was turning them out until 1864.

Edward Bury and his partner James Kennedy began to build locomotives at Liverpool in 1829. They adopted a D-shaped or circular firebox with a domed top, and frames made up of bars of iron rather than the deep plates seen in *Planet* and *Patentee*. 'Bar framing' did not generally find favour in this country, except on Bury's engines, but it was adopted with enthusiasm in the United States and became the normal pattern there throughout the subsequent history of the steam locomotive. At the same time another British invention also crossed the Atlantic, to achieve for a time far greater success there than at home. This was the bogie, or swivelling truck of four small wheels. Placed at the front of the locomotive, it helped to guide it round the curves that abounded on American railways, which had been lightly and cheaply built. In Britain the bogie made very little appearance before 1855, and was rarely applied to express engines until the late 1870s.

This was a golden time for British locomotive manufacturers. Their number multiplied and they often had more orders than they could fulfil, for they were designing and building for the whole Atlantic world. Hawthorn's of Newcastle, for example, turned out four small engines in 1837 much like the Stephenson *Planet*. One of them went to the New York Boston & Providence Railway, two to the Paris & Versailles, the other to the Stockton & Darlington.

In the late 1830s and the 1840s the firms of Stephenson and Bury were strong rivals in the competitive business of locomotive building. Bury's engines had another peculiarity besides those already mentioned. The

2. J. G. H. Warren, *A Century of Locomotive Building by Robert Stephenson & Co.* (1923), 312–13.
3. The usual designation of steam locomotives in Britain is by giving the number of leading, driving, and trailing wheels, in that order.
4. Ahrons BSRL, 264.

great majority of them were carried on four wheels, whilst Stephenson's, following *Patentee*, usually ran on six. A fierce controversy on this matter arose between the partisans of each practice, and it was investigated carefully by the Board of Trade.[5] Bury's firm secured a virtual monopoly of the supply of locomotives to the first of the great trunk lines, the London & Birmingham. In the end that Company's successor, the London & North Western, abandoned his little four-wheeled engines. But they had important merits: they were stoutly built, simple, very economical in first cost, and dependable, within the limits of their power, in service.

Some railway managements pursued a consistent policy of employing small units of power to work their traffic. It was partly a matter of the cost and availability of labour. When it was cheap and plentiful there was no disadvantage in having to use two of these units – or even, on occasion, more – to haul a single heavy train; additional crews could be had at a moderate expenditure in wages. But on the London & Birmingham the policy was brought to an end abruptly after the Company had been merged with others to form the London & North Western in 1846. The new management set itself to find new patterns of locomotive for its growing traffic, as strong and reliable as Bury's but much more powerful. It was not provided adequately with locomotives that satisfied these requirements until 1851–4.

By the late 1840s other railways were using locomotives of a quite different order of magnitude from the Bury engines of the London & Birmingham. The broad-gauge Great Western had started disastrously with a miscellaneous series of experimental machines, almost all of them failures (cf. p. 27); but by 1846 Daniel Gooch had retrieved these errors. In that year he produced a single experimental engine of his own, proudly named *Great Western*. It ran at first on six wheels. In the following year an additional pair of small wheels was added in front, to help to sustain the engine's exceptional weight. In this form, and with a modified firebox, another engine was built, *Iron Duke*, and that established the type. It became the classic broad-gauge express engine, used until the broad gauge itself came to an end in 1892. For its time it was a very large machine. All that Bury built (and was still building) seem puny by comparison. So indeed they were: for here, at one bound, the locomotive had grown about half as big again, and proportionately more capable.

Gooch's great engines were, and in some respects they remained, unique: as unique as the Iron Duke himself. No other railway then imposed tasks on its locomotives of quite the same order as that demanded by the Exeter expresses of 1845–52. True, a train appeared in 1846,

5. PP 1842, xli. 21–3, 227–63.

to run from Liverpool to London in six hours, allowing four hours' business to be transacted there, and returning to Liverpool at night;[6] but its speed was a good deal less. For a moment in 1852 the London & North Western is said to have contemplated putting on express trains between London and Birmingham in two hours (i.e. at 56.5 m.p.h.), and J. E. McConnell, the Company's Locomotive Superintendent at Wolverton, was asked to design special locomotives for them;[7] but the project was dropped – wisely, one must feel, given the brittle state of the permanent way of the time.

These were years of bold experiment. Between 1841 and 1851, not only were current needs entirely reappraised: some glimpses were taken into the far future. Electric traction was tried,[8] the three-cylinder locomotive appeared, and the principle of compounding was foreshadowed;[9] the first railcars were built.[10] These proved no more than flashes in the pan, though the promise of all of them was fulfilled afterwards. One other experiment, full of promise too but marred in the execution, was tried and failed at this time: the atmospheric railway.

The stationary steam engine, tried by a few railways in the 1830s and 1840s, had not found any great favour. In its first application it had been employed to haul trains by cables. Now its power was developed in another form, to work pumps enabling trains to be moved by atmospheric pressure. A tube was laid down between the rails, in which ran a piston attached to the under-side of a carriage. The air in front of it was pumped out, and the atmospheric pressure then propelled the piston forward. The plan was first developed in 1827–36. Samuel Clegg and the brothers Samuda took out their first patent on these lines in 1838 and conducted experiments on a half-mile stretch of track at Wormwood Scrubs two years later. The patentees called their system the 'atmospheric' railway; 'pneumatic' was a term often used subsequently, which indicates the principle of the invention better.

The theoretical benefits it offered were striking. Atmospheric propulsion was clean, free of all smoke and fumes, except in the immediate

6. T. Baines, *History of the Commerce and Town of Liverpool* (1852), 673.

7. Ahrons BSRL, 95.

8. In Scotland, by Robert Davidson on the Edinburgh & Glasgow Railway in 1842. The idea remained alive. Ten years later Herapath was prophesying the application of electricity to railway traction: *Herapath's Railway Magazine* 14 (1852) 381.

9. George Stephenson and William Howe patented a three-cylinder design in 1846, and two such locomotives were built: Warren, *op. cit.*, 101, 392–3. Two locomotives were adapted to something like a compound system, devised by John Nicholson, in 1850–2: Ahrons BSRL, 88–9.

10. Steam railcars were built by William Bridges Adams from 1847 onwards: *ibid.*, 84.

vicinity of the engine house, and comparatively silent; apart from a gentle hissing, the traveller heard no noise but that of the wheels on the rail-joint.[11] The business of starting and stopping became much smoother. Power being supplied from an external source, locomotives were eliminated. That brought down the weight of the train and distributed it much more evenly, which offered a great reduction in the cost of under-bridges and all earthworks. Such gains as these were most important, worth labour and money, time and patience, to secure. Were those resources going to be available?

There was always one outstanding technical difficulty to be overcome. A slot was required along the upper side of the tube, to allow for the passage of the piston. It was closed by a leather flap, strengthened with iron. How was this to be rendered airtight? No satisfactory answer was ever given to that question.

The system had its first public trial on the extension of the Dublin & Kingstown Railway from Kingstown to Dalkey, 1¾ miles long. It was opened in 1844 and continued to be worked on the atmospheric system for 10 years. In England the London & Croydon Railway was worked in this way from Croydon to Forest Hill (later New Cross) for 15 months in 1846–7. The South Devon Railway was similarly operated between Exeter and Newton Abbot for about ten months in 1847–8. The one railway that adopted the system in France, the Paris & St Germain, retained it for a much longer time, from 1847 to 1860.

The invention showed all the merits claimed for it. But it proved unreliable, primarily because the leakage of air was never cured. Most of the stationary engines used were not powerful enough. All the installations turned out to be much more costly than had been expected.

Financially, the most disastrous of these experiments was that on the South Devon Railway. Brunel, its engineer, had estimated the cost of the apparatus required for atmospheric working at £190,000; it turned out to be, first and last, £434,000 – of which no more than £81,000 was eventually recovered through sales when the railway had been converted to conventional steam traction.[12] Nor was that all. The line had been laid out for working on this principle, with abnormally steep gradients between Newton Abbot and Plymouth. Atmospheric trains never ran on that western section. Steam locomotives were called on to work it instead; and it remained a formidable assignment for them as long as steam lasted.

So the atmospheric experiment failed. It brought ridicule on everyone

11. An excellent description of a journey by atmospheric train is given in the standard work on the subject: C. Hadfield, *Atmospheric Railways* (1967), 13–18.
12. *Ibid.*, 172; MacDermot, ii. 107.

who had supported it – and most of all on Brunel. George Stephenson must have chuckled sardonically; he had described it as 'a great humbug' from the beginning. But it deserved a better fate. It had very much to offer. The principle of taking power from an external source, rather than cumbrously moving the apparatus and fuel with the train, was a good one, realised in the end by means of electricity. Had there been time to wait, and a research laboratory available, its defects might have been remedied.

The plan was revived from 1853 onwards in the service of telegraph companies and the Post Office, for the conveyance not of passengers but of bundles of messages and sacks of mails. There it achieved substantial success. It was employed once again, briefly, for carrying passengers, in a tunnel at the Crystal Palace in 1864. This was really a primitive version of a tube railway. In the following year the Waterloo & Whitehall Company obtained powers to construct something that we should call by that name, running under the Thames. Work began in 1865 but was suspended in the financial crisis of 1866 and never resumed. Another effort to build a railway under the Mersey on the same principle also failed at the same time.[13]

Such was the most conspicuous and daring experiment of the 1840s. Even though it did not succeed, it indicated the long views that some engineers were taking. Other new practices established themselves more immediately.

In 1841 Robert Stephenson patented his 'long-boiler' design of locomotive, in which all the wheels were placed in front of the firebox. By this means two advantages were offered: a shorter wheelbase, enabling a larger machine to fit on to the existing turntables and helping it to negotiate sharp curves where necessary; and a greater heating surface, from the longer tubes, as well as one in which the length of the tubes was thought to be better proportioned to their diameter.[14] Locomotives of this kind were constructed in large numbers. In Britain they did not establish themselves for passenger service, but they were built extensively for goods work over the next 25 years. On the Continent they continued in demand much longer: over 600 of the type were running in France in 1886, both in passenger and in goods service, and some were still working in 1950.

Although the long-boiler locomotive was extensively employed in goods traffic – especially in the North-East – the standard type of English goods engine evolved on different lines. It made its first appearance within this same decade: as a six-wheeled machine, with inside cylinders

13. Hadfield, *op. cit.*, 93–102.
14. For a theoretical exposition, see Warren, *op. cit.*, 346–7.

and the rear axle not in front of the firebox but behind. It was solid, steady, capable of long plodding hard work; and in various forms, enlarged in size and even in the twentieth century superheated, it was built for English railways in very great numbers for precisely 100 years. The first of the type emerged in 1848 in engines designed and constructed by Kitson's of Leeds;[15] the last was built for British Railways at Swindon in 1948. Of the 11,500 tender locomotives owned by the railways of England and Wales in 1914, almost exactly half were of this description; there were still over 4,000 of them in the hands of the private British companies when the railways were nationalised.

At the same time another new pattern of locomotive was being developed in England, which also came to enjoy great success abroad. In 1846 a pair of engines appeared built (rather improbably at Whitehaven, for a railway in Belgium) to a design by T. R. Crampton. Like many other engineers of his day, he was convinced that it was necessary to keep the centre of gravity as low as possible, in order to render the engine stable, particularly when running at high speed. He therefore placed the driving wheels of his engine behind the boiler and firebox, which could then be brought lower, so as to rest only on the small carrying wheels. The result was an undoubted improvement in fast service; the Crampton engine swayed and plunged much less than its predecessors, and especially the passenger engines of the long-boiler type. But that gain was accompanied by a serious loss. The adhesive weight – that is, the weight borne by the driving wheels, helping them to grip the rails – was too low; the carrying wheels sustained the engine's main weight, but contributed nothing to its power. After a number of experiments, all the English companies that tried the Crampton rejected it – though some of the type lasted in service up to 25 years on the South Eastern. On the other hand the design was warmly received in Germany and Denmark, and above all in France – so much so that 'le Crampton' became colloquial French for 'a train', and 'M'sieu Crampton' for a railwayman.[16] Nearly 300 were built for service in that country, some of which lasted well into the twentieth century.[17] One, on test there in 1889, attained a speed of almost 90 m.p.h. The main reason for this discrepancy of view between English and Continental engineers was that in England the track was more firmly laid. In France and Germany there was the greatest dislike of concentrating the heavy weight too much on the driving axles, which was apt to cause pitching at speed when the road

15. Ahrons BSRL, 82.
16. G. Esnault, *Dictionnaire historique des argots français* (1965), *s.v.* Crampton.
17. The last on the Chemin de Fer de l'Est was not withdrawn from service until 1922: *Journal of Stephenson Locomotive Society* 30 (1954) 369.

was uneven. And so an English invention became famous abroad when, after trial, it had been found unsatisfactory at home.

The broad-gauge Great Western Railway met its locomotive problems in these years without adopting either the long-boiler or the Crampton design. Its narrow-gauge rival the London & North Western, on the other hand, tried both, giving cautious approval for a time to the first but entirely rejecting the second. Being a very large system, it was split up for administrative purposes into separate units, each with a certain degree of autonomy; and for some time the locomotives on its Northern Division differed from those on its Southern. On the Northern Division Francis Trevithick (the great Richard's son) favoured what came to be known pre-eminently as the 'Crewe type'. He is not to be credited with its invention, which seems to have been due to Joseph Locke and to his assistant W. B. Buddicom.[18] The Crewe type was an engine with outside cylinders, having two sets of deep iron frames, with inclined cylinders fixed between them both. It proved very strong in service. The London & North Western eventually had more than 400 machines of the kind, built down to 1858. The design was taken up elsewhere; the Great Eastern Company was still using it in the 1860s, the Manchester Sheffield & Lincolnshire, in a modified form, 20 years later. It was popular in Scotland, on the Caledonian Railway and on the Highland, which built its last as late as 1901. And under the influence of Buddicom, who went on to build locomotives at Rouen, the type was extensively adopted in France.

The Southern Division of the London & North Western Company had its works at Wolverton, and under J. E. McConnell it settled down in 1851–4 to using machines with inside cylinders and frames. His express engines – nicknamed 'Bloomers' on account of the quantity of 'leg' they displayed – were admirable machines, which continued in service on the faster trains between London and Birmingham until about 1880. His corresponding goods engines were of the type we have noted emerging in 1848. More than 100 of them were built in 1854–63. In 1862, however, the London & North Western decided to concentrate the whole of its locomotive building at Crewe, under John Ramsbottom, who became Locomotive Engineer of the whole railway. As a sign of the scale on which the Company was now operating, and of the growth of standardisation, one may note that his 0–6–0 goods engine (class DX) was built to the number of 943 in 1858–72.[19] By this time the London & North

18. Cf. D. H. Stuart and B. Reed, 'The Crewe Type', in *Locomotives in Profile*, ed. B. Reed (1971–4), ii. 49–72. The claims of Alexander Allan to its invention are decisively disposed of here, pp. 67–70.

19. Eighty-six of these engines were supplied from Crewe to the Lancashire &

Western had achieved what it wanted and left experiment behind – to be taken up again, in different directions, in the 1880s.

The divergence of practice between the two Divisions of this company is worth noticing particularly in one respect. Ramsbottom prevailed over Trevithick, and he imposed his design of placing the engine's cylinders inside the frames. With few exceptions, and in later years none, American engineers did the opposite. So did almost all those on the Continent. In Britain, however, Ramsbottom's inside position was generally preferred throughout the Victorian age. Save for one type designed for special service in 1863, the Great Western Company never commissioned a locomotive with outside cylinders until 1902. The difference of practice established itself early and on many railways besides the Great Western stiffened into a tradition, until the multi-cylinder engine broke it. The British arrangement may have rendered the engine steadier at speed, and it helped to protect the motion from dirt; but then the motion was less easily accessible, and crank axles were rendered necessary, which were often a source of weakness through breaking in service.

The locomotive works of the big companies, headed by those at Crewe, Swindon, and Derby, were very big concerns indeed. Their growth indicates an important change that had now come over this branch of manufacture in Britain. Private firms had, at the outset, played the leading part in the business, both in designing locomotives and in supplying them. The first railway company to appoint senior officers to be responsible for locomotives alone seems to have been the Great Western in 1837. That practice soon came to be generally accepted. The first to manufacture a locomotive for itself had been the Stockton & Darlington, which turned out the *Royal George* from Shildon in 1827. Thereafter, however, it frequently purchased its machines outside. The Grand Junction Company produced the first locomotives from its works at Crewe in 1843; the Great Western started to do the same at Swindon, and the Manchester & Leeds at Miles Platting (Manchester), in 1846. By 1853 nearly all the chief English companies had followed these examples.[20] It thus became the usual practice for the larger British railways to make the locomotives they required in their own shops, though they might at

---

Yorkshire Railway. In 1876 private locomotive builders secured an injunction to prevent the London & North Western Company from manufacturing locomotives or rolling stock for sale or hire (Chaloner, 73). Thereafter, all railway companies were obliged to manufacture solely for their own use, though they might repair the locomotives of another company.

20. The Great Northern is an interesting exception. It established works, equipped to repair and reconstruct locomotives, first at Boston and then, in 1853, at Doncaster; but it did not build its first locomotive until 1867.

any time decide to purchase outside, for a variety of reasons: unusually heavy demand, overloading their own works, which might arise from the opening of an important new line; tempting manufacturers' offers; the availability of good standard designs elsewhere.[21] Some very small companies had works in which they occasionally built locomotives of their own: the Festiniog, for example, and the Maryport & Carlisle. On the other hand a company as large as the Furness habitually purchased its engines outside – nearly all of them from a single firm, Sharp Stewart.

In this matter the British railways differed from most others in the world. Though some American and Continental companies manufactured their own engines – the Pennsylvania, for example, at Altoona, the PLM in Paris and at Oullins, the Est at Epernay – the great majority bought outside. The British policy had much to recommend it, provided that the works were well managed and the flow of orders was adequate and steadily maintained. But it had one deleterious long-term consequence. It helped to make each company very inward-looking, to induce it to maintain its own standards and practices instead of 'shopping around' in search of the best that was currently available. Up to 1850 Britain had played the leading part in the design and supply of locomotives to the world. Thereafter, progress became slower and the initiative went elsewhere. Improvements in design often took place abroad and passed into satisfactory service long before Britain adopted them. Egide Walschaert published the plan of his valve-gear in Belgium in 1844. It was not applied to a locomotive in regular service in Britain until 1881, and it came into general use here only at the turn of the century. Similarly with another Belgian invention, the Belpaire firebox: that was first employed in 1864, but not fitted to a British locomotive until 1891 – and then under the influence of a private firm, Beyer Peacock, which had been making fireboxes of this design at Manchester for the foreign market since 1872.

These statements are not universally valid. The injector, the 'miracle of invention'[22] by the Frenchman Giffard for maintaining the flow of feed-water to the boiler, was announced in 1859 and taken up promptly in Britain. The patent rights were acquired by Sharp Stewart in the following year. Moreover, Britain was still developing and exporting ideas in locomotive practice. In the 1870s the Fairlie double-ended locomotive first proved itself fully in Wales, on the Festiniog Railway, and was then manufactured on a large scale and sent abroad, to make a sub-

---

21. The London & South Western Railway entirely discontinued the building of its own locomotives from 1875 to 1887. On the other hand, the Great Western never bought outside after 1866, except for three experimental machines acquired from France in 1903–5.
22. W. A. Tuplin, *The Steam Locomotive* (1974), 38.

stantial contribution to the economy of many countries, like Mexico, India, and New Zealand.

On balance, however, the railways seem to exemplify the qualities of Mid-Victorian Britain as a whole: a continuing energy, carried over from the tremendous upsurge in the first half of the century, coupled with a serene assumption – sometimes perhaps justified, but often dangerously complacent – that the answers were known, that there was no need to look outside for anything better. The railways had become in a high degree insular, apt to brush aside suggestions for improvement with a quiet assertion that they would not work in Britain.

This attitude was by no means wholly absurd. The track on her main lines was generally better laid and more robust than it was elsewhere – and here she was reaping an advantage that, to some extent, arose from the notoriously high initial costs of construction that had been incurred by her railways in the past. Largely for this reason, higher speeds were regarded as safe in this country – though that assumption was frequently criticised in the light of the numerous accidents of the 1870s (cf. p. 81). A few railways imposed a general speed limit throughout their systems (on the South Eastern it was 60 m.p.h. until after 1900), but nothing of the kind was required by the Government – as it was in France, where no train was permitted to exceed 75 m.p.h. The express locomotive in Britain was therefore expected to run fast and allowed to be heavy on the rails. Though there were sharp curves on some British main lines (the Midland system abounded in them at important junctions) those lines were, on the whole, comparatively straight: hence, in part, the slow adoption of the bogie, which many engineers considered an unnecessary device in this country.

Again, the fuel consumed by locomotives in Britain was usually cheap and good. That statement needs to be accepted critically, for fuel costs varied very much from one railway to another. In 1883 the coal used on the London Brighton & South Coast and the two London underground railways cost about 17s. a ton, while the Manchester Sheffield & Lincoln-shire Company, which served a coalfield itself, was paying 6s. 6d.[23] Compare the position of the Italian railways, which maintained their own fleet of colliers to bring Welsh coal from Cardiff to Genoa, a haul of nearly 2,000 miles, with that of the Great Western, which could afford without the least difficulty to use the top-grade product of that coalfield, the best steam coal in the world. No wonder that, in general, the British railways were so little interested in the principle of compounding for locomotives, when it came to be widely adopted on the Continent. That was not due merely to an obtuse conservatism. Compounding was first and

23. J. S. Jeans, *Railway Problems* (1887), 147.

foremost a device for saving fuel, which was not an economy that many British railways urgently needed to practise: whereas to the French, deprived of much of their coal by the Germans after the war of 1870, it was vital. With one exception, when compounding was tried in Britain it was rejected, in the short or the long run, as offering on balance no useful economy at all.[24]

And finally, to judge the wisdom of British railway managements aright, one must realise the nature of the duties their locomotives had to perform, as compared with those required by Continental and American railways: the density of the traffic (greater than anywhere on the Continent save perhaps in Belgium), the relatively short distance for which British trains ran, in a small country, the far greater frequency of service expected. Devices for economising in *time* were an urgent necessity here. Water-troughs (p. 150) and the slip carriage (p. 269) are cases in point.

It must therefore be recognised that British railways were, in some important respects, different organisms from their foreign counterparts. But equally, the Mid-Victorian age was for them one of conservatism, in the strongest contrast to the dynamic development that had characterised the preceding generation. A distinct change began, however, to appear in the 1880s. To a large extent this was a response to changes in demand that are readily perceptible. The democratisation of travel, which the railways had promoted when they began to carry passengers on a large scale in the 1830s and 1840s, was taken a long stage further as a result of the policies initiated by the Midland Company from 1872 onwards (cf. p. 196). The population of the country was constantly increasing. In the 1870s alone it rose by over 14 per cent; but the increase in passenger journeys was 83 per cent. In the year 1880, 31 railway journeys were made in England and Wales per head of the population.[25] New facilities were being introduced for travellers, copied from foreign example: the Pullman, the sleeping, and the restaurant car all make their first appearance in England in the 1870s. Express trains in consequence grew heavier, and it was not possible to ease the locomotives' task by making them run more slowly. On the contrary, they had to run faster: the competitive principle saw to that. There were now three rival lines from London to Manchester, two to Dover, Plymouth, and Birmingham, two from the north of England to Bristol and the west. As for coal, five

24. The exception was provided by the Midland Railway, which built 45 compound express locomotives in 1902–9, and its successor the London Midland & Scottish, which added 195 more of the same type in 1924–32.
25. The population figures come from the census of 1871 and 1881. Those for journeys relate to 1870 and 1880, since the *Railway Returns* for 1871 are imperfect; they include season ticket holders. PP 1871, lx. 500; 1881, lxxx. 728.

companies fought over the traffic from the Yorkshire pits southward; the London & North Western and the Great Western competed for the long-distance hauls from South Wales.

All this necessarily made new demands upon locomotive departments. They were met at first with caution, even with timidity. The six-coupled goods locomotive had established a standard pattern, which showed no important change in the Victorian age. True, the Great Eastern produced a machine in 1878 that revealed some awareness of current practice in the United States: it had the same six coupled wheels, but what the Americans called a 'pony truck' of two carrying wheels was added in front, and the cylinders were placed outside the frames. Fifteen of these engines were built, but they proved unsuccessful, and the ideas they represented were not pursued much further. When, at the turn of the century, three companies, in urgent need of new locomotives and finding it impossible to get them built in Britain quickly enough, imported machines of similar American type, they all treated them superciliously in service and scrapped them as soon as they could. The eight-coupled tender engine made two appearances here, one in the 1880s on the Barry Railway, the other extensively on the London & North Western from 1892 onwards; but with these exceptions the long-distance freight traffic of all kinds continued to be entrusted almost wholly to the same type of engine as before, a little enlarged in each decade.

The express locomotive took two cautious steps forward, both seen first in Scotland. The bogie had now begun at last to make its way in Britain – sometimes in order to ease running over much-curved lines, sometimes to spread the load on the rails at the front end. Patrick Stirling adopted it for his famous express engines with 8ft single driving wheels for the Great Northern Railway, the first of which appeared in 1870, not because he liked the device in itself – he never used it on any other machine he designed for this kind of service – but because the axles supported 15 tons, nearly 40 per cent of the locomotive's weight, which would have been a quite excessive load to place on a single pair of small carrying wheels.

In 1871 the North British Railway, and two years later the Glasgow & South Western, produced the first examples of what became in later years the most usual type of British main-line express locomotive: a 4–4–0, with inside cylinders, a leading bogie and the frames inside the wheels throughout. The type was taken up in England by S. W. Johnson, who adopted it on the Great Eastern Railway in 1874 and then on the Midland two years later. By the 1880s it had become standard on all the Scottish railways except the Highland, which preferred outside cylinders and the old 'Crewe frames'. The English companies might perhaps have adopted it earlier and more whole-heartedly if it had not been for a small new invention of 1885–6. This was a mechanism for applying sand, under the force of steam pressure, in front of the wheels of a locomotive; and it overcame the tendency that single driving wheels showed to slip round, without holding the rails, when the engine was starting. Since trains had been growing heavier, that tendency had led most railways to abandon locomotives of this kind. Now the single-driver made a spectacular come-back, and between 1887 and 1901 six English railways built large 4–2–2 engines – one of them, the Midland under Johnson, on a considerable scale, to the number of 95.

Some of these engines had great merits. They were free-running, easy to handle, beloved by many of their drivers. Johnson's in particular were very economical in fuel. They were admirably suited to such services as those between Manchester and Liverpool, where the trains were light, fast, and frequent. But though capable of high speed, and occasionally of surprising feats of haulage and of hill-climbing,[26] they were not the solution to the Late-Victorian traffic managers' problem: that of handling fast and heavy trains dependably.

If most British locomotive engineers in the 1870s and 1880s seem insular-minded and perhaps rather unadventurous, one of them provides a notable exception: F. W. Webb of the London & North Western. He was, at any rate, willing to experiment with almost anything (except bogies), to import ideas freely from Europe and America. He worked with conspicuous pertinacity to establish the principle of compounding for locomotives: that is, the double use of steam, first in high-pressure, then in low-pressure cylinders. His main objectives were three – not all necessarily pursued at the same time: to economise fuel; to divide the drive between two axles, in the interests of balance and steady motion; and to get rid of coupling rods, so reducing resistance and allowing the wheelbase to be lengthened with safety – another change intended to make the engines steadier. Webb began work on these lines in 1879 by converting an old engine to the compound system. Then, in 1882, he produced his first new one, *Experiment*. It was followed by nearly 400 more, of various types, built over the next 20 years. They cannot be said to have realised Webb's intentions. When they showed economy in fuel consumption, it was of trifling magnitude. They did perhaps ride more

26. The Great Western's *Duke of Connaught* ran a special mail express from Bristol to London (118½ miles) in 99¾ minutes in 1904; one of the Midland singles took a train of 325 tons over the difficult line from Kettering to Nottingham via Melton Mowbray at an average speed of 51.3 m.p.h. (Ahrons LTW, i. 136); the exploits of the Caledonian single No. 123 between Carlisle and Edinburgh in 1888 are famous – even legendary.

steadily than the simple engines with which they were being compared. But, for the rest, everything told against them. They were complicated machines, and therefore expensive to build;[27] most of them were notoriously recalcitrant at starting and unreliable in service; none showed any great turn of speed or superiority in haulage. Webb's great experiment – interesting though it was, conducted in a spirit of scientific inquiry, and in some respects meticulously recorded – must be accepted as a failure. Directly he retired in 1903, his successor, George Whale, reversed his policy. But then Whale was a practical man, who had himself been responsible for the running of Webb's engines. He turned to building new machines that were studiously simple, in all senses of that word. As for Webb's, he scrapped them as fast as he could, or converted them to simple propulsion.

While Webb was thus engaged, new portents of a different kind appeared in Scotland. David Jones designed for the Highland Railway the first British 4–6–0, a powerful engine with 20-inch cylinders, intended primarily for goods service but yet conveniently employed in passenger traffic on that mountainous line. And two years later J. F. McIntosh put out his *Dunalastair* on the Caledonian Railway, which could claim to be the first express locomotive in Britain to be provided with a really large boiler. These were the true pointers to development, in British conditions; and they quickly came to be accepted as such in England.

We are now in the last phase of development before 1914, and it is one of which the British railways are entitled to be proud. The standards of European express service were rising rapidly, yet Britain still maintained, in most respects, a demonstrable superiority. If she did not impose her example, or lead the world as she had done before 1850, her railways adapted themselves briskly to new demands and showed a sensible willingness to observe and learn from what was going on abroad. British builders continued to supply locomotives to the whole world – competing hotly now with the big manufacturers in Germany, but on fairly equal terms.

The most distinguished work was done on the Great Western Railway. In the Mid-Victorian age that grand and ancient company had been dozing. It moved slowly towards the abandonment of the broad gauge; but the conversion was a costly and troublesome job, and it was spread over more than 20 years (cf. pp. 84–5). Meanwhile, the Great Western's customers had to take it or leave it. Many of them, when they could, left it – in favour, for example, of the London & South Western's rival line to

27. How much more expensive? We cannot tell, since Webb's compounds were built in the Company's own works at Crewe and there are therefore no contract prices for them to be compared with those of commercial builders.

Exeter and Plymouth. But from 1888 onwards an improvement in its
service began. That called for new and larger engines, which William
Dean, its Locomotive Engineer, set himself to provide. In his closing
years the task of forward thinking was taken up by his deputy, George
Jackson Churchward, who succeeded him in 1902. Churchward went on
to endow the Great Western with the most successful range of locomotives, for almost all types of work, that England had ever seen. To
this end he made Swindon a great experimental laboratory, as Crewe
had been under Webb in the 1880s, but with two vital differences: that
most of the experiments succeeded, and that those that failed to prove
themselves were abandoned.

   One of the best features of Crewe's practice had been the standardisation of locomotive designs and components, laid down by Ramsbottom
and carried further by Webb. At Swindon the idea had first appeared
much earlier, adopted by the intelligent young Daniel Gooch about
1840;[28] but it could not prevail over the whole of the Company's large
system until it was all operated on one gauge, and until locomotive
building was concentrated in a single works. Great Western engines continued to be built at Wolverhampton as well as at Swindon, and in some
respects the practice of the two works differed. Churchward concentrated
all new design firmly at Swindon, and the Wolverhampton works ceased
to build locomotives in 1908.

   Like Webb, Churchward was a close observer of the practice of other
engineers, abroad as well as at home. He was willing to look at compounding, and for this purpose bought from Belfort three Atlantic
(4–4–2) locomotives, of types that were performing distinguished work
on the Nord and Orleans systems in France. He built his own simple
locomotives, generally similar. They were tested against one another in
1903–6. The results were observed closely. The compound principle
showed no advantage sufficient to offset the much more complicated
machinery that was required – expensive, and demanding a high degree
of skill on the part of the driver. Churchward proceeded with it no
further. On the other hand the French machines proved notably steadier
in their running, from the use of four cylinders in two pairs (each driving
a different axle), which divided the 'hammer blow', eased the strain on
the rails, and made the engine's passage over them smoother. This was a
new version of a lesson that Webb had tried to teach. It was worth learning, and it led to the building of Churchward's 'Star' class from 1906 onwards, with four cylinders and the same divided drive. They were not
Atlantics but 4–6–0 engines – a pattern that had already proved itself
well in a two-cylinder form. The six coupled wheels provided greater

28. MacDermot, i. 397.

adhesion, and that was especially called for now through changes in operating practice. Long non-stop runs were being introduced, from Paddington to Plymouth and Newport for example. The same locomotive had therefore to be able not only to run fast over the level eastern stretch of the line but equally to surmount the formidable banks west of Newton Abbot and up from the bottom of the Severn Tunnel.

Two other critically important changes were adopted by Churchward in the design of the boiler. From 1903 onwards he began to make his boilers cone-shaped, tapering from the front to the back, to give the largest heating surface near the firebox – a practice he had noted with approval in America. And in 1906 he fitted a superheater to one of his engines for the first time, of the Schmidt pattern from Germany.[29] He subsequently modified it in some respects into what was known as the 'Swindon' type, and this came to be standard equipment for all the larger Great Western engines. When the four-cylinder 4–6–0s were fitted with it from 1909 onwards they became Churchward's masterpiece among locomotives for express service. More than that: these engines must surely be judged the masterpiece among all such locomotives in Britain down to 1914.

It is important to note that though Churchward's engines were still British in character – markedly different from those of Europe and America in appearance,[30] in the materials that went into them and the methods by which they were made, in the fuel they consumed, in the service they were intended to perform – the success of the final result had been achieved by looking abroad and incorporating elements of foreign practice into it, from France and Germany and the United States.

Churchward's matured group of designs (evolved in 1902–11) numbered nine in all, and they covered nearly the whole range of normal service: express passenger, mixed traffic, heavy mineral and goods, suburban and branch-line work.[31] (The railway was already provided adequately with machines suitable for light goods and shunting.) All of these were successful, some outstanding: the 2–6–0 mixed-traffic engines for example, nimble and versatile; the 2–8–0 heavy freight engines, which slogged up on the coal trains from South Wales for nearly 60 years, the class being doubled in size through new building to the same design (of 1903) in 1938–42.

29. He was not the first British engineer to fit superheaters to locomotives. J. A. F. Aspinall had used a rather more primitive version of one on the Lancashire & Yorkshire Railway in 1899.

30. Nothing is said here about the aesthetics of the locomotive. That matter will be touched on in the third volume of this work.

31. An express goods type was added in 1919.

But excellent machines were produced elsewhere than at Swindon, on somewhat different lines. The traditional British 4–4–0 express engine reached perhaps its peak of development in J. G. Robinson's 'Director' class for the Great Central Railway in 1911. The Atlantic type was admirably exemplified, first on the Great Northern, then on the North Eastern, and on the Great Central again. Beside the Great Western's eight-coupled heavy goods engines one may set those of the London & North Western, the North Eastern, and the Great Northern; whilst the Great Central's found uses undreamt of when they were designed in 1911, for in the First World War that type was adopted by the Government as the standard heavy freight engine and built to the number of more than 500 for military service at home and overseas.

In any brief survey of the development of the steam locomotive in this country it is natural to pay greatest attention to the express passenger engine. It was in that type of machine that most of the important innovations were tried and developed first. Moreover, although it is true that receipts from goods traffic were in the aggregate larger than those from passengers, the machines used in handling it were simpler, and much slower to change, than those in express service. There is another kind of locomotive, however, the tank engine, which has scarcely been mentioned but calls for consideration, especially at this point, because it grew more efficient and came to be used much more widely in these closing years. The type was particularly well suited to England and Wales, with their multitude of short-distance services. Carrying its fuel and water with it, the tank engine required no tender and could be driven with equal facility either way: whereas certain risks arose in working locomotives tender first, and the practice was seldom permitted with fast trains. Tank engines had always been employed for certain special services – on the underground railways, for instance, of London and Liverpool; and they had long been found handier for shunting. Nevertheless, some companies had taken them up scarcely at all. In 1886 the Great Eastern had no more than 15, for shunting and goods work, out of a total stock of more than 700 locomotives.[32]

By this time, however, the tank engine was beginning to be used more widely. The London Tilbury & Southend Company tried a ten-wheeled version (4–4–2) in 1880, with immediate and striking success. The first 12 handled the whole traffic of the railway, fast and slow, passenger and goods alike. Thereafter the Company used no others in normal passenger service, building 70, in successively larger versions, down to 1909. Similarly on the Lancashire & Yorkshire Aspinall designed a 2–4–2 tank engine in 1889, the prototype of a series of 330 which ran all over the

32. Ahrons LTW, i. 116.

Company's dense system, in passenger service of every kind.

Another sort of tank engine had a brief efflorescence in the early years of the twentieth century, in the form of the steam railcar, with a very small locomotive built into a passenger carriage. Every major company except the Great Eastern and the North Eastern tried this device, especially in suburban service, in the fierce competition against the newly-arrived electric trams. It was not generally liked, however. The railcars were self-contained, inflexible units, not at all powerful and quite unable to cope with a sudden influx of traffic, say for some big sporting event; and they proved disagreeably hot in summer. Only the Great Western developed them resolutely, till they numbered 100 on the whole system. They continued in service there until, in the 1930s, they began to be displaced by diesel railcars. That was the old world handing over to the new.

Very big tank engines made their appearance, parallel in development with the express tender locomotive, after 1900. The last to appear before the First World War was a magnificent 4–6–4 machine for the London Brighton & South Coast Company, whose huge tanks could hold enough water to take it without stopping over the 87 miles from London to Portsmouth. Even more powerful engines had been built by the Great Central and North Eastern railways in 1907–9 for special work in shunting yards; the Great Central machines were the most powerful locomotive units of any kind at work in Britain before the War.

By 1913 the majority of the locomotives on the Great Western Railway were tank engines; they formed nearly three-quarters of the stock of the London Brighton & South Coast. As for the Rhymney Railway, it had one solitary tender engine, and 122 tanks.

That was in South Wales; and there the tank locomotive made a contribution to the prosperity not merely of one railway company but even, in a sense, of a nation. The railways of south-east Wales presented some features quite peculiar to themselves. Their density was greater perhaps than that of any other comparable tract in the world. They traversed short distances, comprising for the most part lines from the collieries down the valleys to the coal ports on the Bristol Channel. Their passenger traffic was relatively insignificant; coal was their mainstay – above all the steam coal of the Rhondda, which came to be prized more and more highly from 1855 onwards, at home and abroad. Eight small companies shared most of this traffic, and two of them at least (the Taff Vale and the Barry) were among the most profitable railway enterprises in the United Kingdom. These eight were, as might be expected, fierce rivals, often enemies; but they agreed on the use of the tank engine, and especially of one type, the 0–6–2. It first reached South Wales in 1885. When the eight companies came to be merged into the Great Western in 1921–2, nearly 60 per cent of their entire locomotive stock was of this one wheel arrangement. It lent itself admirably to their conditions. It was flexible and easily manoeuvred on the sharply-curved lines of the Valleys and their collieries; its adhesive weight was relatively high; it could provide good coal and water space distributed over its eight wheels. So it became what Plaid Cymru might well claim as the pre-eminently Welsh loco-motive. It is fitting that one, from the Taff Vale Company, should be preserved at Caerphilly today.

The locomotives so far discussed all derived their power from steam, with coal as their fuel. Oil-burning was tried from 1887 onwards by the Great Eastern Railway, the oil being made from a waste product of gas works, including the Company's own. The experiment was thorough: about 60 locomotives were adapted to work in this way. Technically, it succeeded very well. In economic terms it made admirable sense: for the Great Eastern Company was one of those that lay furthest away from a coalfield and had therefore to buy its coal dearly. The plan was defeated, however, by a rise in the price of the fuel, above that of coal; and the effort was abandoned, after a trial of about ten years.[33]

Oil was also used experimentally, on a much smaller scale, in another form. An oil-engined shunting locomotive, designed by W. D. Priestman, was put to work at the North Eastern Railway's Alexandra Dock in Hull in 1894; other oil-engined locomotives were commissioned by the War Office, for use at Woolwich Arsenal, from 1898 onwards. Railcars powered by internal combustion engines running on paraffin or petrol were tried on a number of railways – the Brighton, the North Eastern, the Great Western, the Great Central; there was one in the Isle of Wight. They were under-powered and soon passed out of use, with the exception of the Great Central's car, which stayed at work for 20 years.[34]

Other forms of traction, very much older, continued on railways, side by side with the steam locomotive. The horse, who had played his part in the early development of railways,[35] survived on one regular passenger service in England, the Port Carlisle branch of the North British Com-pany, until April 1914; he was still extensively employed in shunting yards (indeed he was to be seen on this service at Llanelly until 1963 and

33. Cf. Ahrons BSRL, i. 127–9; C. J. Allen, *The Great Eastern Railway* (2nd edn, 1956), 124–6.
34. Dow GC, iii. 318–19.
35. A number of minor lines had been worked by horse-power down to 1860, some for quite long periods of time: the Weston-super-Mare, Heywood, and Southwell branches, for example. The Swansea & Mumbles Railway was worked both by locomotives and by horses in the 1880s and 1890s: C. E. Lee, *The Swansea & Mumbles Railway* (1954), 23, 25.

at Newmarket four years after that). The stationary engine still hauled trains by cable here and there, and one considerable new undertaking of this kind had appeared in 1896, with the opening of the Glasgow Subway – not to mention the short cliff railways that became familiar elements of seaside resorts, like Scarborough, Folkestone, and Lynmouth.

A fair number of railways in Europe and America had turned to electric traction before 1914. It was adopted in England too, but hesitantly and then mainly for one limited purpose: the operation of urban and suburban railways carrying a dense traffic. After minor experiments in the 1880s, in Ireland and at Brighton, and the opening of the first electrically-worked tube railways in London, together with the Liverpool Overhead Railway, in 1890–1900, the larger companies turned to consider the expedient seriously when they found their traffic eroded through the spread of electric tramways. Then it came with a rush: under the Mersey in 1903, in west Lancashire and on Tyneside in 1904, on the Inner Circle of the London underground system in the following year, on the South London line in 1909. In all these cases it answered well. It enabled the main-line companies to recover most, or all, of the traffic they had lost to the trams; it delivered the railways running underground from the nuisance of smoke. Other companies, like the Great Eastern and the South Eastern & Chatham, took powers to electrify their suburban systems, though they did not exercise them, deterred by the high capital cost.[36] Parliament actually imposed on the Midland Railway, when it sought permission to buy the London Tilbury & Southend Company in 1912, the duty of electrifying the system, as a condition of its assent; but the Midland moved very slowly in the matter, and when the War came the obligation was conveniently forgotten. The London & South Western and the London & North Western, however, went ahead with well-laid plans and implemented them in London in 1914–17; the Lancashire & Yorkshire Company introduced electric trains into Manchester in 1916. The Brighton Company was so pleased by its experiments in South London that it decided, in principle, to move by stages towards electrifying its entire system. But that ambitious project was killed by the War.

The total mileage of English railways on which electric trains ran by

36. The Great Eastern remained genuinely unconvinced of the need for electrification. In 1903 James Holden built for it a very remarkable ten-coupled tank engine, *Decapod*, which succeeded in demonstrating that steam could generate a power of acceleration equal to that afforded by electricity. The machine was not used in regular service, however: if it had been, costly engineering works would have been required to fortify the track and bridges over which it ran. (See *Transactions of the Newcomen Society* 28 (1951–3) 269–85; *ibid.* 29 (1953–5) 263–4.) That experiment being abandoned, the Great Eastern turned to the intensification of its conventional service into and out of Liverpool Street.

the end of 1913 was 235.[37] Electric traction had been adopted on these lines under the auspices of 15 different companies; and it had been carried through on at least 12 different systems. The Brighton Company, as well as the Midland (on a short line out of Lancaster), used alternating-current overhead traction; the London Underground, on the Inner Circle, a direct-current four-rail system. On the City & South London and Central London railways the trains were hauled by electric locomotives; on all the rest power was supplied from electric motors built into the trains themselves. These English practices reflected the tentative, experimental nature of electric traction on railways throughout the world.

One other company had quite different ideas again. The North Eastern had been the first railway in Britain to employ this new power in goods service. At Newcastle it had a peculiarly awkward stretch of line, the Quayside branch, which carried no passengers but much freight. It was steeply graded, curved, and in tunnel; the crews of steam engines working it had one of the most unpleasant tasks anywhere on the English railway system. In 1904 electric traction was adopted, with two locomotives built for the purpose. It succeeded admirably, and the Company then determined to electrify another freight line: the stretch of 18½ miles from Shildon to Middlesbrough. Work began in 1913 and the new system was brought into use, with ten electric locomotives, in 1915–16. This was intended to be the first step towards the electrification of the whole main line from Newcastle to York; but that plan, like the Brighton's, foundered in the economic difficulties following the War. Sixty years later the electrification of this great highway of traffic remains a project for the future.

The British railways have often been criticised, then and since, for their tardiness in adopting electric traction. To the Royal Commission on London Traffic in 1905 the advantage was self-evident, the delay indefensible.[38] But then the Commission was not required to devise means of enabling the work to be financed. The capital cost of electrification was extremely heavy, and it could not be shown at that time to bring profit, though it might reduce or avert losses.[39] Looking at the system as a whole, it can be said with reasonable certainty that in 1914 electrification was neither practicable nor desirable, in the general business of the British railways. They had ample supplies of coal, very far

---

37. PP 1914–16, lx. 842. This total excludes the Blackpool & Fleetwood Tramroad. There were no electrified lines in Wales, though the Taff Vale Company was among those which had secured Parliamentary powers to electrify.
38. PP 1905, xxx. 627.
39. The financial achievement of the early tube railways in London was depressing: cf. p. 139.

from exhaustion, and though the Coal Strike of 1912 was a warning of the danger of dependence on one fuel, that threat was overcome; it could surely be overcome if it arose again. On the other side, Britain had no natural sources of hydro-electric power comparable with those of the Alpine countries of Europe. Except for the special purposes that have been indicated, steam locomotives remained not merely adequate but well suited to her needs. Some 21,000 of them were employed on the main-line railways of England and Wales in 1914. Only a crank or a visionary could have foretold that just over 50 years later not one would remain in regular service.

8   Rolling Stock

a. PASSENGER VEHICLES

The Liverpool & Manchester Company afforded the first extensive passenger service yet seen on any railway. The vehicles it provided for the purpose were of two kinds: the first-class carriages, which were clearly derived from the horse-drawn coach, and the second-class carriages, whose forebear was rather the railway goods wagon.

The railway could hardly have looked for its chief models anywhere else. In the conveyance of passengers it was aiming first of all at displacing the coaches, which had been designed to what was (except in small details) a standard pattern. As far as the superstructure of the new vehicles was concerned, which was all that most passengers noticed, it was reassuringly familiar, for in principle it comprised nothing but three coach bodies joined together and mounted on one frame. Even here, however, there were two differences. Each compartment of the railway carriage held six passengers, three on each side in seats divided by armrests, whereas the horse-drawn coach had held only four, cheek by jowl; and on the railway there were no 'outside' passengers on the roofs,[1] though guards travelled up above at first, perched on the high seats they had always occupied before. So the unit, the railway carriage, accommodated 18 passengers, all inside, by comparison with a maximum of 16 – four inside and 12 outside – on the coach.

The body-work was closely similar to the coach's: very naturally again, for it was constructed by coach-builders, trained in an accomplished craft. The Liverpool & Manchester Company employed a young coach-builder, Nathaniel Worsdell, for this work. One of his first tasks

1. Exceptionally, in the late 1830s the Grand Junction Company allowed passengers to travel outside if they chose: N. W. Webster, *Britain's First Trunk Railway* (1972), 103, 106. So did the Newcastle & Carlisle: Tomlinson, 400.

had been to design a tender for the locomotive *Rocket*. He then concentrated on his proper business and continued to be responsible for this department of the railway throughout its life as an independent company. The compartments of his first-class carriages were identical in their outside appearance to the bodies of coaches, with curving side-panels and a pair of quarter-light windows flanking the main one in the door.

Underneath, however, the frames were entirely different. The body was built of the traditional material, timber; the undercarriage was largely of iron, and so were the wheels, though presently they were sometimes given wooden spokes, which seem to have proved less brittle in service. It was of course necessary that the frame should be very much stronger than that of the coach, because of the locomotive's greater power of traction. Here the manufacture of railway carriages began to diverge from coach-building. The Liverpool & Manchester Company indicated as much when in 1836 it bought six first-class carriage bodies from outside makers and fitted them to iron frames made in its own workshops.[2] 'The result has been', said a coach-builder who was benevolently interested in railways, 'that they have separated the branches of the art: the carriage builder for railroads has become a mere wooden box maker'.[3]

The original first-class carriages, though they were well appointed, were evidently not luxurious enough for the railway's wealthier customers, and by 1831 others were available accommodating only four inside, at an extra fare.[4] These were the mail carriages, in one compartment of which seats could be converted into a bed, making the vehicle 'a very desirable one to the invalid or valetudinarian, whom necessity obliges to travel'.[5]

Such was the provision for the well-to-do. But from the outset the railway carried other kinds of passengers, at cheaper rates. The accommodation afforded to them was quite different. The second-class carriages had little in common with stage coaches. They were at first open wagons furnished with wooden benches – passenger trucks, no more. The service the railway offered was much superior to the coaches' in speed, but in comfort it was hardly better, for these passengers, than travelling out-

---

2. Donaghy, 62. Similar practices were also followed elsewhere, e.g. by the London & Greenwich Company: R. H. G. Thomas, *London's First Railway* (1972), 195, 198, 209, 210.

3. W. B. Adams, *English Pleasure Carriages* (1971 edn), 290.

4. Advertisement reproduced in Marshall CH, 69.

5. Donaghy, 60. It is not clear why they were called mail carriages. Ackermann's 'long print' of 1831 shows one lettered as such but devoted entirely to the conveyance of passengers, except for one wooden box on the roof. Can this have held the mail?

side. By 1833 the Company had started to cover in some of these carriages, so creating in effect four classes of accommodation: mail, first, roofed-in second, and open 'third' – though the Liverpool & Manchester never stated formally that it offered a third class until 1844.[6]

It has been contended that railways, by establishing such practices as these, did much to accentuate class distinctions: a generalisation that, critically examined, proves largely untrue.[7] At this point only one element in that discussion need be mentioned. If first-class travel was expensive, and so seemed to widen the gulf between richer and poorer passengers, first-class carriages were expensive too. When prices had settled down into a kind of average, about 1840, it could be said that a first-class carriage cost some £400, a covered-in second only half or a quarter of that sum.[8] The Manchester Bolton & Bury Railway in 1839 put the price it paid for a first-class (18 places) at £480; a second-class (32 places) at £100; and a third-class (36 places) at £60.[9] In other words the capital cost of providing a first-class place there was nearly £27, whilst a second-class place cost just over £3 and a third-class place less than £2.

Perhaps the most frequent discomfort suffered by early railway travellers – it was shared by all classes – arose at starting and stopping, and from rough riding when the trains were in motion. The Liverpool & Manchester Railway showed the way to a good deal of improvement here. Leather-covered buffers had been provided on all its carriages by 1833, and a number of experiments were made with various forms of springs to ease the impact between vehicles. A very notable invention came from the Company's Secretary, Henry Booth, in the screw coupling, which he patented in 1836.

6. Donaghy, 111. It should be added that a few railways also provided for some time a fourth class, so described: the Great Northern, for instance, and the London Brighton & South Coast. But fourth class never became generally established on the British railways as it did on the Prussian.

7. The matter will be discussed in Vol. IV of this work. But the loose thinking that has appeared in its consideration may be illustrated here by one august example, from Elie Halévy's great *History of the English People* (2nd edn, iii. 276), where he singles out the division into three classes as one of the special faults of the railway in this country. That division was in no way peculiar to Britain, however; it was universal in Europe from the start.

8. The Sheffield Ashton & Manchester Railway's expenditure was as follows:

	1st class	2nd class	3rd class
1841	£395	£209–13	£170
1843–5	310	134	97

(Dow GC, i. 107.) Hawkshaw, reviewing the carriages of the Lancashire & Yorkshire Railway in 1850, gave their capital cost as from £161 to £400, with a few that were still more expensive: *Report* (cited p. 146 above), 18–21.

9. PP 1839, x. 319.

Little change took place in the design of British carriages for 20 years after the evolution of these prototypes. The change in the 1840s came through the improvement of third-class travel. The facilities provided for it were first investigated by the Board of Trade in 1842, as a result of the deplorable Sonning accident on Christmas Eve of the preceding year. That had revealed two very serious defects in the construction of the third-class carriages of the Great Western Railway: they were without spring buffers, and the sides of the open vehicles were only 6 ins higher than the seats. As a consequence, when the train (a mixed one, for third-class passengers and goods) ran suddenly into a landslip at night, all the passengers were thrown out and eight of them were killed. Within four days the Board of Trade recommended the Company to remedy these defects; the Secretary replied that it was already engaged in doing so, and undertook to expedite the process.[10]

In reply to the general inquiries of the Board, 21 English companies stated that they conveyed third-class passengers. About half of them fitted spring buffers to their third-class carriages, provided them with seats, and made the sides of them more than 3ft high. As for closing them in with roofs, the Sheffield & Rotherham Company did that with all its third-class carriages but two; the London & Croydon apparently possessed no more than four such vehicles altogether, of which two were closed; on every other English railway the carriages were open, without exception.[11]

The Board made no comment on the returns. But they did not pass unnoticed. The scale of third-class travel was growing substantial. In 1842–3 third-class journeys accounted for 27.4 per cent of all those made in the United Kingdom.[12] Gladstone's Act of 1844 imposed certain obligations on railway managements in respect of third-class service and accommodation (see p. 37), and by the close of that year they were said to have been duly met. Parliament was still not satisfied, however, and in February 1845 it asked for details of the carriages in use for passengers conveyed under the terms of the Act. The replies it received to this inquiry include a comprehensive set of drawings of the vehicles.[13] They show still a wide diversity of practice. The carriages vary in width from 5ft 10ins to 8ft 6ins (on the broad gauge);[14] the inside height from 5ft 2 ins to 6ft 9ins. Rather more than half of them have some glazing, at the

10. PP 1842, xli. 115–16.
11. *Ibid.*, 264–81.
12. *Ibid.*, 333. The contrast between the percentages in England and Wales (22.8 per cent) and in Scotland (42.8 per cent) is notable.
13. PP 1845, xxxix. 33–79.
14. But those on the Brighton, Croydon, and South Eastern railways were nearly as wide (8ft 2ins).

sides, the ends, or in the roof. With two exceptions all appear to be fitted with spring buffers, and all (save in two doubtful cases, where the drawings are incomplete) seem to have their wheels sprung too.

Four of these vehicles are of interest as being larger than most of the rest and running on six wheels: something that no road vehicle had ever done. The six-wheeled carriage did not pass quickly into general use, however. It was heavier, and it did not necessarily ride any better than one on four wheels. Several experiments were made with vehicles mounted on eight, in two pairs of four. Two of these were for Queen Victoria's use on the Great Western Railway, others ran for ordinary passengers on the Eastern Counties and the South Eastern. In 1852 the Great Western put into service a set of six eight-wheeled carriages for its express trains (competing with those on the shorter London & North Western route) between London and Birmingham. They were not a great success, found their way for a time on to the Metropolitan line in 1863, and then retired to suburban service. None of these eight-wheeled vehicles ran on bogies, as many carriages were already doing in America (cf. p. 168), though some side-play was allowed to the pairs of axles at each end.

The carriages of the 1850s and 1860s marked no striking advance on those evolved on the Liverpool & Manchester Railway in the 1830s, though the amenities of passenger travel increased slightly. An oil lamp was usually provided in each compartment; on some railways it was becoming usual to upholster, in a Spartan fashion, second-class seats; footwarmers – metal cans containing hot water – began to be supplied on some lines, for steam heating was unknown in Britain.[15] The riding of the vehicles was improved through the use of the wheels patented by Richard Mansell in 1848, composed of teak segments, with iron bosses and iron (later Bessemer steel) tyres. Though smoking was prohibited on almost every railway, a beginning was made with the provision of special smoking carriages, on the Eastern Counties Railway for instance in 1846, on the North Eastern ten years later, and on the Stockton & Darlington in 1863.[16] The Regulation of Railways Act of 1868 made the provision of smoking carriages obligatory.

The smoking carriages just mentioned were saloons, and that type of open vehicle now began to go into service, in small numbers, side by side with the traditional pattern divided into compartments. It was welcomed for parties, and for families travelling together.[17] Then it was

15. It had however been installed experimentally in a carriage built for the Queen by the London & Birmingham Railway in 1843: Ellis, 45.
16. *Ibid.*, 57–9; Tomlinson, *North Eastern Railway*, 657.
17. The 'family saloon' was widely used in Victorian England, though it began to go

admirable; it was not popular, however, on ordinary occasions, with passengers travelling on their own. The English adhered tenaciously to the carriage divided into compartments; and the few who visited the United States usually disliked the open railroad cars they found there.

Some changes occurred gradually in the old, established patterns that were not mere matters of detail. The vehicles were now longer, and generally contained four or five compartments, not three. Since the accommodation they afforded had also tended to become a little more spacious, this meant that the carriages grew heavier. To make a comparison between the ordinary vehicles of 1845 and 1875, let us take a train made up of six, two of each class. The carriages in 1875 were 24–27ft long, and they were wider (8ft 4ins was a common standard). In 1845 this train would have accommodated 90 passengers and shown a total weight, fully loaded, of 37 tons; 30 years later the accommodation would have been for 122 passengers, and the weight 68½ tons. So the weight of the train had increased by 85 per cent, but it afforded only 36 per cent more seats. In vehicles of every class the paying load, in relation to the total weight, had fallen.[18] The passengers gained; the cost to the railways rose.

Striking changes came in the 1870s, setting standards in the provision of service that continued to rise higher, at an increasing pace, down to 1914. The first sleeping cars in Britain appeared in 1873, on trains running between London and Glasgow: by the East Coast route in April, by the West Coast six months later. They were for first-class passengers only (though the East Coast carriage included an ordinary second-class compartment, for servants); the earlier one accommodated six passengers, the later one 12 – four ladies and eight gentlemen.[19] Both were equipped with lavatories, the first to be provided in any British vehicles running in regular service.[20]

Here was a major innovation, a sign for the future. It attracted custom and established itself, being extended to trains running from Euston to Holyhead and Liverpool in 1875,[21] and reaching the Great Western, for a service between London and Plymouth, two years later. But at the same moment a different kind of sleeping car, in some important

---

out at the beginning of the twentieth century. A late example, including even the luxury of a bath, was put into service on the Great Northern Railway in 1906, but it was not much patronised: F. A. S. Brown, *Nigel Gresley* (1975 edn), 25–6.

18. Cf. the table in J. W. Barry, *Railway Appliances* (4th edn, 1884), 236.
19. Neele, 191. Ellis (85) gives the accommodation for gentlemen at six, but this seems to apply to a later vehicle.
20. There had been sanitation in a few royal, invalid, and family saloons since about 1850: cf. Ellis, 47–52, 211.
21. Neele, 204.

respects superior, was making its way on another system, the Midland. The Midland's new routes were in general longer than those of the established railways, and physically they were harder to work. If the Company was to make them pay, it would have to attract custom by superior service. Its decision in 1872 to carry third-class passengers by all its trains, including every express, was unprecedented, not in Britain alone but on the Continent. It was followed by what was in some respects a complementary decision two years later: to abolish second class altogether, reducing first-class fares and (for the first time in Europe) providing upholstered third-class seats.[22]

The grounds on which this decision was defended, against critical Midland shareholders and the Company's scandalised rivals, were that the provision of accommodation in only two classes would simplify the marshalling of trains and reduce the rising costs of operation. In itself, this argument was valid; but its force was weakened by another step the Midland Company took at the same time. Allport had visited North America in 1872, and he had taken a shrewd and discriminating view of the railways he found there. In particular, he liked the Pullman cars, which had started to run in 1865 and were by then appearing widely. He also liked the American provision for sleeping on long night journeys. On his advice the Midland Company introduced Pullman cars on to its system in 1874. The first of them ran between London and Bradford, affording sleeping accommodation by night but convertible into 'parlor' cars in the day-time. More then went into service, to Manchester and Liverpool and on the new Midland route to Scotland in 1876.

Being American, these cars ran on bogies. They were the first true bogie carriages seen in Britain in ordinary service, though experiments had been made in that direction more than 20 years earlier.[23] They were 58ft long and they weighed 21½ tons – nearly twice as much as the British second-class carriages of the time. The total weight of the Midland trains, though it was reduced by the suppression of second class, was at the same time increased by the corresponding provision required for more third-class passengers, and in the case of these principal expresses by the inclusion of the heavy new Pullman vehicles. It could

22. It is true that a few British railway companies had never offered second-class travel. The largest of these was the Great North of Scotland; but then neither it nor any of the others that followed a similar policy had ever run what could be called, by any sensible use of language, an express train.
23. The Great Northern Company also undertook to build some bogie carriages in 1874, but this was clearly as a *riposte* to the new Pullman cars on the Midland: the earliest reference to the plans for them occurs on 8 May (F. A. S. Brown, *Great Northern Locomotive Engineers*, i, 1966, 182), by which time the first two Pullmans had made demonstration runs, going into regular service on 1 June.

well be argued that all the Midland had done was to create a new three-class structure of Pullman, first, and third – though this applied only to the services on which the new cars operated: they never ran, for example, on the main line from the north to the west, between Derby and Bristol. When the use of Pullmans spread to other railways, such as the London Brighton & South Coast, which retained second class, the number of classes there rose to four.

The first Pullmans, together with their immediate successors, offered British travellers amenities they had never previously known. Their bogies afforded an incomparably smoother ride. They were heated by hot-water pipes – a vast improvement on the crude footwarmers, which were all that had hitherto been available, even to the richest passengers;[24] lighted by kerosene lamps, which gave a much better illumination than the usual small pot-lights; and provided with lavatories. The sleeping-car supplement was six shillings; that for day travel varied according to distance from one shilling to five.

And yet the Pullmans were only a partial success.[25] The supplementary charges in the parlor cars were resented, and the open saloon did not become popular. On the Midland they lasted, in various forms, down to 1888, when the Company bought Pullman out. They were adopted by five other English companies in 1875–1914,[26] and by two in Scotland.[27] They met with varying fortunes; on a number of railways they came and went. Only the Brighton Company took them to its heart and used them on a large scale.

The 1870s had one more big development in store. Hitherto, no meals had been available to travellers on any ordinary train service. The first luncheon baskets had been offered at Derby in 1875, and at Chester in the following year.[28] Three years later a dining car made its appearance, running between Kings Cross and Leeds on the Great Northern Railway. It was a Pullman car and the catering was done, not by either the railway company or Pullman but by private contract. A supplement was charged for travelling in the car, on top of the cost of the meal.

24. Described with care by Findlay, 188–9; cf. 388–9. The West Coast sleeping cars remained entirely unheated until 1883 (Neele, 278), the East Coast cars for ten years after that (Ellis, 141).
25. G. Behrend, *Pullman in Europe* (1962), 25–7, 34.
26. In chronological order, the London Brighton & South Coast, Great Northern, London & South Western, London Chatham & Dover, South Eastern & Chatham, and Metropolitan.
27. The Highland and the Caledonian. They also ran on the North British Railway north of Carlisle, as part of the service by the Midland route between London and Edinburgh.
28. Midland Company's handbill, National Railway Museum, York; Neele, 214–15.

As far as accommodation in express trains is concerned, we have suddenly moved by 1880 from the Middle Ages of railway travel into the beginning of the modern world. Each of the elements in it that we should regard as essential had by then been exemplified in England, though no single train combined them all, and one at least had appeared and disappeared. A Pullman train on the Midland had offered intercommunication between one car and another in 1875, but with the failure of the parlor cars to attract custom the train-sets were broken up and the cars distributed one by one among the standard vehicles of the railway company, each of which continued to be self-contained.

Although Pullman cars had only a limited success in Britain, their influence made itself felt. The Midland Company began building bogie carriages of its own. Fine new rolling stock (quite apart from the Pullmans), running on six-wheeled bogies, was provided for its Scottish services in 1876. In succeeding years the eight-wheeled vehicle spread steadily. The cautious London & North Western adopted it as a standard for main-line trains in 1883; but it rejected bogies in favour of Webb's radial trucks, which allowed a little play only to the outer axles of each pair.[29] The Great Northern, on the other hand, for all its early experiments in this direction, continued to favour the six-wheeled vehicle. It was partly a matter of money. In 1875 Patrick Stirling contended that a bogie carriage cost £1,030 to build, or £25 15s. for each seat provided, against £483 for one running on six wheels, at £14 4s. a seat. Later in the same year he and his colleague C. R. Sacré of the Manchester Sheffield & Lincolnshire Company summed up the case like this: 'In considering the bogie carriage, we are at once agreed that there is a needless amount of weight per passenger carried and a great increase in the cost of maintenance, and we are of opinion that the bogie system is not likely to make great progress in this country'.[30]

That prophecy proved false, and indeed both the companies represented by these engineers were soon to build bogie carriages of their own. But the Great Northern remained much under Stirling's influence in this matter, and the hard-riding qualities of his six-wheeled vehicles were long remembered.[31]

At the same time Stirling's reiterated contention that the bogie carriage was expensive was quite true. Its adoption, by the time it had

---

29. Their mechanism can be studied in the West Coast postal sorting carriage of 1885 in the National Railway Museum at York.
30. Brown, *Great Northern Locomotive Engineers*, i. 184, 186.
31. Ahrons (LTW, i. 1) even suggested that the wheels were octagonal. Anybody who travelled on the special train, composed of these vehicles and hauled by one of Stirling's engines, in 1938 should understand what Ahrons meant.

got well under way, was one element in the notable rise in working costs that appeared in the 1890s. There were others, linked with it: the spread of heavy dining and sleeping cars, and above all the adoption of the corridor. That first appeared, in the 'bellows' form familiar to us, with the gangway enclosed, in 1891–2, on the Great Eastern and the Great Western railways. Their trains were different, and each offered something important that the other did not. The Great Eastern set (used on the boat train from Harwich to the North of England) comprised three vehicles only, which included dining accommodation for passengers of all three classes: a striking innovation, for that had previously been offered only to the first class. The rest of the train consisted of non-corridor vehicles. The Great Western's train, which ran between Paddington, Birmingham, and Birkenhead, lacked a dining car, but it had a corridor throughout. True, that appliance was less useful than one might expect, since the practice was to keep the end doors communicating between the carriages locked – probably from a fear that third-class passengers might trouble their social superiors; but at least every passenger in the train enjoyed access to a lavatory.

The new idea caught on at once, to reach its logical conclusion on 1 July 1893, when corridor trains appeared on the afternoon services from London to Edinburgh and Glasgow both by the West and by the East Coast lines. They were corridor trains throughout, first and third class (no second was offered), and carried dining cars, to which passengers of both classes had access *en route*. The West Coast train made such an impression that it instantly became known to the men on the line simply as 'The Corridor', and it kept that nickname for many years, long after corridor trains had become familiar throughout England. So the express train, as we think of it today, had arrived. But there were still variations. The Midland, for instance, though liberal with its dining cars, did not give passengers much chance to move in or out of them on the way; they were often unconnected with the adjoining carriages. Diners could occupy their seats the whole way from St Pancras to Bradford or Manchester, and if the car was full the rest of the company had to fast. On the Great Western dining cars began to run in 1896, but they were first-class only; the second- and third-class passengers did not get them on that system until 1903.

These improvements were welcome, and highly appreciated by travellers. Where there was competition between two companies – from London to Birmingham or Manchester, for instance, from Bristol to Glasgow – passengers could now select their service not only for speed and convenience, but also for the amenities offered on the journey. From the management's point of view, however, all these developments were a source of difficulty. The increase in the weight of the carriages that had been marked in 1845–75 continued at the same pace, if not faster, over the next 40 years. The first Pullman cars in England had weighed 21½ tons; the first cars used on the 'Southern Belle', when it started to run under that title between London and Brighton in 1908, weighed virtually twice as much – 39–42 tons. The six-wheeled main-line carriage had now given place to the eight-wheeled carriage, weighing 27–30 tons. And the ratio of paying load to weight hauled had grown much more unfavourable: for the corridor involved a sacrifice of two seats in every compartment; dining cars with all their kitchen equipment were very heavy, and accommodated relatively few passengers;[32] as for sleeping cars, those built by the Midland Company in the Edwardian age carried 11 passengers each and weighed 37 tons.[33] So these trains grew inexorably heavier, and even if they were well filled their profitability decreased.

Most secondary and branch-line services were maintained, wholly or in large part, with express stock that had been displaced by the newer models. The growth of traffic was so great, however, from the 1870s onwards that it became impossible to cope with it in this way, and the more respectable railways turned to building new stock, designed for this purpose, and especially for suburban service, on a large scale.[34]

Much of this new stock was entirely traditional in character: long sets of four-wheeled vehicles, with four or five compartments each. On some railways they were formed into permanent sets, coupled closely together to reduce the length of the trains and so allow the very maximum number of carriages to stand at existing station platforms. Most of the companies with a dense London suburban traffic built many trains of such vehicles. Much ingenuity often went into their design. By the 1890s, for example, the South Eastern was building 13-coach sets for this purpose weighing 138 tons, to seat 478 passengers.[35] James Holden on the Great Eastern split his four-wheelers down vertically and inserted an additional section to enable them to seat five passengers, instead of four, a side. These were expedients designed to deal with a continually increasing business. The North London, on the other hand, conservatively-minded and handling a stationary or declining volume of traffic, clung to its well-established

32. On most railways, indeed, the inclusion of a dining car added nothing whatever to the seating capacity of a train, for it only accommodated passengers already seated elsewhere.

33. Ellis, 225.

34. The less respectable at this time included the South Eastern (see Ahrons's inimitable description of its 'travelling panoramas' in his LTW, v. 3–5), the London & South Western (Williams LSWR, ii. 321) and the Lancashire & Yorkshire before its regeneration got under way in the 1880s.

35. O. S. Nock, *The South Eastern & Chatham Railway* (1971 edn), 134.

habits. It went on building its hard little carriages of the traditional pattern, scarcely changed from 1863 until the last of them appeared in 1910.[36] Superbly constructed, they had 'a certain quality of apparent immortality'.[37] The North London never owned any vehicle running on six wheels, let alone bogies. All the London companies with a large suburban traffic had still to provide for three classes (except the London Tilbury & Southend Railway, which discontinued second class in 1893). Bogie vehicles, also close-coupled, made a gradual appearance, but only the London & South Western seems to have braced itself to a decision in these years to provide them for all its suburban traffic.

Such were the vehicles used for the dense suburban services in London. But there were other suburban services that were not dense, where the companies' need was to offer dignified comfort to the commuter who was well-to-do. Among them the design of these carriages afforded a competition in excellence: won surely by the Great Central, whose five-coach sets of 1911 must have been the best supplied for service of this kind anywhere in Europe. Each set cost nearly £7,000[38] and seated 2.2 passengers per ton of dead weight, whereas the South Eastern four-wheeled sets just mentioned seated 3.5 – with this important difference, that in the rush hours the South Eastern trains were also crammed with passengers standing, whereas on the Great Central from Marylebone out to, say, Gerrard's Cross hardly anyone can ever have needed to stand at all.

Meanwhile, however, a new kind of suburban train had made some headway. On the first tube railways of the 1890s the vehicles were not divided, in the traditional English manner, into compartments. The cars (so they were called, with a significant American inflection) were open from end to end. The same principle of design was followed on the Liverpool Overhead Railway in 1893 and in 1904 by the Lancashire & Yorkshire Company, in the trains it built for its new electrified service to Southport, as well as by the North Eastern on Tyneside. It appeared again when the Metropolitan and District lines were electrified in 1905, and on all the subsequent tube railways. The open car, in its earlier Pullman form, may not have been liked everywhere. For these services, however, it proved acceptable. The same design was used for the steam railcars (cf. p. 185) of the Edwardian age.

Electricity had its influence on carriages in another way too. By this time it was coming to be used for lighting them. The first tentative step

36. Ellis, 78–9.
37. M. Robbins, *The North London Railway* (4th edn, 1953), 23. When no longer used on the North London, they were sold for other service and dispersed all over England and Wales.
38. Dow GC, iii. 314.

in this direction had been taken as far back as 1881. On 14 October of that year the Pullman car *Beatrice* made a trip from London to Brighton and back, lighted by electricity: 12 incandescent lamps, taking current from a cumbrous battery mounted underneath its floor. This was the first installation of electric lighting on any train in the world. The experiment succeeded, but it had little immediate result. Most companies were moving at the time away from oil lighting to gas; and once they were committed to that change they did not feel inclined to switch to something different – expensive, clumsy in its original form, and very little proven. Two rather small English companies, altogether backward in the matter, gained eventually from this new development. The North Staffordshire and the London Tilbury & Southend continued to light their carriages by oil until electricity was established and then went over to it straight away, without ever using gas at all. What did perhaps most to determine the change in the end was a consideration of safety. Gas lighting caused a fire in an accident at Clapham Junction in 1892. It was a factor in other mishaps. And then the Midland Company, which had continued to put its faith chiefly in gas, had two appalling experiences, in accidents to its Scotch expresses on the wild Pennine moorlands, at Hawes Junction in 1910 and at Ais Gill three years later. That really settled the matter. By 1914 every major company in England had accepted electric lighting as its standard for the future, though gas continued in use for a long time to come.

The Edwardian age, as one would expect, provided a climax of opulence in the development of carriage design; even adding to it something of real grandeur. The Great Western turned out stately vehicles 68–70ft long and 9ft 6ins wide. They were the largest that ever ran in ordinary service in Britain before 1914. They were also among the most economical of their kind: the third-class carriages seated 80 passengers each and weighed only 33 tons. To carry 2.4 passengers per ton of dead weight in a corridor vehicle represented a remarkable achievement. The London & North Western's carriages included the special stock built for the American boat trains to Liverpool. The Great Central's were as splendid in main-line as they were in suburban service. The Great Northern began experimenting in 1907 with 'articulated' rolling stock: two carriage bodies, that is, mounted on three bogies, instead of four, to reduce dead weight.[39]

Early in the twentieth century the London & North Western provided for King Edward VII and Queen Alexandra two of the most sumptuous carriages that have ever run in this country: 12-wheelers, each self-contained, equipped for travel both by day and by night. These vehicles,

39. Brown, *Nigel Gresley*, 24–5.

built at Wolverton in 1903, weighed 46 tons each – more than any that had ever been seen in Britain before. Those were magnificent carriages of a special kind. This brief survey may end with another, provided for ordinary travellers, first and third class, and – like those two, as well as Queen Victoria's most beautifully furnished saloon – still to be seen today in the National Railway Museum at York.[40] It was built by the Midland Railway at Derby in our very last year, 1914, for service between St Pancras and Glasgow. It is a 'Dining Carriage' – the words firmly emblazoned on its waist-line – 65ft long, and carried on two six-wheeled bogies. The seating provided is in two compartments, for 12 passengers and for 18. One is intended for smokers and – how times had changed since 1868! – it is the larger of the two. The vehicle is heavy, weighing 39 tons. But then it is a self-sufficient unit, with its own kitchen, which includes a cooking range – not to mention all the *batterie de cuisine*, the utensils in copper, pewter, and iron that belong to its time. The lighting is electric, the cooking by gas; electricity was not adopted for both purposes together until the 1920s.

In all its appointments the carriage reflects the dignity and comfort of its age. It is not in the least grandiose. Everything is uniformly, and thoroughly, good. The seating cannot be called luxurious; instead, it is well designed, and properly shaped to the human frame. Every detail is pleasant to the eye and touch, from the brass racks and handles to the framed photographs, delicately tinted, of the landscape of Ulster. The prevailing tone throughout is of the richest red: on the outside of the vehicle the Midland's crimson lake, on the inside dark mahogany. The furnishing has been handled not just by machines, but by men trained in the traditions of the coachbuilders' craft. That craft had contributed much to the railways at the beginning of their great age. It was still handsomely displayed on them in 1914.

b. FREIGHT VEHICLES

Like the passenger carriage, the goods wagon of 1830 had established ancestors. But though in origin it owed something to the farm cart, its true forebears were not road vehicles. They were vehicles designed for use on railways, worked by horses and serving the coal mines, above all in the North-East and in South Wales.

Each of those two regions had its own pattern, depending on the method adopted for discharging the coal at the end of its journey from

40. The royal saloons of 1903 are not, internally, in their original condition. They were much altered to suit the needs and taste of King George V and Queen Mary.

the pit. In the North-East the sides of the wagon sloped inwards; a door was fitted to its bottom through which, when the wagon had been pushed on to a staith, the coal could be shot into a vessel or into a 'cell' in a coal-yard. Such wagons held a chaldron (a Newcastle chaldron, of 2 tons 13 cwt) each; hence their usual name of 'chaldron wagons'. Although in their original form they have passed out of service long ago, their modern descendants are still to be seen in collieries; and the principle they embody is exemplified in the hopper wagon used widely, for a variety of purposes, today. In South Wales the coal was discharged by tipping the vehicle. Accordingly, it was rectangular, with its doors in the short sides of the rectangle. All these wagons were built of wood throughout, except for their iron wheels and axles. They were entirely unsprung.

Such vehicles jogged along well enough behind horses. They were not suited, however, to intensive handling by powerful locomotives. The Stockton & Darlington Company soon cast about for improvements on the traditional pattern, and in 1828 it commissioned Robert Stephenson's works to build one mounted on springs.[41] Either this did not succeed or the expense was thought unnecessary, for the unsprung wagon continued to be standard on that railway, as well as on the Liverpool & Manchester, which, in this as in many other respects, paid attention to its predecessor's experience.

But coal traffic did not form an important part of the Liverpool & Manchester Company's business. It had other kinds of freight to handle, for which different types of vehicle were required: timber had to be carried on flat trucks, general merchandise in high-sided open wagons, livestock in covered cages. The Company even built two well-appointed horse boxes in 1833.[42] It experimented with the use of boxes to stand inside wagons – what today we should call containers; but that plan did not prove successful.[43]

The broad-gauge Great Western Railway offered some interesting new practices in the 1840s. Some of its wagons ran on six wheels, not on four. Towards the end of that decade they came to be made entirely of iron.[44] They were equipped with spring buffers, and some of them with brakes; the 'brake van' makes its appearance among them soon after 1850.[45]

No other English company seems to have adopted the iron wagon at this time as the Great Western had done. The Gloucester Wagon Com-

41. Tomlinson, 158–9.
42. Donaghy, 64, 67–8.
43. PP 1845, xvi. 8–9.
44. They were not, however, the first iron wagons to be built. Vignoles was experimenting with some on the St Helens & Runcorn Gap Railway as early as 1832: Diary (BL Add. MS. 35071, entries for 2 Jan., 27 Mar. 1832).
45. MacDermot, i. 450–1.

pany built one for the Exhibition of 1862,[46] but it remained a show-piece only. However, though the bodies of almost all English wagons continued to be made of wood, the frames of a good many were built wholly or partly of iron.[47] In the 1850s it became the generally accepted practice to fit them with spring buffers. And there the matter rested for the remainder of the Victorian age. The open timber-built wagon, rectangular in shape with doors in its long sides, resting on an iron frame, with a hand brake and with springs to the axles and buffers, was standard on most British main-line railways by 1855. Sixty years later it was standard still. Nothing better illustrates the conservatism of the railways; one might almost say of Britain itself.

Conservatism here can be accounted for on grounds other than those of mere resistance to change. Many people have observed that the British goods wagon was a very small unit of carriage. Its average size rose a little, from say 5–6 tons' capacity in the 1850s to 8–10 in the 1880s; but there it stayed for some time. Not surprisingly it was argued then, and it has often been argued since, that the unit was far too small, and that this was a cardinal weakness in the operation of goods traffic in Britain. Americans, in particular, were scornful of the puny wagons used in Britain, comparing them with their own freight cars, carrying 25–30 tons apiece. Two explanations, however, need to be considered.

In the first place, though anyone could see that a larger unit would often be more economic, that was no more than a theorist's comment unless the load was of a size to fill a larger wagon. Acworth put the matter thus, with his customary downright common sense, in words ascribed to an imaginary English goods manager, looking across the Atlantic in 1889:

> You see our trade and that of America are totally different. American lines carry corn from the North-West, beef and bacon from Chicago, cotton from the Mississippi valley, and so forth in hundreds of train loads and tens of thousands of tons, half across a vast continent, down to the great towns upon the Atlantic seaboard. Thirty-ton trucks are in their right place there, but what should I do with them to carry a couple of tons, say, from Bradford to Southampton? If our English customers would be satisfied with goods trains run at the American speed of 12 or 15 miles an hour, it would be a different matter; we then might possibly load goods for different places in the same truck, and stop to unload and fill up again *en route*. But that won't do for English people; if the goods were not alongside the wharf in Southampton next

---

46. *A History of the Gloucester Carriage & Wagon Company* (1960), 9.
47. Nearly 60 per cent of the Lancashire & Yorkshire stock was of this description in 1850: Marshall LYR, iii. 100–1.

morning, the Bradford manufacturer would soon transfer his custom to one of our competitors.[48]

It was, one might say, among the curses entailed on British railway managements that they had to handle very small quantities of goods, in short hauls, maintaining comparatively high speed.

But it can surely be argued that *some* consignments were large and regular; and especially that when the railway was handling commodities for its own use it might have done so more efficiently. Locomotive coal, for instance: why should the companies not have conveyed that in large units, having nothing but their own convenience to consult? Again the matter looks simple, but is not. This contention is valid in respect of the train when it had reached the company's line. But it had to be loaded with its coal in the colliery, on the colliery's own tracks, and they were often laid out on curves too sharp to allow a vehicle with a long wheel-base to traverse them. The bogie vehicle was only a partial answer: for vehicles of very different sizes – 30-ton bogie wagons and 8-ton 'British' wagons – often combined awkwardly in one train and when being shunted in marshalling yards. Still, all that said, it surely ought not to have taken the Great Northern Company until 1906 to venture on introducing large wagons of this sort for the brick traffic between Peterborough and London, where none of these objections applied.[49]

The greatest difficulty that confronted railway managements in Britain, in trying to handle their goods traffic, has yet to be mentioned: the problem of the privately-owned wagon. The railway companies' Acts of Parliament permitted anyone to use their tracks for the conveyance of his own vehicles, on payment of a toll. Privately-owned goods vehicles came on to public railways from the beginning, and came to stay. Some obvious dangers had to be guarded against. The companies were given power to refuse to convey wagons that were ill constructed or in bad repair;[50] but those that wanted to attract and keep their customers' business, especially when they were faced with competition, had often to overlook defects they would not have tolerated in vehicles of their own.

The practice of admitting private wagons sharply differentiated the British from all European railway systems, except the Belgian. Great administrative complexities were involved. The wagons had to be taken back empty to their owners' works or collieries; and when improvements in design were introduced, in buffers or brakes or lubrication, much of the effect of them was lost through the difficulty of imposing them on

48. Acworth RE, 185.
49. Brown, *Nigel Gresley*, 22.
50. Under the Railways Clauses Act (1845), 8 Vict. cap. 20, sects. 118–20.

private owners. Those owners included many small men, working on a narrow capital, whose stock comprised no more than a few wagons each. They would naturally spend as little as they could in this direction; and as usual the strength of the chain depended on its weakest links.

Some improvement may perhaps have come about with the growth of big wagon-building firms, with a reputation to lose if they supplied their customers, on the cheap, with vehicles that proved unsatisfactory in service. Much of this business came to be centred in and around Birmingham, as an offshoot of the iron trade of the Black Country. Joseph Wright of Saltley made a name for himself very early, not only as a manufacturer but also as a hirer-out of wagons and sometimes as a contractor: he ran the entire North Staffordshire Railway on behalf of that Company for ten years (1849–59).[51] As this implies, his business was a large one. He sold out at a profit to a new Metropolitan Railway Carriage & Wagon Company and left Birmingham, to live at Surbiton; he retained an interest in the new concern, however, and was one of its directors. Its nominal capital in 1868 was £300,000.[52] The Birmingham Carriage & Wagon Company was a rival enterprise on a similar scale at Smethwick, run entirely by local men – one of its founders was a coffin-maker of Bordesley.[53] A third Black Country firm was the Railway Carriage Company of Oldbury. Every one of these concerns was to some extent linked, through common directors, with the Staffordshire Wheel & Axle Company of Spring Hill, which was somewhat larger, in terms of capital, than any of them.[54]

These businesses all came to be organised, on this scale and in this form, from 1860 onwards. The Gloucester Wagon Company was launched at the same time and soon came to take a leading share in the trade. And in 1862 the well-established business of John Ashbury in Manchester passed out of his hands to become the Ashbury Railway Carriage & Iron Company Ltd. These were among the giants, and they helped to set standards – though not to impose standardisation: as late as the 1880s and 1890s hardly any two designs executed by the Gloucester Company for private owners were the same.[55] They also hired out wagons on a large scale. The railway companies built wagons for themselves, as they built carriages. But they could not always keep pace with the demand. The Birmingham Company, for example, supplied every major railway

51. Christiansen and Miller NSR, 162–3.
52. BRSM 1869, 449.
53. Its surviving records – sadly discontinuous – are in the Staffordshire Record Office: D8 31.
54. BRSM 1869, 449.
55. See *Historical Model Railway Society Journal* 5 (1966).

in England in this way from 1864 onwards except the Manchester Sheffield & Lincolnshire, which went to the Gloucester Company,[56] and the London & North Western, which built all its own.[57] And other firms proliferated, to meet the endlessly expanding demand – at Lancaster and Hartlepool, for instance, at Crigglestone, Llanidloes, and Bullo Pill.

The difficulties presented by the privately-owned wagon were by now very well recognised. The Royal Commission on Railways of 1867 discussed them at length. It admitted fairly enough the owners' interests in the matter as well as the railways'; but though it shrank from recommending compulsory purchase it urged that the companies 'should avail themselves of every opportunity of obtaining possession of the railway plant used on their lines'.[58] The advice was reinforced by some of the Inspectors, reporting on accidents caused by the faulty workmanship or maintenance of goods wagons.[59] But it was not heeded, or at least not acted on, until 1881, when the Midland Company began to purchase the privately-owned wagons working on its lines,[60] proposing to hire them and its own vehicles out alike to its customers in future. The Caledonian adopted the same policy in Scotland. Neither company carried it through to the end. No others moved any appreciable distance in the same direction.

The companies as a whole preferred to act in a different way, through the Railway Clearing House. In 1885, following an accident at Penistone caused by the breaking of an axle on a privately-owned wagon, the Board of Trade began to hint at Government intervention, in order to force upon the companies the duty of rigorously inspecting every wagon taken on to their lines. The rules were very clear;[61] but they were not put into force effectively by all the companies alike. A well-defined set of specifications was required, accepted by all the railways and enforced on the owners. This was achieved at the Clearing House later in the same year in respect of 8- and 10-ton wagons. It extended not only to dimensions but also to the quality and character of the materials to be used, and in 1887 the companies agreed to impose it on every owner dispatching wagons on to their lines. A rumpus followed, organised by the Railway Carriage & Wagon Builders' Association and the Association of Private Owners of Railway Rolling Stock. They fought a long and on the

56. Dow GC, i. 222.
57. Staffordshire Record Office, D8 31: Records of Wagon Hirers.
58. PP 1867, xxxviii (i) 70.
59. Cf. cases cited in Bagwell RCH, 199–200, 202.
60. The charges the Company might make for hiring wagons out are defined in its Act of that year: LPA 44 & 45 Vict. cap. cli, sect. 52.
61. Cf. the procedure laid down on the London & North Western, described in Findlay, 196–8.

whole successful action against accepting these Clearing House requirements. In 1889 the field of battle was extended, when the companies tried to insist on the reconstruction of wagons fitted with dumb (i.e. unsprung) buffers. There were said to be some 200,000 of this type running in coal traffic alone. The Gloucester Company challenged the Great Western on the issue before the Railway and Canal Commissioners in 1894, with an indecisive result that gave it, in practice, the victory. At last in 1903 the companies moved in this matter, announcing that they would not accept dumb-buffered wagons any more after the end of 1909. But they were disunited. The London & North Western and the Scottish companies were not prepared to take the issue to its conclusion, and when war broke out in 1914 the prohibition had still not been enforced.[62]

The private ownership of wagons was also in part responsible for the very long delay in extending the provision of continuous brakes from passenger to goods trains. They were made compulsory on passenger trains by statute in 1889 (see p. 228); they were still fitted to only a small number of goods vehicles when the railways were nationalised 60 years later. In this matter Britain stood alone, among all the countries of the world carrying a dense railway traffic, and the explanation is provided in part by the impossibility of requiring this costly apparatus to be fitted to the private wagons. It would not be just, however, to leave the statement there, as if the private owners were the villains in the piece: for the railway companies moved very slowly in the business themselves. The Cambrian Company began to order cattle trucks equipped with continuous brakes in 1897.[63] The Lancashire & Yorkshire was building covered wagons of various types, for fish and refrigerated meat as well as for cattle, similarly fitted, at the same time.[64] But the Great Western did not fit continuous brakes to any of its goods vehicles until 1903.[65] Negligible progress was made with the task on the railway system as a whole before 1914.

The consequences were lamentable. It was not only – perhaps, in this case, not primarily – a matter of safety. This deficiency affected the whole operation of the line. The only brakes available on an ordinary goods train when in motion were those of the engine and tender and of the brake van, controlled by the guard. Hand brakes were fitted to the wagons individually, but they could be applied only when the train was running very slowly, or at rest. A heavy goods train about to descend a steep gradient had therefore to stop while as many of the wagon brakes

62. Bagwell RCH, 201–8.
63. Christiansen and Miller CR, ii. 138.
64. Marshall LYR, iii. 121–2.
65. MacDermot, ii. 306.

as was necessary were pinned down, one by one, throughout the train: a procedure enforced, for example, on every such train running south from Birmingham to Bristol when it reached the top of the Lickey incline near Bromsgrove, with the consequent delay to any passenger train that might be following it. Working under limitations of this sort, and able to be brought to a stop only very gradually, through insufficient brake power, British goods trains necessarily moved at a restricted speed. But passenger trains now ran very fast, and faster still from the 1880s onwards. Without continuous brakes on goods trains, only two solutions to this difficulty were available. They could be shunted, or diverted into loops, to allow passenger trains to pass them, which of course reduced their overall speed; or the number of tracks could be increased to provide for 'fast' and 'slow' running. This costly expedient was adopted by almost all the large companies on substantial parts of their main lines (cf. p. 92). The Midland Railway provided itself with the longest continuous stretch of four-track line in the country, in the 75 miles from St Pancras to Glendon South Junction, just beyond Kettering; and it proclaimed the reason by reserving the two additional lines for goods traffic alone, providing no platforms on them for passengers at wayside stations. This very heavy capital expenditure was not incurred solely to keep goods and passenger trains separate, but that was in large measure the reason.

In sum, therefore, we are faced with what seems almost a paradox. Goods traffic accounted consistently for a higher proportion of the railways' revenue than that from passengers. Yet the instruments for handling it – even, in terms of service, the treatment it received – were notably behind the times in Britain, where the passenger service was, taken all round, as good as any in the world. At the heart of it all lay the vehicles, their design and equipment. The great majority of those that ran on the railways of the United Kingdom – about 1,350,000 in 1907[66] – were almost identical in design with those that had been in service 50 years before.

The great majority, but not all. A multiplicity of special vehicles had

66. In that year the Railway Clearing House estimated the number of private owners' wagons at 600,000, and the *Railway Returns* show 743,995 as belonging to the British railway companies (596,166 to the companies in England and Wales): PP 1908, xcv. 135–41.

An exact census was taken of private owners' wagons on 1 Aug. 1918, when it was found that there were 626,223 registered to run on the railway companies' lines. Of these 61.3 per cent belonged to colliery proprietors, and a further 23.4 per cent to 'coal factors, merchants, and other distributors': so something like three-quarters of all these private wagons were employed in the coal trade. E. A. Pratt, *British Railways and the Great War* (1921), 692.

appeared, some of them embodying new ideas, called for by new kinds of service that were coming to be required. Many examples might be given.

Most of the large companies built some big wagons, if only to show that they were willing to make the experiment, to learn from examples abroad. The Great Western tried a 25-ton wagon, mounted on bogies, in 1888, but found it impossible to get it more than half full, and tried no more.[67] Bogie wagons on steel tube frames (an American idea) were used on several railways – the Furness, the Great Northern, the Lancashire & Yorkshire.[68] The 30-ton wagon made some progress, on the Midland for coal, on the Lancashire & Yorkshire in connection with the Continental traffic brought into Goole.[69] A few very big low vehicles were built for the carriage of girders and long bars of steel.

Though some of the companies hardly gave the experiment a full trial, building large-capacity wagons singly or in very small numbers, others went further: the Lancashire & Yorkshire commissioned 50 of the big eight-wheelers. It cannot be said, however, that foreign example demonstrated its usefulness, in this instance, to the companies at large. Again, as with locomotives (cf. p. 177), the railway managers argued that conditions in Britain were different. Their contention was disputed, but it also won powerful support. The Board of Trade's Chief Inspecting Officer of Railways, Lt-Col. Arthur Yorke, visited the United States in the autumn of 1902 and gave particular attention to this matter. His conclusion was that no great economy resulted from the use of the large wagon. 'The important factor in the case', he pointed out quite truly, 'is not the length of the car, but the carrying capacity of the car in relation to its weight.' The Americans were getting a load of about 2 tons for each ton of deadweight hauled. In Britain the proportions were less favourable,[70] and they could be improved. But the London & North Western and the Great Western companies were already building 20-ton wagons, on four wheels, weighing no more than 8 tons empty. 'For ordinary trade purposes in this country', he concluded, 'the four-wheeled wagon, of improved design and increased capacity, is, I believe, the best suited.'[71]

Tentative experiment had also gone on in other directions. Containers, for example, after their first trial on the Liverpool & Manchester Railway, had been favoured by Brunel on the Great Western and used for a time at Gloucester during the crisis over the break of gauge there (pp. 28, 204).

67. MacDermot, ii. 306.
68. R. J. Essery *et al.*, *British Goods Wagons* (1970), 26.
69. Marshall LYR, iii. 122.
70. In the 1880s a careful commentator had reckoned the load-weight ratio in Britain as, on average, 1.6:1, compared with 2.13:1 in the United States: E. B. Dorsey, *English and American Railroads Compared* (1887), 10.
71. PP 1903 lx. 851.

Later in the century private owners, particularly furniture removers, made use of what were called 'lift vans' – virtually wagon bodies without wheels, which could be placed on flat trucks. Coal was carried in boxes by several companies, where it was especially important that it should not crumble through breaking. The London & South Western carried china-clay in the same manner in the 1890s.[72]

The range of vehicles built for special purposes is endless: for fish and banana traffic, for refrigerated meat, for milk and margarine, for gas (to illuminate country stations and to replenish the stores needed for lighting and cooking in trains), for tar and oil. The London & North Western built 100 wagons exclusively for the glass traffic of St Helens.[73] Beyond these demands, which arose in the normal economic life of the country, we reach out into the bizarre: the tiny hearse wagon (still to be seen today), painted black and crowned with four urns, used for bringing down bodies for burial from the hills on the narrow-gauge Festiniog Railway;[74] the animal vans of Barnum's Circus, based at Stoke-on-Trent, brilliant yellow and lettered in red 'Barnum & Bailey – Greatest Show on Earth'.[75]

And finally the brake vans, from which these slow-moving traditional trains were supervised and, in some degree, directed. With them every company went its own way.[76] At first it seems that the guard, or brakesman, simply sat in an open wagon. Then, by the late 1840s, the enclosed van made its appearance, reserved for his use. In time it acquired certain conveniences: a stove – most of the guard's work was stationary, and bitterly cold in winter; platforms, even enclosed verandahs at one end of the van or both; look-outs, shallow bay windows ('duckets') or bird-cages in the roof, to enable the guard to observe his train and check the signals. Some were mounted on six wheels, which enlarged the braking surface. Certain companies, like the Great Western, favoured the use of sand to increase resistance, poured on to the rails through gear controlled by the guard; the Midland, on the other hand, wholly rejected the practice.[77] To give additional brake power without employing two guards the Great Northern and the South Eastern & Chatham companies used pairs of brake vans, close-coupled together.

Whatever the pattern adopted, the essential purpose of the brake-van was the same: to provide a control over the movement of the train, at the opposite end from the centre of power in the locomotive. Save in the

72. Essery *et al.*, *op. cit.*, 92–3.
73. *Ibid.*, 111.
74. J. Simmons, *Transport Museums* (1970), 138–9.
75. Christiansen and Miller NSR, 251.
76. See the extraordinary table of variants in Essery *et al.*, *op. cit.*, 140–1.
77. *Ibid.*, 118.

special case of a goods train descending a steep gradient, with the hand brakes on some of its wagons fastened down, these were the only controls that were provided, until continuous brakes began to make their slow progress. The goods guard cuts no great figure: he can never be a folk-hero like the driver of the engine. But his work was responsible, it was monotonous, it needed endurance and sometimes courage. It is worth while to reflect on the qualities required, in the 1880s, of the three-men crews – driver, fireman, and guard – who took the Midland express goods train from London to Manchester at a running speed of 28 m.p.h. over an almost continuous switchback, rising to 1,000ft at Peak Forest.[78] The wagons were small, the means of controlling them very imperfect. That the train made its eight-hour journey, night after night, in safety is a tribute to the civil and mechanical engineers, but also to those men's skill.

78. See the train's schedule in Foxwell and Farrer, 31.

9   Dangers, Precautions, and Controls

The express goods train just considered, running from London to Manchester, exemplifies the fully-developed Victorian railway in its ordinary routine. It is time now to examine some parts of the mechanism by which the railways were operated, above all the contrivances that made it possible for that train to pursue its long journey steadily and safely.

In any study of operation, safety devices are paramount. For railways were always potentially dangerous, and that consideration underlay the whole of their management. Stringent codes of rules were adopted very early, which were enforced by the sharp punishments of fine and dismissal. Some of these related to general conduct and discipline within the companies' organisation, but the most important were concerned with safety – the safety of passengers, of the goods carried, and of the railway servants themselves.

Some rules were needed from the outset for ensuring that the trains kept a proper distance apart; and they were all the more essential because the locomotives hauling them broke down frequently. It was not enough to draw up a timetable and insist that it must be adhered to. Other precautions were necessary on the line itself: some form of signalling. That was provided by hand at first, with the aid of lamps at night and in fog. Flagpoles were installed on the Liverpool & Manchester Railway by 1833, the flags and lights on them raised and lowered by hand. At the rear of each train was a revolving lamp, which showed red when the train was in motion but was turned round by the guard to blue when it stopped; with the result, we are told, that 'the engineer of the next train instantly sees this change and is enabled, by checking the velocity of his engine, to avoid a collision that would be tremendous'.[1] It appears to us very haphazard; especially since it was often impossible for the drivers to observe any signals at all if smoke or steam was beating down

1. *The Railway Companion . . . By a Tourist* (1833), 24.

Fig 4. *Signalling on the Midland Counties Railway, 1840. Red flags are shaded, white clear. (A) Caution; move slowly. (B) White flag, all clear; red flag, stop. (C) 'Brought to the shoulder as the train passes.' (D) Both flags held above the head, across the line: assistance wanted*

or if the weather was thick. There was a serious accident caused by fog at Rainhill in 1832, when one train ran into the back of another standing still, and several people were killed. The directors then laid it down that in such conditions the policeman at the station should 'immediately run 300 yards behind the train' to warn any other that was following; if no policeman was available, then this duty fell to the fireman.[2] Worked in such a way, it is extraordinary that the Company seems to have experienced only one major accident arising from causes of this sort.

Hand signalling, on posts with flags or lamps, continued to be the method employed on almost all railways in the 1830s – even for example at a complicated junction like Brockley Whins, between Gateshead and Sunderland.[3] The Midland Counties, a link in the first trunk railway between London and the North East, opened in 1840 with hand-signalling still, to rules that were quite its own.[4]

The development of the railway system in the 1840s, the multiplication of junctions, and the increasing provision of express trains, running at three or four times the speed of stopping trains – all these things imperatively demanded a more sophisticated system of signalling. A new instrument was now available for the purpose: the electric telegraph. Cooke and Wheatstone developed it largely in conjunction with the railways as they grew. It became an essential part of the equipment for

2. Donaghy, 120–1.
3. Tomlinson, 411.
4. This figure is re-drawn from the back cover of the *Guide or Companion to the Midland Counties Railway* (1840).

running the London & Blackwall Railway, worked by cable haulage, from the beginning in 1840. That was a very short line, and peculiar in its operation. The Yarmouth & Norwich, a complete railway 20 miles long, run in the normal way with locomotives, employed the telegraph throughout from its opening in 1844. Here was the means of communicating from one point of control to another, of reporting train movements, and of transmitting information about anything that was happening out of course. The companies varied greatly in the speed with which they made use of it. It was set up by the London & South Western between London and Gosport in 1845. The London & North Western began to lay it down between London and Rugby in the following year, chiefly in order to increase the capacity of the line without the addition of further tracks.[5] On the other hand, when the long Great Northern line was opened between London, Lincoln, and Doncaster in 1850, it was not furnished anywhere with the telegraph, which was erected between London and Peterborough only in 1852.[6]

The advantages of the telegraph to the public service and to private persons were obvious, and the companies responsible for developing it pressed ahead with their profitable work. Its value in railway operation was not universally accepted. Lardner devotes a chapter of his *Railway Economy* in 1850 to the telegraph, but in the course of it he never mentions the contribution it could make to the railways themselves. The Great Western Company, having been the first to allow it to be laid down, from Paddington to West Drayton, made no use of it there for its own purposes, and it was removed in 1849. But next year the Company changed its mind, and entered into an agreement with the Electric Telegraph Company to install it all over the system.[7] Like nearly all the new mechanical devices now to be discussed, the telegraph seemed dangerous to some people on the ground that it reduced the need for human vigilance. There was truth in this argument: a blind faith in the telegraph was largely responsible for an accident at Ponders End, on the Cambridge line, in 1851.[8] Everything depended on the way in which it was used.

In the 1830s and 1840s the general practice was to impose a time interval in the dispatch of trains. On the Great Western, for example, the 'danger' signal was displayed for three minutes after each train had gone

5. Gourvish, 238.
6. C. H. Grinling, *The History of the Great Northern Railway 1845–1902* (1903), 140.
7. MacDermot, i. 328; Sir Daniel Gooch, *Memoirs and Diary* (ed. P. B. Wilson, 1972), 45–6.
8. See the remarks of the Inspector: PP 1852, xlviii. 142.

by.[9] But signals were usually installed only at stations, and on the Great Western line stations were as much as 11 miles apart – 20 minutes' travelling in a fast train. Much could go wrong in 20 minutes, and the engine-driver would have no warning until he saw trouble confronting him ahead. Before very long a new idea came to be considered: the adoption of a safety interval based not on time but on space. This seems to have been employed first in tunnels, units of fixed length and especially difficult to work because of their darkness and smoke. Telegraph posts could be erected at the mouths of the tunnel, enabling the entry and exit of the train to be instantly signalled from one end to the other, and a rule established that no train should be allowed to move into the tunnel until the preceding train was out of it. This arrangement was brought into use on the Great Western Railway in the Box Tunnel in 1847 (with incomplete success), and in other tunnel sections in 1846–52.[10] It was also introduced quite early at the Clayton Tunnel on the Brighton main line. But the risks that attended the working of a single section of a railway in this fashion, with the remainder run on a time-interval system, were dreadfully exemplified in that very tunnel in 1861, when one train ran into the back of another and 23 people were killed. The responsibility for the accident was divided. It was caused in the first instance by the defective working of an automatic signal at the south end of the tunnel, which failed to move into the 'danger' position directly a train had passed it. That naturally fortified the arguments of those who disbelieved in mechanical devices. But the accident was also due to the 'time-interval' system, which allowed trains to be dispatched too closely behind one another.

The space-interval idea was quickly developed much further, notably on the Southern Division of the London & North Western Railway, to Edwin Clark's plan, in 1855. This divided the line into sections 2 miles in length, and it was a primitive block system.[11] But in the language used later, the system was 'permissive', not 'absolute', block, and there lay its central weakness. Under a permissive system a second train might be allowed to enter a block section at the same time as a preceding one, the signalman at the beginning of the section first stopping it and then instructing it to go on with caution. An absolute block system forbade two trains ever to be in one section together. The London & North Western experiment, bold and costly as it was, did not serve to prevent accidents, and it came under severe criticism from the Inspecting Officers for its shortcomings. They were justified, but the Company should be given

9. MacDermot, i. 313, 319–20.
10. *Ibid.*, i. 320–2.
11. It is carefully described in Neele, 82–9.

credit for the progress it made. As in other matters – and especially perhaps on this railway: we shall see something similar in considering continuous brakes – there was progress up to a point, to a better but still imperfect system, and then a long hesitation in moving to the final improvement, the logical conclusion.

The adoption of the block system went forward irregularly, at the will of each individual company. The South Eastern is said to have been the first to equip the whole of its main line in this way, the work being complete by 1851.[12] That again was on the permissive system. The first line to be worked throughout on the absolute block system was the Metropolitan, from its opening in 1863.[13] It was followed by the Bristol & Exeter in 1871.[14] Elsewhere, much slower progress was made in this direction, or none at all. So busy and important a piece of railway as the original Liverpool & Manchester (by now part of the Northern Division of the London & North Western) was not even supplied with the telegraph as late as 1859.[15] On the Great Western and the companies amalgamated with it in 1862–3, the South Wales and the West Midland, a few sections of single line were worked on the permissive block system, but scarcely any double lines until after 1870.[16] Then, however, the Company went ahead with the installation fast. By 1873, 44 per cent of its mileage was worked on absolute block.

Alarmed by a series of spectacular accidents that had occurred since 1865, Parliament had now come to the support of the Board of Trade Inspectors in the strictures they constantly passed on the companies' management and operation. By the Regulation Act of 1873, returns were required annually from each company, showing the length of its line worked on the block system. Three substantial companies were then able to show that the whole of their lines were worked in that way: the London Chatham & Dover, the North Staffordshire, and the South Eastern. Of the biggest companies, six (the Great Eastern, Great Northern, Great Western, Lancashire & Yorkshire, Manchester Sheffield & Lincolnshire, and North Eastern) had less than half their lines thus equipped, the lowest proportion being on the Lancashire & Yorkshire (24.2 per cent) and the Manchester Sheffield & Lincolnshire (12 per cent). By 1880, under pressure from the publicity these returns afforded, the change was striking:[17]

12. G. M. Kichenside and A. Williams, *British Railway Signalling* (1963), 8.
13. C. E. Lee, *The Metropolitan Line* (1972), 13.
14. MacDermot, ii. 97.
15. PP 1859 (sess. 1), xxv. 661–2.
16. MacDermot, ii. 264.
17. PP 1874, lix. 221; 1881, lxxxi. 433.

TABLE 7. PERCENTAGE OF TOTAL MILEAGE
WORKED ON THE BLOCK SYSTEM,1873-80
(ENGLAND AND WALES)

Year	Absolute block	Permissive block	Worked by telegraph not on the block system	Total
1873	48.9	2.3	18.4	69.6
1880	80.8	0.7	5.2	86.7

Here was a great contribution to public safety; but it had necessarily been expensive, and that figured in the comments made on the matter at shareholders' meetings. Some companies made an excessive and discreditable commotion about it. The Lancashire & Yorkshire – nearly the most backward of all the large ones – grumbled bitterly. Thomas Barnes, the chairman, asserted in 1883 that the installation had cost £660,000. He clearly regarded it as an iniquitous tax, which had 'been imposed by the Government, and had reduced the dividend by over a half per cent'.[18] He remained a stubborn reactionary; but, happily for the Company's customers, when he made these remarks he was about to go out of office.

By this time the system of signalling trains had also greatly advanced. The 'policeman' making his signals by flags in his own hands had quickly been displaced by indicators mounted high on poles: discs, crossbars, square boards, circles, diamonds, but from the 1850s onwards, to an increasing extent, semaphores. Each railway devised its own plan, and that could be a cause of difficulty to drivers who worked their engines, under running powers, from one company's system to another. True, that was not a common practice; where a through train ran on to another company's line it was usual to change engines and crews. But there were from the beginning some lines that were jointly worked – like that between London and Redhill, on which Brighton and South Eastern trains both ran; and the number of 'foreign workings' from one railway to another presently grew. There was a wide measure of agreement on some practices: that red signified 'danger', green 'caution', and white 'all clear'. But even that elementary set of rules was not invariable. Where the London & Greenwich and London & Croydon trains parted, at Corbett's Lane, a red light meant 'all clear' for Croydon trains, a white one for Greenwich. Similarly, at Brockley Whins, white indicated 'all clear' for trains of the Brandling Junction Railway, red for those of the Stan-

18. Marshall LYR, ii. 241-2.

hope & Tyne. The Great Western used a red disc to indicate 'all clear' by day, though a white light at night.[19]

Semaphores came into use slowly. What is thought to be the first was installed by C. H. Gregory at New Cross in 1841. They are found, in a form that later became widespread, on the Manchester Sheffield & Lincolnshire Railway in 1849, the arm being movable into three positions: horizontal to indicate danger, pointing downwards at 45 degrees for caution, and disappearing within a slot in the post for 'all clear'.[20] When the absolute block system was adopted, the three-position signal was not needed, and it became the usual practice for 'all clear' to be indicated by the diagonal position. This had the important merit of always giving a positive indication to the driver, eliminating the negative

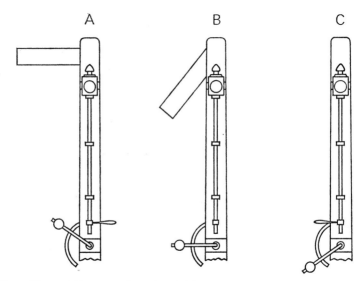

Fig 5. *Three-position semaphore signal:* (A) *Danger.* (B) *Caution.* (C) *All clear* (*arm within a slot in the post*)

one provided by a semaphore that had disappeared into its slot. At the same time, however, trains were travelling faster, and there came to be a need to warn drivers that there might be a danger signal ahead at the next block, to give him time to slacken speed gradually. For this purpose the separate 'distant' signal – already in use here and there for some time[21] – was developed. Even so, it was differently interpreted from one

19. O. S. Nock, *The South Eastern & Chatham Railway* (1971 edn), 24–5; Tomlinson, 411; MacDermot, i. 314–15.
20. Dow GC, i. 135.
21. *Ibid.*, i. 136; Williams LSWR, ii. 304.

railway to another. The Great Western and the London & North Western had exactly contrary practices here, and since they operated a number of joint lines – from Shrewsbury to Hereford, for example, and from Chester to Birkenhead – this was a source of serious danger. The Railway Clearing House made efforts to get the companies to consider a common code, but with not much success.[22]

As the movements governed by signals and points grew more complex, it became desirable to group together the levers controlling them in the charge of a signalman. This was first done at Bricklayers Arms Junction on the South Eastern Railway in 1843. Then, in 1856, at the same place, another historic piece of equipment was installed: a frame in which the levers and their wires were so arranged that signals and points could not be moved in conflict with one another. Here was the start of interlocking, which later became a fundamental part of the British railways' safety equipment. It was due chiefly to John Saxby, a foreman in the locomotive works of the Brighton Railway, who had developed the plans in his spare time and had taken out a patent for the purpose earlier in the same year. Six years later he resigned from the Brighton Company's service to set up in business on his own, with a partner from the same company, J. S. Farmer. Saxby & Farmer became perhaps the best-known of all the manufacturers of signalling equipment, side by side with other firms like McKenzie & Holland of Worcester. They were consulted, and their products purchased, by railways overseas as well as at home, in India, Australasia, and South America.

The system of interlocking represented a very great advance. Naturally it took some time for this complicated technique to gain acceptance. To begin with it was established and developed entirely in and near London. Austin Chambers improved it, in an installation at Kentish Town on the North London Railway in 1860. The first railways to adopt it on all their lines, in conjunction with absolute block working, were the Metropolitan and the District. The South Eastern, having proved the plan at Bricklayers Arms, went ahead to extend its use; and the London Chatham & Dover, impecunious though it was, did the same. But their neighbour the Brighton Company moved faster than they, or any other large line. Having installed an improved version of the 1856 prototype at Victoria in 1860, and another at Brighton very soon afterwards, the Company pressed ahead with extending the system, and by 1877 the whole of its lines were controlled by interlocked equipment.[23]

Even when signals and points were interlocked, and signalmen therefore unable to cause their movements to conflict, there was still room for

22. Bagwell RCH, 224–8.
23. Marshall SR, 230.

some human error. Though under the absolute block system it was forbidden for a second train to enter a block section if a preceding train was still within it, a signalman could make a mistake, like anybody else. He might forget the first train altogether, or fail to note that the man in the next box had not yet accepted it. W. R. Sykes came up with an answer, which was to take the matter out of the signalman's hands by making it impossible, through an electrical device, for him to clear the line for the second train until the first was 'out of section'. This was what came to be called 'lock-and-block'.

Sykes put his proposal before J. S. Forbes, the Chairman of the Chatham Company, in 1874, asking to be permitted to equip three adjoining signal boxes at Brixton in this way. Forbes pooh-poohed the idea, and refused. However, he was overborne by the joint opinion of the four Board of Trade Inspectors, and the experiment was allowed after all. Sykes took out a patent for his new device in 1875, in which the expression 'lock-and-block' occurred. It succeeded and was quickly extended on the Chatham Company's system, first in the London suburban area and then down the whole main line to Dover by 1882.[24]

Nearly all the leading railway administrators took up the same attitude to these improvements as Forbes. They were understandably anxious at the cost of adopting them, and they mistrusted their effects in reducing human responsibility. Even very wise managers like James Allport of the Midland shared this second fear.[25] As we have seen, there was something in it; but of course it was a question of balancing the advantages and possible dangers against one another. As soon as a mechanism had been devised that proved itself over a reasonable period of time, it was generally the best course to adopt it, hoping perhaps to improve it further with experience. This is what the Board of Trade urged, and in the 1880s, under steady pressure from it, from the Government and from public opinion, the new signalling systems came to be accepted. The results sometimes impressed foreign observers profoundly. 'It is astonishing to see the blind faith the English engine-driver places in his block signals', wrote an American, E. B. Dorsey, in 1887. 'In dense fogs, when he cannot see 100ft ahead on dark nights, . . . he runs at full speed and generally on schedule time, feeling sure that he is perfectly safe because his block signals have told him so, and they cannot make a mistake or lie. . . . The English Government, through the Board of Trade, obliges all English railroads to adopt the block system, and run their trains by it, and we should follow their example.'[26] That last remark is particularly

24. *Ibid.*, 355.
25. Parris, 193, 196, 200.
26. E. B. Dorsey, *English and American Railroads Compared* (2nd edn, 1887), 13.

striking, for Dorsey was by no means favourably disposed towards British railways in general. In almost everything else he thought American practice best. It may perhaps be added that although the French engineer Regnault devised a space-interval system of signalling for the Ouest Company as early as 1847, the term generally used in France to describe such arrangements in later years was 'le block-system'.[27]

Such were some of the devices introduced during the Victorian age to control the movement of trains. But they all presupposed that when danger was signalled ahead, the train could be readily brought to a stop. That condition was not satisfactorily fulfilled. Locomotives with tenders – the great majority – carried no brakes themselves. It was thought that the application of them, when running at speed, would subject the driving axles to dangerous torsion. Brakes were therefore fitted to the wheels of the tenders only. Some tank engines at first had no brakes at all, but it became the usual practice with them to fit brakes to the rear pair of wheels. If they were coupled, that strained the coupling rods. One sometimes wonders why tank engines made such slow progress in Britain – for example, why the Taff Vale Company, whose longest run was less than 30 miles, should have rejected them entirely for 25 years.[28] Here is in part the explanation.

Otherwise, the only brakes on a train were those worked by a guard, fitted to the wheels of one of the vehicles. Brunel described them in 1841 as 'tolerably useless'.

What then happened when the driver of a train, travelling at normal speed, saw a danger signal ahead of him, or an obstruction on the line? He shut off steam, applied the tender brakes, whistled for the guard to apply those he controlled, and perhaps, if the emergency was grave, risked putting his engine into reverse gear. Even when these manoeuvres succeeded, the experience was bound to be uncomfortable and alarming to the passengers; but they quite often failed, and it was a common cause of derailments.

George Stephenson gave his mind to the problem in retirement and described in 1841 a self-acting sledge-brake to be fitted to every carriage.[29] Two years later a paper was read to the Society of Arts containing an embryo notion of the continuous brake – that is, one continuous throughout the whole train and not confined to one or more guard's or

27. P. Lefèvre and G. Cerbelaud, *Les Chemins de fer* (1888), 262.
28. D. S. Barrie, *The Taff Vale Railway* (2nd edn, 1950), 33.
29. PP 1841, viii. 125.

brake vans. Though nothing came of these suggestions, the idea went on simmering, and in 1852 James Newall, Carriage and Wagon Superintendent of the East Lancashire Railway, patented the first continuous brake that displayed its efficacy in service, on the steep Baxenden bank near Accrington. It was demonstrated to officials of several companies shortly afterwards, in what was the earliest of a long series of 'brake trials' held over the next 30 years. That stimulated Charles Fay, Newall's counterpart on the neighbouring Lancashire & Yorkshire Railway, to patent an alternative version of his own in 1856.[30] Both passed into general use on their two companies' systems, which were merged in 1859. It was bad luck that a shocking accident should have occurred at Helmshore, on the same Baxenden bank, to a train not fitted with any continuous brake in 1860. And it was creditable to the Lancashire & Yorkshire Company that it should have decided, in consequence, to equip all its trains with continuous brakes forthwith.

Other companies were also favourably impressed by these inventions. The London & South Western began to use Newall's brake, in the light of tests made almost as soon as it was patented.[31] But not all companies, by any means, thought the same. When an accident even worse than that at Helmshore had occurred in 1858, also on an incline, at Round Oak on the Oxford Worcester & Wolverhampton Railway, that company considered adopting the new brakes used in Lancashire and held trials of them near Evesham.[32] It decided nevertheless to stick to the brakes already in use, operated by hand.

Further experimentation followed; patentees were busy and numerous. The Fay and Newall brakes had been purely mechanical, operated by wheels and screws. In 1864, for the first time in Britain, atmospheric pressure was used, acting on a piston, to apply the brake. The designer was Charles Kendall and the device was tried on the London Chatham & Dover Railway, where it was said four years later to have worked with unfailing regularity.[33]

But these were only isolated efforts, here and there. In the 1860s the need for effective continuous brakes throughout each train began to be stressed by the Board of Trade Inspectors, in language that grew stronger as the years passed. For some time the great companies paid little heed to it. The first of them to move in this direction was the London & North Western, and it selected a design that offered an important advantage, went ahead with installing it at considerable cost, and then found it had

30. Marshall LYR, iii. 55–6, 102–3.
31. Williams LSWR, i. 240.
32. MacDermot, i. 274.
33. Marshall SR, 354

chosen an unsatisfactory type, which required it eventually to change to another, at much further expense. G. P. Neele, the Superintendent of the Line, tells the story – his narrative of it coloured by bitter subsequent experience. The system adopted was Clark's, later improved by F. W. Webb, the Company's Locomotive Superintendent, an indefatigable patentee, and it was tried out first in 1868. It made no use of pistons or air pressure but was actuated by a chain controlled by the guard – not the driver. The locomotive engineers had a rooted objection to placing it in the driver's hands: 'don't have all your eggs in one basket', said Ramsbottom.[34]

The grim sequence of major accidents in the late 1860s and early 1870s underlined the need for more effective brakes, especially on inclines and for trains running at high speed. There seemed, however, to be objections to every existing design, devised not only in Britain but also elsewhere. The need for satisfactory brakes was evident. It was not the Board of Trade's business to impose one system. Had it attempted to do any-thing of the kind, it would have met with howls of protest from the companies. But it could, and did, insist that each company ought to adopt *some* system, which could be shown to be efficient. A Royal Com-mission on Railway Accidents was appointed in 1874, and to help its investigation of brakes the Midland Company offered to hold extended trials of different designs, fitted to the trains of a number of railways, on its own system. They were carried out near Newark, on its level line between Nottingham and Lincoln, over a week in June 1875. Six com-panies – five English and one Scottish – took part. The results could scarcely have been decisive, for the basis of scientific comparison was absent. The trains differed from one another in weight and design; the weather varied, and this was especially important because there was a great difference between the performance of brakes on dry and on wet rails. Still, it was clear that the American air brake devised by George Westinghouse was a highly efficient one. It ought to have been no less clear that the Clark and Webb one was not. On its trial the train equipped with it broke in two; the operation of the brake not being automatic, the first part proceeded on its way, leaving the second behind. Neele sums up the consequences caustically: 'Each of the patentees went away from the refreshment tent at Rolleston Junction self-satisfied that their own system was the best. And so it came to pass that for years afterwards our rolling-stock was fitted up with the encumbrance of the chain brake'.[35]

The debate continued. Further trials of a similar sort were held in 1880 at Gisburn, again on the Lancashire & Yorkshire line, and on the

34. Neele, 168–9.
35. Neele, 206.

narrow-gauge Festiniog Railway.[36] Then in the next year the Government made its first intervention in the business, requiring each company to make a half-yearly return showing the proportion of its passenger stock fitted with continuous brakes, and the number of trains it ran on which those brakes were not provided; specifying at the same time – a warning here to the rival patentees – the cases in which any such brake had failed.[37]

The first returns showed how properly the Inspecting Officers had criticised the companies for their dilatoriness. In June 1880 the Board sent a circular letter to them all, observing that the matter had been under discussion since 1857 and that it now appeared that by the end of 1879 only 23 per cent of locomotives on British railways and 28 per cent of carriages were fitted with continuous brakes. Furthermore, some of the brakes in use were highly unsatisfactory. Patiently the Board spelt out what might be wrong with them: 'Some are only sectional, not being continuous throughout the train; some can only be applied by the guard or guards, and not by the engine-driver; . . . whilst others are not automatic, that is, capable of self-action when a train from any cause becomes divided'. The circular then went on to hint, in veiled but quite unmistakable terms, at the possibility of Government action if the companies failed to act themselves.[38]

The irritation produced by this letter can be detected in the replies made to it by some of the companies. Only two of the large ones – the Great Eastern and the London Brighton & South Coast – responded straightforwardly, reporting their progress and indicating that the task was well under way. They had both settled on the Westinghouse brake, and they stuck to their decision. The others pointed out, with some justification, that there was no agreement among experts on the best system; and since there was much through running between one railway and another, it was desirable that neighbouring companies should agree. What could a railway like the North Staffordshire do, when it exchanged rolling-stock with four large companies, each of which had adopted a different braking system? The Great Western suavely asked the Board if any brake yet designed had fulfilled all its requirements satisfactorily 'and has proved itself reliable in working, and is reasonably economical'; if so the directors would 'give their best consideration' to the pattern the Board recommended.

There was force in the companies' line of argument, and humbug too. The North Eastern pointed out, quite truly, that the Westinghouse

36. The Festiniog trials are analysed in detail in PP 1880, lxiv. 344–5.
37. 41 Vict. cap. 20.
38. PP 1880, lxiv. 339–40.

brake (which it had adopted) was being constantly altered and improved, and that that had delayed progress in fitting it to all the Company's engines and carriages. It is a familiar type of difficulty – exemplified again on the British railways when they undertook electrification in the twentieth century. The brakes *were* still in an experimental stage of development: so much so that the Midland Company, having decided on the Westinghouse system and moved a considerable distance towards applying it to the whole of its stock, felt obliged to abandon it and turn, at considerable expense, to a vacuum brake instead.

When all this has been allowed for, it remains true that the companies moved slowly, and that they did so because they were anxious to reduce or defer expenditure. These were difficult years for them. A number had reached a peak of prosperity about 1872 and were now declining from it: the Great Western paid 6 per cent in 1872–3 and $3\frac{3}{4}$ per cent in 1879, the dividends of the North Eastern and the Lancashire & Yorkshire fell in these same years by 3–4 per cent. The main explanation – here at least there was no room for doubt – lay in the rise of their working costs, attributable in part to the expenditure they had undertaken on safety equipment. To which their critics replied that it was wrong for them to try to keep up dividends at the expense of the passengers' safety.

All through the 1880s the Inspectors maintained the pressure. They were strengthened by the railways' critics in Parliament, gunning for them for other reasons but always glad of an additional weapon against them. Looking back, it seems at first strange that the Government, which had stepped in to regulate the railways' business a good deal more closely in the 1870s, did not exercise its authority now. For this, however, there were two good reasons: one political, the other technical. The railway interest in Parliament, though now very evidently on the defensive, was still strong, and no Government wished to antagonise it superfluously. The companies were moving at a steady pace towards the adoption of effective safety precautions. Understandably, the politicians preferred to leave the business in their hands. They were also handicapped by the discordant opinion of the experts, and particularly reluctant to approve any one system as effective and prescribe its use. That had been done in one case earlier, and the system had then proved faulty (cf. p. 231). The Government's inaction therefore was not merely supine. It was in a real difficulty, which it hoped that time and patience would solve.

That seemed to be happening. By the end of 1888, two-thirds of the locomotives and carriages at work in the United Kingdom were fitted with a continuous automatic brake that fulfilled the conditions laid down by the Board of Trade; over 90 per cent with a continuous brake of one kind or another. But that was not enough. Fate then struck. A fearful accident occurred on the Great Northern Railway of Ireland at Armagh on 12 June 1889. The disaster, in which 80 people were killed and as many again seriously injured, revealed the hopeless inefficacy of the non-automatic brake the train carried; and it was made even worse than it would otherwise have been by the absence of the block telegraph system on this section of the line. The Conservative Government decided at once to legislate, giving the Board of Trade power to compel all railway companies to fit their passenger trains with continuous brakes, and to adopt the absolute block system.[39] At this point, Mr Rolt observed, 'the old happy-go-lucky days of railway working came to their ultimate end and the modern phase of railway working as we know it began'.[40]

There was one other type of safety appliance, the want of which seldom caused accidents, though it often aggravated the distress arising from them and from other irregularities in railway travelling. From very early days it had been apparent that some means of communication was needed between the driver, the guard, and the passengers in a train when it was in motion. The Liverpool & Manchester Company had placed the guards on the carriage roofs – a natural continuation of the practice of the coaches; and the London & Birmingham did the same. That was a singularly bleak position, exposed to the engine's cinders, and dangerous when the train passed under a bridge. The practice was soon abandoned and the guard placed inside. If he was no longer to keep the train under surveillance, who would notify the driver if anything went wrong? Accidents occurred, asking that question pointedly. Perhaps the most dramatic of them was the one that happened to the Countess of Zetland on the Midland Railway in 1847. She was in her chariot, carried on a flat truck in the middle of the train, and it caught fire a little way south of Leicester. She and her maid, who was with her, screamed 'fire' and waved handkerchiefs. The guard and driver did not see them, the railway policemen beside the line took no notice. (In the absence of the telegraph, what could they have done?) The maid eventually jumped or fell off the truck, gravely injured; but Lady Zetland held on until at last the train reached Rugby.[41]

That accident, befalling a peeress, created some stir. It demonstrated the hazards of railway travel at their most terrifying. The first steps were being taken, as it happened, just at this moment to guard against such calamities. Earlier the same year the Great Western Company decided to

39. Regulation Act, 1889: 52 & 53 Vict. cap. 57, sect. 1.
40. L. T. C. Rolt, *Red for Danger* (1966 edn), 193.
41. See Lady Zetland's own account in D. Lardner, *Railway Economy* (1850), 345–6.

send a Travelling Porter with each express train. He was to sit, facing backwards, on the engine's tender, and to communicate with the driver if he saw a signal from the guard or any mishap. The plan was thought to succeed, and it was extended to other trains running for long distances. The men were provided with hooded seats, which they nicknamed 'iron coffins'.[42]

The Commissioners of Railways gave their attention to the problem twice, in 1847 and 1851, and the Board of Trade, to which their duties then reverted, continued to keep it under review.[43] For a time the Board favoured making use of the footboards of carriages as a means of communication – as in Belgium, where the guards moved along the train in this way. It consulted the Railway Clearing House, which set up a committee to examine this plan and reported against it, because it might be dangerous to those who made use of it, but also on other grounds too: it would render the unprotected female liable to assault, and allow passengers to move into carriages of a superior class, unobserved.

Meanwhile, other experiments were being made on the Continent, and they were examined in England. The French had tried 'voltaic' (i.e. electric) communication, a mirror, and a rope attached to a bell or to the engine's whistle – a device also favoured on the Dutch and some German railways. The first two had failed. The third was open to serious objection. Either the rope would be accessible to the train crew only – which would indeed be something, but would do little to help a passenger in trouble; or, if the passengers had access to it, they might misuse it, moved by 'fear or levity'. A Committee investigating this problem in 1853 recognised that most of the passengers' personal anxieties could be removed at once if the American design of open cars were adopted, instead of the now-familiar compartments; but it thought that this plan was 'so opposed to the social habits of the English, and would interfere so much with the privacy and comfort which they now enjoy, that these considerations . . . would forbid its adoption in this country'.[44] It cautiously recommended the use of a cord or wire running from the back of the train to a bell on the tender, but on condition that Parliament should guard against the abuse of the appliance by making that a penal offence.[45] Two Committees of the House of Commons said loudly, in 1853 and 1858, that some communication should be made compulsory; but they were not more

42. MacDermot, i. 366.
43. The history of the subject from 1847 to 1865 is excellently reviewed by one of the Inspectors, Capt. H. W. Tyler, in a report to the Board of Trade: PP 1865, l. 17–29.
44. *Ibid.*, 36.
45. *Ibid.*, 37.

specific than that. The bell-and-rope system was widely adopted, in default of anything better, but it proved unreliable when trains were long, and it could do little to prevent 'outrage in railway carriages'.

That was a real fear to many travellers, and not without reason. Women were often exposed to assault and failed, like Lady Zetland in different circumstances, to attract the guard's attention.[46] Some railways – the Great Western and the South Western, for instance – provided separate ladies' compartments, or were willing to reserve such on request;[47] here again the Americans were ahead of the English, as Dickens noted in 1842.[48] But this danger worked both ways. 'Unfounded charges of indecent assault have been very common of late', wrote William Hardman in 1866 – having just escaped one, as he thought, himself.[49] *Punch* demanded in the same year that 'unattended females' should be segregated in compartments of their own and forbidden to enter any other, to avoid 'the danger of extortion to which male passengers travelling singly are exposed'.[50]

Other dangers, equally or more dreadful, could arise. In July 1864 a patient far gone in smallpox was put into a train with other travellers at Gloucester, and when the stationmaster at Cheltenham was remonstrated with he said he could do nothing about it.[51] Twice, at this time, passengers were set upon by savage lunatics, shut into compartments with them.[52] These experiences coincided with the murder of Thomas Briggs by Franz Müller in a train on the North London Railway. The victims in these cases were unable to call for assistance. So travellers could only be advised that, especially when passing through tunnels in unlighted trains, it was 'always as well to have the hands and arms ready disposed for defence, so that in the event of an attack, the assailant may be instantly beaten back or restrained'.[53]

That was hardly satisfactory, and the railway companies now found themselves called upon peremptorily to find a solution to the technical problem. Any train, after all, might get into difficulties through the

46. Cf. for example *The Times*, 10 Nov. 1845, p. 7.
47. MacDermot, i. 370; G. Measom, *Guide to the London & South Western Railway* (?1866), Notice to passengers in prelims.
48. *American Notes* (Everyman edn), 61.
49. *The Hardman Papers*, ed. S. M. Ellis (1930), 153–4. Wilkie Collins felt the same. 'Danger from virtuous single ladies whose character is "dearer to them than their lives" is serious', he remarked to his mother. 'I won't travel alone with a woman – I promise you that': K. Robinson, *Wilkie Collins* (1951), 211.
50. *Punch* 51 (1866) 70.
51. *The Times*, 20 July 1864, 12.
52. Bagwell RCH, 194; *Annual Register*, 1864, Chronicle, 118–19.
53. *The Railway Traveller's Handy Book*, ed. J. Simmons (1971), 75.

failure of a single axle or tyre, which could be observed by passengers who yet were unable to summon any help. Two such cases occurred within eight days of each other on the Great Western between Didcot and Reading. In both instances, as it chanced, well-known engineers were among the passengers and able to give clear accounts of what had happened.[54] Such things could not be allowed to continue unchecked. Disraeli's Conservative Government laid it down in the Regulation Act of 1868 that every passenger train travelling more than 20 miles without stopping must include 'such efficient means of communication between the passengers and the servants of the company as the Board of Trade may approve', adding the final clause demanded long before, subjecting any passenger who misused the appliance to a fine of up to £5.[55] That was all very well, but what system could honestly be approved? The General Managers of the companies told the President of the Board of Trade that they considered the bell-and-rope system devised by T. E. Harrison of the North Eastern Railway could be adopted with safety. He accepted this advice, and the Act went into force on 1 August 1869.

The Inspecting Officers of the Board of Trade had not agreed with the Managers and had advised the President against Harrison's device. They were soon shown to be right. It proved quite undependable: to such a point that in 1873 the Board of Trade was obliged to revoke the approval given to it. So now, in terms of the Act of 1868, the companies were obliged to provide the communication that the Board approved – but the Board would approve none. It is surprising that neither *Punch* nor the young W. S. Gilbert spotted this farce.

The companies that had adopted Harrison's device went on using it, *faute de mieux*. But new thinking was under way. The Brighton Company produced an electrical system of communication that the Board of Trade felt able to approve in 1877, and the South Eastern did something similar.[56] The ultimate solution had to wait on the interminable discussion of the continuous brake. When that instrument was perfected, either on the Westinghouse or the vacuum systems, it became possible to connect a cord or chain to it and so to permit the guard or any passenger to apply it in case of necessity – still, of course, under the penalty for misuse enacted in 1869.

By the end of the nineteenth century the British railways had struggled through to attain a safety system that appeared to many people to be

54. PP 1865, xlix. 173, 177.
55. 31 & 32 Vict. cap. 119, sect. 22.
56. Marshall SR, 230; J. W. Barry, *Railway Appliances* (4th edn, 1884), 291–6.

complete: as perfect as any system could be that still had to be operated by human beings. Not a single passenger was killed in an accident anywhere in the United Kingdom in the year 1901. It was the first time such a record had been set. But there was no cause for complacency. A run of misfortune followed. There were at least a dozen major accidents in 1903–15, ending with the worst that has ever occurred in Britain, at Quintinshill on the Caledonian. Not all these disasters were due to the failure of safety precautions: the extraordinary series at Salisbury, Grantham, and Shrewsbury in 1906–7 were all caused by excessive speed over sharp curves, maintained by the drivers in a quite inexplicable defiance of stringent regulations. Every year the accidents tirelessly investigated by the Inspectors showed that deficiencies in the system continued. In the years preceding the First World War important new developments took place, some of which looked forward to radically different practices in the future.

The consequences of human error, of forgetfulness and momentary inattention, could still be grave – as at Hawes Junction on the Settle & Carlisle line in 1910, when a signalman forgot the presence of two stationary locomotives. The engineers' efforts were directed more and more towards still further reducing the human element, or eliminating it altogether by automation. One such device was the track circuit: a closed electric circuit installed on a stretch of line, which was broken as soon as wheels moved on to it, with the effect of locking a signal or releasing some other safety appliance. This had first been experimented with in the 1860s; it was installed with success in one of the tunnels outside Kings Cross in 1894. The logical conclusion to which it led was completely automatic signalling, actuated by the train in its passage. Although that did not become established in Britain until the 1950s, the railways were moving towards it before 1914. In 1901–5 automatic signalling was installed on two stretches of two main lines: the London & South Western between Woking and Basingstoke and the North Eastern between Darlington and York. Experiments were also made with an automatic warning system, by which a ramp in the track caused a whistle or bell to sound in the driver's cab if he passed a distant signal at danger. That was first tried out on the Henley branch of the Great Western Railway in 1906. After further experiment it was installed on the whole main line between Paddington and Reading in 1908–10. This still left the driver with the responsibility of applying his brake. The next stage forward was clear: to make the application automatic. That, however, was an elaborate and costly task – it was estimated after the War that it would cost £4 million to install and £750,000 a year to maintain[57] –

57. O. S. Nock, *Fifty Years of Railway Signalling* (1962), 62.

and there was no agreement on any system that was totally efficacious: so for the moment it lay in the future.

There were other new devices coming into use in these years, some of them to reach their fulfilment in the system of our own time. Power signalling, that is operation not by hand but by electricity or air power, was first installed in this country by the London & North Western Railway at Crewe in 1898 and by the Great Eastern at Spitalfields in the following year. It effected a great economy in time and labour and made it possible to control long stretches of line from a single point. The Midland Company moved over to a form of centralised control, exercised by telephone, from 1907 onwards. These were both devices imported from America. But signal engineers in Britain were still making their own contributions to the general stock of experience. The first illuminated track diagram ever devised was put in by the District Railway at Acton Town station[58] in 1905. Today that is an essential element in every new power-signalling installation.

Such developments as these had far-reaching consequences. They were sketched by A. F. Bound, the Signal Superintendent of the Great Central Railway, in a remarkable paper delivered to his professional colleagues early in 1915. For him the block system, evolved with such pains in the nineteenth century and accepted in England as the foundation of the railways' safety, was 'discredited'. 'With its codes, rules, instruments, and confusion', he cried, it should 'be swept away' in favour of a wholly new system based on the track circuit.[59] There was no chance, as he well knew, of realising his plans at the moment, when the country was engaged in a war. But his cogent criticism of current practice, and his clear view of the right course to follow in the future, are still deeply impressive. His arguments provide a characteristic conclusion to this story, at the point to which we take it here: a story of endless experimentation, of discontent with existing methods, fearlessly voiced as soon as they proved to be faulty, of mechanical ingenuity applied in the service of the railways' most necessary instruments of control.

This account has drawn heavily on the work of the Inspecting Officers of the Board of Trade, the experience they accumulated and the judgments they passed on the accidents they were set to investigate. It is right to look now at the work they performed.

58. Then called Mill Hill Park.
59. Bound's paper and the protracted discussion on it are extensively summarised in Nock, *op. cit.*, 32–43.

Broadly speaking, it fell into two parts. Both were very important, though in time one came to be overshadowed by the other. The first Inspectors were appointed by the Board of Trade under the Regulation Act of 1840,[60] with the duty of examining new lines before they were opened, to ensure that they were safe for public traffic.[61] But they also concerned themselves with accidents. They were given no clear statutory power to do so.[62] Indeed the first investigation of the kind was conducted into an accident that had occurred on the Hull & Selby Railway before the Act of 1840 was passed. The companies made no attempt to resist these inquiries; they may have felt a little protected under the Regulation Act of 1844, which laid it down that no Inspector should 'exercise any power of interference' in their affairs.[63]

In the 1840s and 1850s, when the railway system was growing most rapidly, the Inspectors' work in examining new lines took first place. The Inspectors had to learn the job and they were sometimes criticised or ridiculed for their ignorance, real or supposed.[64] But most of the men appointed were well chosen and showed that they were willing to learn.[65] They could on occasion be fooled,[66] and their authority set at defiance.[67] But that did not happen often. They soon made themselves respected, even by the companies, which they often had to criticise. The South Western Company went so far as to name a set of locomotives after them.[68] David Davies – an uncomfortable man to fall foul of – paid one of them a striking tribute at the opening of the final section of the line from Pencader to Aberystwyth in 1867: 'We had the honour of having one of the oldest and most strict [Inspectors] of the day – I mean Col. Yolland. I am told that he rarely does pass a railway on the first examination. However, he has passed this'.[69]

60. 3 & 4 Vict. cap. 97, sects. 5 and 6.
61. The Act of 1840 authorised the Board to require an inspection of any railway; that of 1842 applied only to railways that were to be used for the conveyance of passengers.
62. Cf. Parris, 34. The second chapter of Dr Parris's book gives very much the best account we have of the first Inspecting Officers, their appointment and the work they undertook.
63. 7 & 8 Vict. cap. 85, sect. 15.
64. Parris, 30.
65. For comments on them, from different points of view, see [F. R. Conder,] *Personal Recollections of English Engineers. By a Civil Engineer* (1868), 320–1; Neele, 44.
66. Cf. Dow GC, i. 227.
67. E.g. on the Birmingham & Gloucester Railway in 1840 (Lewin I, 133) and at Radstock in 1877 (R. Athill, *Somerset & Dorset Railway*, 1970 edn, 110).
68. Marshall SR, 171.
69. I. Thomas, *Top Sawyer* (1938), 87.

The Inspectors were invariably officers of the Royal Engineers. They needed to be, and in general they were, men of tact, feeling their way into what became a delicate relationship with the managers and boards of the companies. It was their duty to indicate clearly, in reporting on accidents, what they believed to have been the cause of each. But if that cause reflected badly on the company, there were many different tones of voice in which the Inspector could express his censure. Whatever the defect might be, it was his first object to get it put right, in order to avoid further accidents of the same sort; and quite often the Inspector evidently considered that end would be attained by carrying the company along with him, not by publicly attacking its inefficiency or neglect. On the other hand, there were occasions on which he had to speak right out, loud and clear. So we find one assailing the Great Northern Company's 'very objectionable and dangerous practice' of turning rails (cf. p. 145) in 1860.[70] Another in the following year pillories the London & North Western for 'adopting vicious modes of working, and setting itself against improvement'.[71] A copy of the Inspector's report was transmitted to the company concerned, which sometimes tried to defend itself, showing resentment at his criticisms.[72] In due course all the reports were published. The number of them is very large. In the bad years 1871–5 it rose to an average of 165 a year, in respect of accidents in England and Wales, with the highest number of all, 209, in 1872.

The range of information the reports afford is very wide. Much of what they discuss is technical. They examine, for instance, the behaviour of metal in boiler explosions[73] and in the failure of rails and tyres;[74] the design of locomotives – the enginemen's dislike of the Cramptons on the London Chatham & Dover Railway,[75] the danger of employing tank engines on fast trains.[76] All branches of signalling practice come under review here: not merely the design and operation of signals and points, but the difficulties the men might have in working them, because perhaps the signals were sited in such a way that they could not easily be seen at a distance. The reports reveal at times an entire irresponsibility, or at least an amazing carelessness, in railway management: on the Lancashire &

70. PP 1860, lxi. 83.
71. PP 1861, lvii. 143.
72. Cf. for example the lengthy comments of the Midland Company's General
    Manager, James Allport, on the Inspector's report on the Long Eaton accident
    of 1869: PP 1870, lix. 190–2.
73. PP 1861, lvii. 201–6.
74. PP 1860, lxi. 99–100.
75. PP 1863, lxii. 764.
76. PP 1863, lxii. 825; PP 1898, lxxxi. 289–90.

Yorkshire at Bolton[77] or the North Eastern at Carlisle,[78] in the 'wild runs' down the Seven Mile Bank of the Brecon & Merthyr.[79]

One of the reasons for the last of these deplorable accidents, which happened to a goods train and killed four footplate men, was that all the men travelling with the train were worn out with over-work. The Inspectors came to have a great deal to say about this aspect of railway employment. One of them, Capt. Wynne, raised it with a Commons Committee as early as 1858. The Inspector reporting on the Clayton Tunnel accident on the Brighton line in 1861 drew attention to it, in the case of the signalmen involved. It came up again at Wakefield on the Lancashire & Yorkshire Railway two years later, when the Inspector found the signalman regularly on duty for 37 hours at a stretch; it soon became a common theme in the reports and by this means publicly notorious, attacked by commentators as diverse as *Punch* and Karl Marx.[80] In the long battle that followed the Inspectors were always on the side of the limitation of hours, in the interests of public safety. It was the same thing in the fight to secure the interlocking of points and signals and the adoption of effective continuous brakes: the Inspectors were determined (though patient) and well aware of the effect of a sudden strong observation. So, for instance, in 1872 Capt. H. W. Tyler appended to one of his accident reports a 'statement of a few of the worst accidents that have occurred on railways from defective signal and point arrangements and want of interlocking' – 26 examples, taken from every year since 1867. In the end Parliament supported the Inspectors and secured the victory.

Throughout all this argument, the position of the Inspectors remained the same. Neither they nor the Board under which they worked had any power to compel the companies to adopt the practices they recommended. At first sight this seems absurd. When the case was so clearly made out, why should the old practices have been allowed to continue, with the casualties they entailed? The principle laid down so categorically in 1844 that they were to have no authority to interfere in the running of the railways was always maintained; and in the end one may feel that was wise. The Inspector's relations with the servants of the companies, from chairmen to boy porters, continued to be external. He was free to say just what he thought right for the very reason that his responsibility was limited. It was a grave responsibility, to scrutinise with intelligence, and

77. PP 1874, lviii. 485.
78. PP 1881, lxxx. 570–2.
79. PP 1878–9, lxii. 216–22. Cf. D. S. Barrie, *The Brecon & Merthyr Railway* (1957), 134–5.
80. *Punch* 51 (1866) 221; *ibid.* 61 (1871) 206; Marx, *Capital* (Everyman edn), 255.

to report fairly. It was better that the other responsibility, of implementing or not implementing the recommendations he made, should rest clearly elsewhere. The Inspector's detachment was a valuable part of the authority he came to wield.

The Inspectors often defended the conduct of the men involved in these accidents. There too it was easier for them to speak when they had nothing to do with management. Like many just judges they were apt to be abused from both sides. From the nature of their office, they could never be popular with the companies, and those belonging to the railway interest might attack them.[81] But the men sometimes saw them as part of 'the Establishment'. Here is the way they appeared to a disgruntled ex-stationmaster in the 1870s:

> What a satisfaction it must be to the public when an accident *has* happened to know that 'a real gentleman', appointed by the Government, goes down to the spot, taking luncheon in a saloon carriage on his way thither, accompanied by the officials of the line on which the accident has happened, and whose very frown or hint beforehand, accompanied by their presence, will undoubtedly have the effect of 'the whole truth and nothing but the truth' being laid before the inquiring Colonel or Captain Inspector, and that he will report so that no more accidents of a like nature may occur, or in other words that he will actually sit in a stationmaster's office and have the men in one at a time, and ask them to state what they know about it, and that he will write it down.
>
> How likely it is that after Inspector Bull has been to the men and tutored them as to what they ought to say, and pointed out that if they say 'so and so' it must end in their dismissal, that they will convict themselves and the company. Pooh! don't believe it.[82]

A slight reading of the reports themselves shows that as a travesty. But, even so, it needs to be remembered. The Inspectors were really the men's friends, often interpreting their needs and difficulties, sometimes even explaining their shortcomings with humanity; but they were, in the long run, true friends to the companies too, with their just and constructive criticism. Their object was to secure a safe and efficient service. Like their fellows in factories and mines, these Inspectors were engaged in a subtle and difficult exercise. Over the years they performed their part in it well. The country owed them a great debt. So did the whole railway

81. Cf. for example E. D. Chattaway, *Railways: their Capital and Dividends* (1855–6), part 2, 105.
82. E. J. [*recte* H. A.] Simmons, *Memoirs of a Station Master*, ed. J. Simmons (1974), 77–8.

service, the companies and their employees alike. The student of history has reason to be grateful to them too. Their reports, which have not yet been studied with anything like the care they deserve, are a gold mine for the knowledge not only of the railways' working but, more broadly, of life and labour in the Victorian age.

10   The Companies

The railway system of England and Wales was entirely in the hands of joint-stock companies.[1] The Government never owned any of them until 1948. To understand the way in which the system was actually made to work, it is necessary to look at these companies more closely, at their organisation, their management and practice. Such things were by no means uniform between one company and another. Sooner or later most of them developed characters of their own – sometimes a strong individuality. That needs to be appreciated too.

Their number fluctuated considerably. In 1854 there were about 180 in all, of which perhaps a third could be regarded as independent entities;[2] 12 years later the total was 366, and that was the highest figure ever attained.[3] Thereafter the number gradually fell, owing chiefly to amalgamations, though at the turn of the century it rose slightly for a little while again. When the War came in 1914 the Government assumed control of 106 railway companies in England and Wales, under the terms of the Regulation of the Forces Act, 1871. Of these, 13 were joint lines;[4] 30 were very small companies, worked and controlled by larger ones; and

1. There were, or had been, a few exceptions to this statement, in railways that belonged to private individuals: such, for example, as the Edenham & Little Bytham in Lincolnshire, which was entirely owned and worked by Lord Willoughby de Eresby (see *Locomotive* 14, 1908, 196–7, 216–18), and the Londonderry Railway, south of Sunderland (cf. G. Hardy, *The Londonderry Railway*, 1973). But they were very small, and in relation to the whole system quite insignificant.
2. The number can only be approximate, since in some cases it must be a matter of judgment to decide whether to include certain companies, closely associated with others, or not.
3. BRSM 1867, 1868.
4. That is, lines owned by two or more companies. Four of these comprised systems more than 100 miles long: the Cheshire Lines, the Great Northern & Great Eastern, the Midland & Great Northern, and the Somerset & Dorset.

seven were light railways, built since 1896. In addition, 43 companies were left uncontrolled, all of them very small indeed in mileage, yet including one important group, the underground railways of London. The number of independent companies in England and Wales in 1914, large and small, may be taken as slightly over 100.[5]

Four of these corporations stood out from the rest, as they had done continuously since the middle of the nineteenth century: the Great Western, the London & North Western, the Midland, and the North Eastern. Taken together, in 1913[6] these four owned about 53 per cent of the system, in terms of miles; and the capital they had raised, in shares and loans, amounting to £435 million, represented about 46 per cent of that of the railway companies in the aggregate.[7] At the other end of the scale comes the Easingwold Railway in Yorkshire, with a single line just under $2\frac{1}{2}$ miles long and a capital of £15,800.

This disparity between the large companies and the small had inevitably grown greater with the passage of time, as the large ones became first giants and then mammoths. The disparity was a characteristic of the British system, in contrast to that of France, where the State played a part so much more directly important in the planning, as well as the finance and administration, of railways. Going back to the 1830s, the companies for building the first trunk lines, like the London & Birmingham and the Great Western, were established by the authority of Parliament side by side with such enterprises as the Aylesbury, the Taw Vale, and the West Durham, with lines $2\frac{1}{4}$–7 miles long. Those three little railways were all presently absorbed into larger concerns; but some of the early companies had a long history as independent entities. The most remarkable were perhaps the Taff Vale, to be discussed in a moment; the Maryport & Carlisle, incorporated in 1837 and still cheerfully independent in 1914; and the North London, dating from 1846 – though its working was taken over by the London & North Western, which had always exercised a strong influence over it, in 1909. All these companies enjoyed, at least for part of their lives, great prosperity. The Maryport & Carlisle

5. All these companies are listed in E. A. Pratt, *British Railways and the Great War* (1921), 54–6.
6. The last year before the War for which full returns are available: PP 1914–16, lx. 643–846.
7. These figures apply to England and Wales. A perfectly precise statement is impossible to make because all three companies had substantial interests in Scotland and Ireland too. The Midland held almost a third of the capital of the Forth Bridge Company, for instance; the Midland, again, and the London & North Western were partners with two Scottish companies in the Portpatrick & Wigtownshire Joint Railway; all three companies – and especially the Midland – had interests in Ireland.

Ordinary shares paid an average dividend of nearly 7 per cent between 1844 and 1922, rising as high as 13 per cent in 1873. Other very small companies, not so prosperous but very long-lived, included the Southwold and the Bishop's Castle, the Isle of Man Railway and the companies in the Isle of Wight, the Festiniog and the Corris in Wales.

Since these companies differed so greatly in size, it is rash to make generalisations about them. Let us consider a sample of seven, made up of two of the largest, the London & North Western and the North Eastern; one of the smaller of the leading companies, the London Brighton & South Coast; the North Staffordshire and the Taff Vale, soundly-established companies of the second rank; the Metropolitan, an urban and suburban system in London; and the Colne Valley & Halstead, a rural company in Essex, which kept its independence until 1922. Table 8 (p. 242) summarises a few particulars of their work and their varying fortunes over the years.

At first sight it appears that there was almost nothing identical between these seven units: the tiny company, never paying a dividend, its whole receipts at one time inadequate to meet its expenditure; and the two great ones, well founded and carefully managed, able to maintain their position surely even in times of adversity. But they did have a good many things in common. They were all subject to a body of general legislation, such as the Companies Act of 1844 and the measures establishing the principle of limited liability in 1855–62. Railway companies as such were governed by a series of Acts relating specifically to their business, passed between 1845 and 1911; and their conduct was shaped by the Regulation and Railway & Canal Traffic Acts of 1840–94. In addition, they had of course to conform to the whole body of legislation that affected them as providers of a public service and as employers of labour – concerning compensation for injury or death in accidents, for example, or the carriage of dangerous goods, or the rehousing of working-class tenants displaced by the extension of their lines.

More particularly, each company was regulated by the Local and Personal Acts that had set it up in business or altered and extended its powers. These measures became very numerous. Taking account of all the railways it had absorbed, the London & North Western was subject to about 470 of these Acts by 1914. Even a much smaller undertaking, the North Staffordshire, was regulated by 42. The first Act setting up a railway company to provide a public service had been passed in 1801, in respect of the Surrey Iron Railway. With that model before them, promoters and legislators hammered out a long series in the years that followed. They all constituted the company as a public corporation,

TABLE 8. THE BUSINESS OF SEVEN COMPANIES 1857–1913 [8]

[*1857*]

Co.	Miles open	Capital			Traffic receipts				Expend. £000	Working exp. %
		Paid-up shares £000	Loans £000	Divi- dend %	Pass. carried 000*	Pass. £000	Freight £000	Total†		
LBSC	185	5854	1936	6	9429	611	138	749		
LNW	657	24092	10467	5	11566	1680	1822	3506		
NE	720	14863	5759	5	7551	707	1129	1837		
NS	129	3996	1204	4	1491	99	155	254		
TV	51	887	267	8	412	20	202	222		

[*1873*]

Co.	Miles open	Paid-up shares £000	Loans £000	Divi-dend %	Pass. carried 000*	Pass. £000	Freight £000	Total†	Expend. £000	Working exp. %
CVH	19	152	58	nil	76	3	5	9	9	101
LBSC	345	14091	4741	3¼	29322	1164	390	1618	832	51
LNW	1594	43530	19368	7½	47282	3608	5045	8768	4586	52
Met.	13	5850	1946	2¼	56127	429	18	478	185	39
NE	1339	34809	11474	9¼	31288	1625	4299	6041	3140	52
NS	183	5479	1778	2⅝	4159	149	347	619	331	53
TV	74	1353	436	12	1917	67	377	510	303	59

[*1890*]

Co.	Miles open	Paid-up shares £000	Loans £000	Divi-dend %	Pass. carried 000*	Pass. £000	Freight £000	Total†	Expend. £000	Working exp. %
CVH	19	87	414	nil	194	4	8	13	10	77
LBSC	435	17819	5882	7	56610	1801	608	2572	1261	49
LNW	1877	76421	27617	7¼	96307	4718	6667	11591	6229	54
Met.	38	8442	3343	3	89263	626	41	706	302	43
NE	1612	44723	14219	7¼	50058	2157	4946	7290	4053	56
NS	194	5981	1937	5	8598	217	444	744	360	48
TV	113	6652	996	3	13710	131	520	714	411	58

[*1913*]

Co.	Miles open	Paid-up shares £000	Loans £000	Divi-dend %	Pass. carried 000*	Pass. £000	Freight £000	Total†	Expend. £000	Working exp. %
CVH	19	87	429	nil	185	6	11	18	16	89
LBSC	447	22525	7176	5¼	80426	2636	860	3534	2174	62
LNW	2009	85864	39022	7	127350	7214	8865	16327	10544	65
Met.	83	12508	5537	1⅝	197526	689	81	830‡	523	63
NE	1733	56814	24097	7	86867	3819	7375	11315	7221	64
NS	212	8082	2846	5	11022	293	723	1059	661	63
TV	112	8295	1526	4	14511	245	722	967	576	60

* Ordinary passenger journeys + number of season-tickets multiplied by 600 (cf. p. 277). Some uncertainty arises through different methods of reckoning workmen's weekly tickets.

† Total from all sources, including e.g. hotels and ancillary services.

‡ Excluding revenue from Surplus Lands.

8. Source: *Railway Returns*. The figures for 1857 are from those printed in PP 1857–8, li.

defined its powers, laid down the procedure by which it could acquire the land it needed, and afforded some protection to the public against damage or nuisances or dangers that the railway might occasion. By the 1840s, when this class of legislation had grown large, it began to assume something like a standard form.

But the Acts never became stereotyped. Let us take one simple illustration of the differences between them. Most companies' Acts (though not all: there is no uniformity here) include a section to prescribe the amount of luggage that passengers in each class should be permitted to take with them free of charge. Gladstone's Act laid it down in 1844 that passengers by Parliamentary trains might take with them 56lb of luggage ('not being merchandise or other articles carried for hire or profit') free of charge; but that is the only regulation of this matter to be found in a general statute. Provisions quite discordant with one another were introduced into Acts of Parliament passed at the same time. In 1846, for instance, one company was required to allow 150lb of luggage free in the first class, 100lb in both second and third; another only 112lb first class, 60lb second, and 40lb third – so that in this instance the third-class passenger was entitled to less than a Parliamentary one, even though he paid more for his ticket.[9] Here, at least potentially, was a source of worry or annoyance to travellers making long journeys from one company's lines to another; and one must remember that the middle-class Victorian traveller habitually took with him quantities of baggage inconceivable today.[10] Gradually, as the companies grew into larger units, a standard practice of a sort emerged, allowing 150lb, 120lb, and 100lb in the three classes respectively; but even in 1906 it could only be laid down that these were the amounts 'usually allowed'.[11]

The railway companies were not, indeed, all made to a single pattern. Consider some more of the Acts passed in that busiest of all years, 1846. Some are very much more minute than others, prescribing for instance the first directors by name instead of leaving it to the shareholders to choose them. In the London & North Western Company, formed by amalgamation in this year, it was laid down, with penalties, that the offices of Treasurer and Secretary were never to be held by the same person:[12] perhaps a reflection of the suspicions and jealousies felt by

9. LPA 10 & 11 Vict. cap. 135, sect. 66 (Leicester & Hitchin Rly); cap. 223, sect. 29 (Manchester & Birmingham & North Staffordshire Junction).
10. In 1862 the *Railway Traveller's Handy Book* (1971 edn, 40) suggests that railways running to manufacturing districts were more liberal in this matter than those in the south-east, with a large holiday traffic; but no such principle of difference can be discerned in the original Acts.
11. G. B. Lissenden, *The Railway Passenger's Handbook* [1906], 37.
12. LPA 9 & 10 Vict. cap. 204, sect. 59.

the amalgamating companies towards one another in the past. Some of the Acts make an evident attempt to forbid the companies to engage in any business except their prime one of running railways; and yet the Manchester Sheffield & Lincolnshire was specifically authorised to sell water to the companies supplying Manchester, Salford, and Stockport – a provision much criticised subsequently.[13]

That criticism arose from the desire to keep the railways within bounds. From the outset the scale of their operations, in terms of the capital required, was far bigger than any that had ever been seen before. By its first Act of 1835 the Great Western Company was authorised to raise, in shares and loans, a total of £3.3 million. Given supplementary powers, it increased that amount to £6.3 million in less than seven years. When the London & North Western Company was formed by amalgamation in 1846, its capital was almost £23 million. Such entities were completely out of scale with any others in the country. What limits could be set to the power of corporations backed by such enormous wealth?

Hence, at least in part, the restrictive nature of much early railway legislation; and especially the evident desire to prevent these companies from engrossing other people's business. Again and again they tried to secure powers to own and run steamships. In the 1840s only two of them succeeded, both at the second attempt: the Chester & Holyhead, an unusual kind of railway (cf. p. 31), and the London & South Western. That company managed for a time to do what it wanted without Parliamentary powers, by means of a company indirectly associated with it, formed in 1841. But this undertaking, and another that succeeded it, were under-capitalised. The railway sought power to take over the business itself, which was refused by Parliament in 1844 but granted on a fresh application four years later, against the strong opposition of steamship companies.[14] The South Eastern Company acquired similar powers in 1853. In the 1860s Parliament abandoned its hostility to proposals of the kind, to allow in the end all the railway companies serving ports of any consequence to enter the steamship business direct.[15] It was a sign that the companies had come to take a well-recognised, assured place in the country's economic life. It was also a sign of something else: the strength of the position they had built up for themselves in Parliament.

13. LPA 10 & 11 Vict. cap. 279, sect. 20; Dow GC, i. 113.
14. Williams LSWR, i. 202–6.
15. The chief dates are: London Chatham & Dover Company, 1861 and 1864; London Brighton & South Coast, 1862 and 1864; Great Eastern, 1863 and 1867; Manchester Sheffield & Lincolnshire, 1864; Lancashire & Yorkshire, 1870 and 1900; Great Western, 1871; North Eastern, 1905.

In the 1840s something had appeared there that was reckoned as 'the railway interest', comparable with the East India interest that had been powerful there for a long time past. Already by 1847 it comprised some 80 Members of the House of Commons.[16] In the next two decades the railway interest grew much bigger. 'There are said to be 200 "Members for the railways" in the present Parliament', wrote Bagehot in 1866.[17] There was some exaggeration here, and loose thinking. Dr Alderman's very careful recent analysis brings us much closer to the facts. It shows us that the total number of railway directors in the House of Commons elected in 1865 was 157, of whom 41 sat on the boards of major companies and could therefore be considered to represent powerful railway concerns, to form 'the efficient interest'. In the House of Lords there were 49 railway directors, but only 11 of them belonged to the more important group.[18] Thenceforward the numbers fluctuated. They can be summarised as follows:[19]

TABLE 9. THE RAILWAY INTEREST IN THE HOUSE OF COMMONS, 1868–1914

Period	Average number: total	Average number: 'efficient interest'
1868–84	124	42
1885–91	85	36
1892–1905	73	40
1906–14	42	18

There will be more to say on this matter in the fourth volume of this work. Here we may note that down to 1905 the railways enjoyed a considerable representation. Too considerable, many people thought. 'Railways and railway gentlemen are far too strong in the House of Commons', said *Punch* in 1873, with a general election coming into sight. 'The candidate not to vote for on any account is a railway chairman, director, official of any kind.'[20] By that time the companies were growing widely unpopular. For this there were various reasons, but underlying them all was the fear and mistrust of their economic and political power. Before 1868 the general trend of legislation had been to facilitate their business, to aid its enlargement. From that year onwards the opposite became true.

16. Alderman, 25.
17. *The English Constitution*, chap. iv: *Works*, ed. N. St J. Stevas, v (1974), 274.
18. Alderman, 25–6.
19. Averages calculated from the detailed figures given in *ibid.*, 232–48.
20. *Punch* 65 (1873) 195.

In one field after another new burdens were imposed on them, their free-dom of action was curtailed by the State.

The structure of management in the companies developed a common character, with some notable variations. At the top of the hierarchy stood the board of directors, presided over by a chairman it elected. In some companies the chairman was a very powerful, even a dominant, figure, remaining in office for many years and keeping a close eye on the whole organisation. Sir Richard Moon, Chairman of the London & North Western Railway from 1861 to 1891, is one striking example; Sir Daniel Gooch, who presided over the Great Western from 1865 to his death in 1889, another. But between those two there was an important difference. Moon had had no experience of railways before he was chosen a director of the London & North Western Company in 1847. He came of a Liverpool merchant family. Gooch, on the other hand, had been inti-mately involved in railways for the whole of his working life, except for the brief interlude of less than 18 months in 1864–5, when he was con-cerned with the laying of the Atlantic cable. On the face of it, one might have expected that Gooch would be a common type of chairman. In fact, he was nearly unique. Very few other chairmen had ever had anything to do with the working of a railway themselves. That was generally thought to be a positive advantage. Bagehot, who knew a great deal about business management and had a pair of the most observant eyes in Mid-Victorian England, remarked:

> The most successful railways in Europe have been conducted – not by engineers or traffic managers – but by capitalists; by men of a certain business culture, if of no other. These capitalists buy and use the services of skilled managers, as the unlearned attorney buys and uses the services of the skilled barrister, and manage far better than any of the different sorts of special men under them.[21]

If we allow Gooch to be a distinguished exception – a 'special man' in a highly peculiar chairmanship – Bagehot's rule is well borne out. The only other chairmen of importance in the Victorian age who had been brought up in the railway service were Edward Watkin and his rival J. S. Forbes, and they had a most malign influence on the companies over which they presided. It was noted as something altogether exceptional – a rare and high compliment – that the London & North Western board should have tried to persuade its General Manager Sir George Findlay to succeed

21. *The English Constitution,* chap. vi: *Works,* v. 330.

Moon on his retirement.[22] But Findlay was too wise to accept the honour and soldiered on until he died at his post two years later.

The general practice was to keep direction and management firmly apart. When these companies had settled down after the hectic 1840s, they attracted to themselves some exceedingly able servants. The wiser chairmen and boards trusted them implicitly and allowed them to run the railway, intervening as a rule only when financial questions arose. There were exceptions. In early days John Easthope, Chairman of the London & Southampton Company, meddled incessantly in the operation of the railway, which brought him into collision with the engineer Joseph Locke and with his fellow-directors, who forced his resignation in 1840.[23] Later, the Great Northern board included some masterful directors, who thought they knew more about the business than the Company's senior officers.[24] Conversely, there were managers who, to a large extent, took the control of the whole company into their hands. Samuel Swarbrick of the Great Eastern was one[25] – though it must be allowed that he had good reason to distrust both the competence and the integrity of some of the directors of that company. Later in the century, Cornelius Lundie engrossed to himself almost every office of importance on the Rhymney Railway and directed it with hardly more than formal attention to his board.[26] It was not unusual to elect a General Manager to the board on his retirement. The London & South Western Company made it a regular practice, and in 1904 its directors even broke the firm Victorian rule by choosing a former General Manager, Sir Charles Scotter, to be their chairman. The Midland accorded Allport the honour of election to its board twice, in 1857 when he left it briefly for shipbuilding, and in 1880 at the end of his long and distinguished second tenure of the General Manager's office.

A modern device often adopted to try to secure the best of two worlds is the appointment of a Managing Director. Only one English railway company of any importance took that step before 1914: the Furness, which was served in this way by (Sir) James Ramsden from 1866 to 1883.[27] But its circumstances were unusual. It was much the largest railway company that could be regarded as a proprietary one: an appanage of the dukes of Devonshire, and in a lesser measure of the

22. *The Times*, 27 March 1893.
23. Williams LSWR, i. 39–40, 215–16; S. Fay, *A Royal Road* (1882), 39–40.
24. Cf. F. A. S. Brown, *Great Northern Locomotive Engineers*, i (1966), 82–3, 121–2, 205–10.
25. *Great Eastern Railway Magazine* 13 (1923) 22–3.
26. Cf. the amusing sketch of him in Ahrons LTW, iv. 105.
27. Sir George Gibb, however, tried out the idea on the North Eastern board in 1905, without success: Irving, 265.

dukes of Buccleuch. (What other railway company ever had two dukes on its board at the same time?) Ramsden had worked as an engineer on the construction of the line, and soon after it was opened in 1846 he began the development of the new town of Barrow: a task that came to share his abundant energies with that of managing the railway and its docks.[28]

The administrative structure of most of these companies was fairly uniform. Where there were significant differences, they were usually to be explained in terms of personality, of the relative strength of individual officers.[29] The boards of directors of the large companies settled down in the end to numbering 20 members or less and met, as a rule, once a month. They divided their business between committees – finance, traffic, locomotive, and so on – to each of which one chief officer was responsible. The administration was usually headed by the General Manager. In some of the smaller companies, like the Brecon & Merthyr and the Furness, the same officer was also Secretary – i.e. secretary to the board itself; but the large companies all kept these two posts distinct. Under the General Manager there was a division between goods and passenger traffic. The normal practice was to stick to 'Manager' as the title of the officers responsible for goods business, using 'Superintendent' for those on the passenger side: 'Superintendent of the Line' was a common description of the chief passenger officer.[30] The system was split up into 'Divisions' or 'Districts'. On the biggest railways these were numerous: there were 13 District Goods Managers on the Great Western, ten on the London & North Western. The London & South Western, on the other hand, had only three Divisions, based on London, Eastleigh, and Exeter.

The technical equipment of the railway was in the charge of two chief officers: the Chief Engineer and the Locomotive Superintendent.[31] Here there were some material differences in the companies' practice. In a number of them the relations between these officers were notoriously hostile – one more reflection perhaps of the lamentable jealousy that divided civil from mechanical engineers so conspicuously in Britain. On

28. Cf. S. Pollard and J. D. Marshall, 'The Furness Railway and the Growth of Barrow': *JTH* 1 (1953–4), 109–26.
29. The structure described here relates to the year 1914, set out in detail for each company in BRSM 1915.
30. On the North Eastern Railway, however, where the post was not created until 1892, its duties included the supervision of freight train operation also: Tomlinson, 773, Irving, 217.
31. By 1914 several companies styled him Chief Mechanical Engineer—e.g. the Great Central, Lancashire & Yorkshire, London & North Western, Midland, North Eastern, and South Eastern & Chatham. The Lancashire & Yorkshire had initiated the practice, in 1886.

the Great Western the Chief Engineer, J. C. Inglis, was on bad terms with G. J. Churchward, the Locomotive Superintendent. In that company these two chief officers were not subordinate to the General Manager; they reported directly to the board. In 1903 Inglis became General Manager himself. He soon set about a major reorganisation of the administrative structure of the company at the top, moved especially by the rising costs incurred in operation and the urgent need to keep them down. His plan was to bring the Great Western into line with most other companies by making the General Manager the sole chief executive, who should be able to impose a co-ordination on the work of all departments, which in his view had been lacking. The scheme was steadily resisted within the Company, not by Churchward alone. Though it was formally accepted by the board in 1910, it was not then implemented. Inglis's health broke down under the strain of the battle, and he died in 1911. His plan was taken up again after the First World War, and realised at last in 1921–3.[32]

Such jealousies and rivalries were not peculiar to the Great Western, or to railway companies: they arise in all human organisations. They were to be found at the same time on the North Eastern, whose very able General Manager, George Gibb, aroused a good deal of antagonism;[33] and on the Midland, where a real feud developed between R. M. Deeley, the Locomotive Engineer, and Cecil Paget, who became the Company's General Superintendent in 1907.[34] In earlier days they had been no less common. The Great Northern board, for example, had had frequently to adjudicate between Patrick Stirling, who was responsible for its loco-motives and rolling stock, and F. P. Cockshott, the thrusting Super-intendent of the Line, anxious to see that the Company lost no points in the hot competition to improve passenger facilities in the 1870s.[35] Occasionally, even the men took a hand in the business. When Alexander McDonnell came from Ireland to succeed Edward Fletcher as Locomotive Superintendent of the North Eastern Railway in 1882 he found methods and equipment that he regarded, with good reason, as antiquated, and set about their replacement energetically. The reorganisation he initiated was permanently valuable;[36] but the footplate men disliked the innova-tions on his locomotives, and his position became so uncomfortable that he resigned after only two years' service.[37]

32. Cf. O. S. Nock, *The Great Western Railway in the Twentieth Century* (1971 edn), 10–11, 43–9, 93–4.
33. See Irving, 265–6.
34. See J. B. Radford, *Derby Works and Midland Locomotives* (1971), 190–5.
35. Brown, *op. cit.* i. 176–80.
36. Irving, 90–2, 95.
37. See Ahrons LTW, i. 76–9.

Some of the chief officers of the great companies remained in their posts a very long time. C. A. Saunders was Secretary and General Superintendent of the Great Western Railway from 1833 to 1863, and when he retired three officers were appointed to do his work, a Secretary, a Financial Secretary, and a General Manager. Allport on the Midland Railway and Henry Tennant on the North Eastern both served as General Managers continuously for 20 years; G. P. Neele was Superintendent of the Line on the London & North Western from 1862 to 1895. There was a good deal of movement from one company to another, sometimes induced by the offer of higher salaries. When William Stroudley, for example, was offered the post of Locomotive Superintendent of the Brighton Company in 1869, at £800 a year, the Highland Railway was obliged reluctantly to let him go since it could not afford to promise him any immediate increase on the £500 it was paying him.[38] As might be expected, the very large companies mostly filled their important posts by promotion from within their own service. An extreme case was that of the Great Western, which only once in 50 years appointed a chief officer from outside. The exception then was Louis Trench, brought in from the London & North Western as Chief Engineer in 1891, and he resigned after little more than 18 months. The board replaced him by Inglis, who had spent his early years in the Company's service and worked much for it as a consultant. And it never went outside again.

In their early days railway companies had of necessity to look for their staff – at all levels, from the top of the administration down to the merely mechanical – to those who had no experience of railways at all. In management, they frequently sought officers from the armed forces, accustomed to command: for theirs had always to be a strictly-disciplined organisation. Military and naval men occupied prominent positions in the railway companies in the 1830s and 1840s: Moorsom and Huish and Bruyères on the London & North Western; Laws on the Lancashire & Yorkshire and the Great Northern; O'Brien on the North Eastern; Gretton, Superintendent of the Manchester Sheffield & Lincolnshire; Coddington at the Railway Department of the Board of Trade, until he was tempted away by the Caledonian Company with a salary nearly three times as large.[39] This is an important element in the early railways' direction – the more perhaps because the Board of Trade's Inspectors were always recruited from the Royal Engineers, and they could naturally make easy contact with fellow-officers, from other branches of the services. But conspicuous as these men were, they were only a small

38. *The Highland Railway* (Stephenson Locomotive Society, 1955), 26.
39. Parris, 111.

minority. A much larger number of the companies' early officers were civilians, brought in from other branches of commercial life.

Many of them were recruited from older transport undertakings, from coaching and road haulage and from canals. When Chaplin and Baxendale, two of the big men in the road transport industry, moved into railway management, they brought over some of their employees too. The first stationmasters at Woking and Richmond, for example, on Chaplin's London & South Western Railway, had both worked under him in the coaching business.[40] Pickford's supplied a number of the officers responsible for goods traffic: such as the brothers Moseley, who went from that firm's Manchester office to the Eastern Counties Railway.[41] James Meadows, Principal Agent of the Peak Forest and Ashton Canals, stepped across to become Clerk and Secretary of the Sheffield Ashton & Manchester Railway in 1847 and General Manager of the new Manchester Sheffield & Lincolnshire Company in the following year – though he did not establish himself in that position, resigning before the end of 1848.[42]

For the rest, the origins of the railway officers were diverse. Henry Booth of the Liverpool & Manchester had been a corn-merchant (an unsuccessful one) before he found his true vocation in the railway business.[43] Saunders, educated at Winchester, had also been a merchant, in Mauritius, before he went to the Great Western. Samuel Smiles started out as a country doctor and then became a journalist until he was caught up in the Mania and was appointed Assistant Secretary of the Leeds & Thirsk Railway in 1845. W. D. Phillipps, who had a long career as General Manager of the North Staffordshire, began life as an engineer, apprenticed to John Scott Russell. These are almost random samples, to indicate the range of experience on which the early railways drew. As soon as they were well established, however, they ceased almost wholly to look to other professions for their officers, except in highly specialised business like hotels and marine undertakings. It can very nearly be said that, at the level of management, they came to constitute a closed service.[44]

It was only at the end of the nineteenth century that one company – the North Eastern, moved by Gibb – began deliberately to recruit staff for management, taking in young men from the universities and training

40. Williams LSWR, i. 227.
41. Neele, 8. This matter is explored by Dr G. W. Turnbull in his 'Note on the Supply of Staff for the Early Railways': *Transport History* 1 (1968), 3–9.
42. Dow GC, i. 81, 121.
43. R. Smiles, *Memoir of Henry Booth* (1869), 19.
44. On the well-recognised path of promotion in the Great Western Company see H. Holcroft, *Outline of Great Western Locomotive Practice* (1971 edn), 79–80.

them under one of the chief officers.[45] None of the other companies followed this example before 1914.

On most early railways clerks, and even porters, were appointed only after an interview with the board.[46] On some of them the directors exercised the right of patronage in turn: a procedure thoroughly accepted in large administrative bodies, following the august pattern of the East India Company. The Liverpool & Manchester acted in this way, so did the London & South Western and the Great Western.[47] Directors were thus constantly exposed to pressure,[48] and sometimes to odium. As the railway system grew, and patronage of this sort fell out of fashion, other practices prevailed. At all times, however, in the Victorian age the railways retained one pre-eminent characteristic. They were a family service, in which brothers joined, and fathers came to be followed by their sons. Here are Seymour and Frederick Clarke, for example, who entered the Great Western service in 1837 and 1839 and left it together when their salaries were reduced during an economy campaign in 1850, one to become Manager of the Great Northern, the other first of the South Wales Company and then of the London & South Western. Or again the Worsdells: the Quaker coachbuilder who went to the Liverpool & Manchester Railway and passed into the employment of its successor the London & North Western, with his two sons who followed one another as Locomotive Engineers of the North Eastern.

In a railway town it was very difficult for a newcomer to get employment with the company unless he was a member of a family already working for it.[49] Here was one important factor in that *esprit de corps* which became so notable in the railway service. It was a sentiment that could cut very deep: as in the moving gesture of the Manchester Sheffield & Lincolnshire men, at Mexborough and other depots, who offered to forgo a week's pay as a contribution to the loss sustained by the Company through the Hexthorpe accident in 1887. Had this proposal been accepted, it might have paid nearly half the bill for compensation; but the directors properly and gratefully declined it.[50]

45. Irving, 215–16.
46. The system is described in the *Handbook Guide to Railway Situations* (1861), 8–10. For a racy account of an interview see E. J. [recte. H. A.] Simmons, *Memoirs of a Station Master* (1974), 2–9.
47. Donaghy, 138; Williams LSWR, i. 227, ii. 338; *Handbook Guide*, 8.
48. For example from those who thought themselves entitled to reward for having accorded them their political support. Lord Sondes, as Chairman of the East Kent Company, was lobbied in this way by a Mr C. Johnson of Canterbury in 1859: Kent Archives Office, U791/06, bundle 2.
49. K. Hudson, *Working to Rule* (1970), 61.
50. Dow GC, ii. 204–5.

That is perhaps the most extraordinary indication of the strength of goodwill in the railway service to be found anywhere in the Victorian age. But there are others: for example in the attitude taken up towards Daniel Gooch by the Great Western community at Swindon[51] – an attitude unimaginable today, for it recognises and frankly respects a paternal kind of government.

That attitude is also a reflection of something else: of the character railway companies bore as employers. To understand this matter, it must be seen in the light of the changing ideas of the Victorian age – certainly not in accordance with our own, which are quite different. In their early days the railway companies were considered good to work for, their servants fortunate men. Not that they paid very highly, except at the top, and by no means always there. What they had to offer, above all, was the expectation of steady, continuing work; and that was more valuable than anything to most people, anxious to achieve an income that was certain. Like all other employers they could hire and fire, and they did, particularly in the hectic early days. But then, by the same token, a man who lost or gave up his job with one railway could often – if the circumstances were not disgraceful – find work with another. The Eastern Counties Company was able to break an engine-drivers' strike in 1850 by securing men from the London & North Western and the North British; the North Eastern did the same thing on a large scale, and partly at least by formal arrangement with other companies, in 1867.[52]

Those circumstances were exceptional. In the ordinary way, once the railways had settled down to their business, their servants could expect to retain their jobs and if they showed enterprise to secure some modest promotion. It is true that in times of economic stress they were liable to have their wages reduced, as in 1849–50;[53] but that was a danger to which Victorian employment of every kind was exposed. These men enjoyed an unusual degree of security, arising from the very nature of the railway's business, which had to be carried on whether times were good or bad. That was a great thing; and as the years went by the companies came to offer their servants a good deal more. They supplied them with uniform clothing – something not given in a factory. They built houses for them, to be occupied free or at a moderate rent, even if these were

51. Cf. the address to him, thanking him for securing the 54-hour week, in 1871, to be seen in the Great Western Museum at Swindon.
52. P. L. Kingsford, *Victorian Railwaymen . . . 1830–70* (1970), 78, 80.
53. See the examples of fluctuations of wages in the traffic grades down to 1880 given by Dr Kingsford: *ibid.*, 89–96.

available to no more than a minority.[54] Some companies offered medical benefits[55] and assisted provident societies and savings banks. A few accorded some of their servants modest pensions.[56] In other words, the railway companies played their part – and it was a greater one than that of many other employers – in the growth of organised welfare. It has to be remembered, in this connection as in all others, that they were commercial enterprises, not in any sense benevolent institutions. Their directors and senior officers had a clear duty to the shareholders, who were liable at any time to hold them peremptorily to account for it. Such provision as they made for improving the conditions of employment of their staff had to be justified economically, as maintaining an efficient service.

Here too, as in so many other respects, a great change can be seen emerging in the Mid-Victorian age. The railway companies did not become, in any important sense, worse employers; but the community came to raise its expectations of employers in general, to show itself inquisitive into these companies' harshnesses and shortcomings, and vocally critical of them.[57] We have seen how they were attacked for the long hours of work they imposed on some of their employees (p. 236), which engendered a widespread fear for public safety. Though the men themselves protested on this subject – trying as early as 1861 to invoke the aid of the State in their cause – the most effective pressure was put upon the companies from outside, from the Board of Trade, from Parliament and public opinion, rather than from within the service itself.

By 1914, then, the railway companies had many critics and enemies, few friends. An increasing number of people were becoming convinced that their day was over, that the whole railway system should be unified under the control of the State. This doctrine was accepted in the Labour party; but support for the idea of nationalisation came from other quarters too. It had had its protagonists back in the Mid-Victorian age: Rowland Hill and Arthur Helps, for example;[58] S. R. Graves, Conservative M.P. for Liverpool and director of the London & North Western;[59] Sir Henry Tyler, a former Chief Inspecting Officer of the Board of

54. *Ibid.*, 127.
55. See for example the development of the railway's medical service at Swindon from 1847 onwards (VCH *Wilts.*, v. 243–4, ix. 135, 141–2) and at Crewe from 1844 (Chaloner, 55–6).
56. Kingsford, 159–60.
57. Cf., as an example, Alderman, chap. 4, on employers' liability.
58. PP 1867, xxxviii(i). 108–13; Helps, *Brassey*, 336.
59. See his *Railway Amalgamations* [1872]; *Journals of Lady Knightley* (1915), 227.

Trade.[60] Early in the twentieth century the matter began to be considered by local government bodies. Following the strike of 1911 an effort was made to induce the Town Council of Northampton to resolve in favour of nationalisation, on account of the 'dislocation of trade caused by the tyrannical attitude of the railway companies towards their workmen'.[61] It did not prevail, but it was a straw in the wind. By that time the issue was a matter of general public debate. Nelson's commissioned two volumes to argue the case for and against the nationalisation of the railways.[62] There were those in railway management who had come to accept the idea too. Sir Charles Scotter of the London & South Western served on the Viceregal Commission on Railways in Ireland in 1906–10 and sided with the majority in advocating state purchase.[63] Even Sir George Findlay, though he remained opposed to nationalisation (partly on account of the enormous new patronage it would put into the hands of the Government), and though, unlike Scotter, he rejected the policy in Ireland, went so far as to indicate the lines on which state purchase might be put through, as if he recognised that sooner or later it would come.[64]

Nevertheless, the companies' power remained in 1914, threatened but not fundamentally shaken. What did most to destroy it were the two wars that ensued. And for all the disturbance and anger that had surged up over the preceding generation, they still commanded a great deal of loyalty and devoted allegiance among their officers and servants. The proof of that is to be seen both in the war of 1914–18 and in the protracted and sometimes bitter process of amalgamation that followed it.[65] These things lie beyond the scope of the present study; but when a full judgment on the work of these companies, their achievements and failings, comes to be attempted, it will have to look back at them from the 1920s.

---

60. PP 1872 xiii (i). 657–62, (ii). 95–7.
61. *Minutes, 1910–11*, 434.
62. A. E. Davies, *The Case for Railway Nationalisation*, and E. A. Pratt, *The Case against Railway Nationalisation*, both published in 1913.
63. Marshall SR, 143.
64. Findlay, 289–94. Cf. his *Irish Railways and State Purchase* (1886).
65. A simple anecdote exemplifies the tenacity of this feeling, with the precision of a snapshot. After 1923, following on an agreement between the Great Western and the Southern companies providing for co-operation in the territory they served in common, the General Manager of the Southern Railway, Sir Herbert Walker, sent one of his senior officers to make a tour of the districts affected. Having explained the new policy to a group of railwaymen, he asked if it was understood. 'Yessir', came the reply from one of them immediately, 'we'm to give they Great Western bastards 'ell'.

In the end, the close student of the Victorian railways is bound to see each of these companies as having attributes of its own, like human beings. That has sometimes betrayed those who have written about them into a mistaken partisanship. The London & North Western Company has been repeatedly subjected to carping criticism. Mark Huish, its first General Manager, appears in half-a-dozen histories of other companies as nothing but a bully, a crafty blackguard. We can now see him, thanks to Dr Gourvish,[66] as one of the ablest railway administrators of his time, forward-looking, asking some of the chief questions that ought to arise in the developing management of railways and persistently trying to answer them. Dr Gourvish does not hide his mistakes. The element of the bully certainly was there, and most clever men expose themselves to being thought crafty by their opponents – particularly by those they outwit. Huish's decline and fall is a sad story, reflecting ill on those he served. But at the end of this long and careful study we are left above all with a view of the working of a great corporation. In that Huish played a larger part than anyone else. After his dismissal, the Company went on. The institution was greater than the man.

Again in later days, when the London & North Western had become, on most tests, the leading railway company in Britain, its grandeur provoked envy and jealousy, as success will always do in other human beings; and the envy and jealousy have been transmitted to some of those who have written about the Company and its rivals long afterwards. We know more about the London & North Western than about any other railway company in the Victorian age. A number of its servants chose to describe and analyse its work, from different points of view; and that is something exceptional, indeed almost unique. On the whole, the documentation of these companies is official, impersonal. We have often to infer motives and consequences, to put together explanations of policy ourselves, guided only by formal statements and decisions. Some private papers remain, and there will certainly be others to be discovered; but even they may not tell us very much. In the case of the London & North Western, four writers – all well informed, and three of them officers of the Company – set out to describe its work, in books published between 1849 and 1904.[67] Here and there one detects a tone of complacency in them, as if they were setting out to show other people –

66. T. R. Gourvish, *Mark Huish and the London & North Western Railway* (1972).
67. Sir F. Head, *Stokers and Pokers* (1849); Sir G. Findlay, *The Working and Management of an English Railway* (six editions, 1889–99); C. J. Bowen-Cooke, *British Locomotives* (1893); G. P. Neele, *Railway Reminiscences* (1904). I have discussed two of these works, and their place in the literature of the subject, in introductions I have written to reprints of Findlay's book (1976) and Neele's (1974).

and especially other railway companies – how things ought to be done. Reflecting on some of the Company's mistakes, such as its persistent use of the inadequate Clark and Webb chain brake (cf. p. 225), one smiles wryly as one reads, perhaps bitterly. But how difficult it seems to be for modern partisans to appreciate the merits displayed here!

A fair appraisal of the London & North Western Company, after its formative years under Huish, would perhaps run somewhat on these lines. It acquired a large territory, in the Midlands, north Wales, and north-western England, which it made wholly or mainly its own. Elsewhere it competed with others as an invader, in South Wales, in the east Midlands, in Yorkshire. Whether as monopolist or as competitor it was always tough, and very tenacious; rarely volatile, as its rivals the Midland and the Sheffield companies were apt to be. When put on the defensive, it could act with disconcerting energy – as in the Race to Scotland in 1888, when 'this dignified corporation started up with the animation of a schoolboy',[68] or when, over the last 20 years before the First World War, it put out its best efforts to retain the American liner trade for Liverpool, in competition with Southampton and Fishguard.

The greatness of the Company arose in large measure from prudence and caution, from the pursuit of sterling qualities like punctuality as well as from that economy in management which was the watchword of Sir Richard Moon, its strongest chairman.[69] So also did its failings. Under his guidance the Company pressed economy much too far, and through his prejudices it missed business that might have been profitable. He did his best to prevent his officers from promoting excursion traffic, for example, at a time when it was substantially enlarging the revenues of more liberally-minded railways. Moon was opposed, in all his instincts and sympathies, to the democratising tendencies of his age. It was a standpoint worthy of respect in itself, but questionable in the chairman of a railway company, and by the 1880s it was clear enough that he was unwilling – perhaps he was not able – to read the signs of the times.

It cannot be said that by sticking to old-fashioned methods, cautious but tried, his company afforded a better service to its customers than its rivals: certainly not in the fundamental article of safety, for its record of accidents was not always a good one (cf. p. 81). And it must be doubtful whether even Moon's pursuit of economy was as effective as it appeared.

68. Foxwell and Farrer, 14.
69. Moon has been judged almost as unfairly as Huish. That is understandable. Harsh, puritanical, autocratic, he can never be a sympathetic figure. But he was devoted, intelligent, effective both as a driving force and as a guide; and, for at least 20 of his 30 years as Chairman, the Company owed him a debt beyond computation.

Like other economists of his sort, he was always ready to be taken by new devices for saving money, which might or might not turn out to be genuine contributions to that end.

A more successful pursuit of economy was undertaken by the North Eastern Company, in the opening years of the new century. Dismayed by the steep rise in operating costs, George Gibb and his colleagues set themselves first to analyse thoroughly what was happening, by much more sophisticated methods than had ever been used by a railway company in Britain before, and then to reduce expenditure wherever that could be managed without impairing the quality of the service. In 1900–12 the mileage of trains run by the Company was reduced by 15 per cent, while at the same time the volume of each separate division of its business notably increased: by 18 per cent in minerals, by 35 per cent in goods, by 29 per cent in passengers.[70] The North Eastern did not, of course, stand alone here. All the chief British companies, facing similar difficulties, made efforts in the same direction; but the North Eastern's were demonstrably the most effective.[71] It had taken its own path, and exposed itself to a good deal of sniping from disgruntled competitors.[72] Its achievement in the end was notable. There can be no doubt that, as Dr Irving puts it, 'the North Eastern in 1913 was a leaner and fitter company than in 1900'.[73] By then it could claim with some justice to be the best economist of them all.

Such were two of the giants among these corporations. But there were dwarfs too, who also deserve remembrance. No traveller, surveying the system laid out before him in Bradshaw's *Guide*, could possibly guess the difficulties encountered by some small companies in providing a regular service of any kind. In north-eastern Wales, for example, the Wrexham Mold & Connah's Quay Railway had endless trouble in maintaining even a minimal stock of locomotives in repair: in 1874 it possessed a total of eight, of which five were out of commission. It hired and borrowed others that frequently turned out unsuitable: one proved too light for its work; another, offered by the Metropolitan, too heavy for the track. Throughout its life it made do with a strange assortment of engines, which it tinkered about with in improbable ways until at length, ramshackle as

70. Based on figures in Irving, 293–9. The passenger figure includes estimated contract journeys.
71. See the comparison in respect of freight train mileage in *ibid.*, 280.
72. *E.g.* in its policy towards the trade unions after 1890. The North Eastern's insistence on the use of ton-mile statistics was assailed with scorn, even with personal venom. Cf. the tone of the exchange between W. D. Phillipps of the North Staffordshire and the *Statist* in 1901: G. Paish, *The British Railway Position* (1902), 266–9.
73. Irving, 245.

ever, it passed into the control of the Manchester Sheffield & Lincoln-shire Company in 1890.[74]

A number of these companies were, and remained for years, hopelessly insolvent (cf. pp. 75, 110). It is surprising that their creditors refrained from pressing their claims to a conclusion – and still more surprising that in some cases they managed to get further credit, at least indirectly, to-wards retrieving their fortunes or even extending their lines. The Somerset & Dorset Company was in the hands of a receiver from 1866 to 1870 and released only because the Court of Chancery accepted a highly dubious financial arrangement; yet in 1871 it secured Parliamentary powers to build a 26-mile extension over the Mendips to take it into Bath. Stranger still, a respectable contractor was found to undertake the work, and the line was completed quickly, in 1874.[75] Again, when the Midland & South Western Junction Railway went bankrupt in 1884 there were two parties among its creditors and shareholders. One urged that the Company should be wound up and its property sold for what it would fetch, with the almost certain consequence that all service would cease on the line then open between Swindon, Marlborough, and Andover. The other contended that the only hope for the Company lay in further con-struction, of a railway already authorised, to join the Midland at Chelten-ham. Here, it was argued, lay a chance of giving the Company a viable system. Again, the adventurous view prevailed. Some creditors accepted debentures; further debentures were authorised by an Act of 1887 and – much more remarkable – taken up.[76] In 1891 the task was completed, and in the following year the Company had its one stroke of good fortune, when it secured the services of the young Sam Fay, lent by the London & South Western, to put its affairs into order. He did so with impressive success. The Company was freed from receivership in 1897 and pursued its business, adequately if without any return to its Ordinary shareholders, until it passed into the enlarged Great Western system in 1923.

These 100 companies, then, present between them a very broad spectrum, from surely-founded efficiency and lively enterprise to feebleness, muddle, and bankruptcy. Nobody could call it a satisfactory way of constituting a railway system for one of the chief industrial nations of the

74. J. M. Dunn, *The Wrexham Mold & Connah's Quay Railway* (1957), 18, 25; Dow GC, iii. 46–79.

75. R. Athill, *The Somerset & Dorset Railway* (1970 edn), 56–9.

76. T. B. Sands, *The Midland & South Western Junction Railway* (1959), 12. Cf. also C. G. Maggs, *The Midland & South Western Junction Railway* (1967), 37–40.

world. Yet the system worked: not as smoothly or conveniently as might
have been desired, certainly not always to the contentment of its users
and servants, but still in normal times regularly, in accordance with
advertised arrangements. For that a good measure of the credit was due
to two institutions that did not get much credit from the public: the
Railway Clearing House, which regulated many of the dealings of the
companies with one another from 1842 onwards, and the Board of Trade,
which enjoined irritating and costly practices upon them but also
afforded them, large and small alike, the advice that arose from the
collective experience of railway business, not only within the United
Kingdom but in some matters also from overseas. No other system but
one based on independent joint-stock companies would have been
acceptable to Britain in the 1830s and 1840s. It expanded quickly on
these lines and then set hard in a mould. In due time many people became convinced that some other system would be better, based on a
fresh amalgamation or on outright State control. But on 4 August 1914
the 100 companies stood. With all their shortcomings and faults, they
faced up well to the test that then began for them, the severest in their
history.[77]

77. Although it lies outside the limits of this book, a brief reference ought to be
made here to E. A. Pratt's copious work *British Railways and the Great War*
(1921). Dry, factual, hardly at all interpretative, it yet provides an admirable
record of much of the work performed by these companies in the last years of
their independent existence.

Conclusion

These last few pages afford at once a conclusion and a prologue: a conclusion to this volume and a prologue to those that are to follow it.

The railway system has been described here, its growth, and something of the way in which it was operated and managed. All this development reflects most faithfully the changing attitude of the Victorian State and of individual citizens towards an economic enterprise that grew rapidly in magnitude, threatened for a time to become even a dominant force, and then, in the opening years of the new century, began here and there to move into retreat.

On the Continent and in America, these things emerged differently, and were managed in other ways. Everyone there who was interested in the establishment of railways had the advantage of being able to observe how they had developed in Britain, and to draw lessons from that. Her example had been studied for a long time: back in the eighteenth century in France,[1] in Sweden,[2] and in Prussia;[3] more often, and more extensively, in the 1820s and 1830s when Americans, like William Strickland and Horatio Allen, arrived, as well as visitors from Europe.[4] The observation of these men was concentrated chiefly on techniques and mechanism. The management of railways, their place in the public life of the country, did not concern them much. It was natural to treat them all, down to and including the Stockton & Darlington, as elements in the coal trade, or in the other industries with which they were associated. With the Liverpool & Manchester Railway that was impossible. It did

1. Cf. G. Jars, *Voyages métallurgiques* (1774–81), and B. J. F. de St Fond, *Travels in England and Scotland, 1784* (1907).
2. See the observations published in 1740 and 1776, noted in M. J. T. Lewis, *Early Wooden Railways* (1970), 154, 177, 312.
3. *Ibid.*, 263, 330.
4. The study of early British railways abroad is excellently summarised in chap. 18 of Dr Lewis's book.

not serve the coal trade, and for some time after its opening served industry only in the second place. Its main task was the conveyance of passengers; and that business, carried on by mechanical traction, at once raised new issues of great magnitude. Here was a joint-stock company with a working capital of nearly £800,000, 30 miles long, carrying 80,000 passengers a week, as well as bags of mail for the Post Office, driving out all the coaches running on parallel roads; regulating its traffic – disciplining its customers, one might say – more strictly and minutely than any transport enterprise had ever done before: all this under the authority of Acts of Parliament framed, in some important respects, with a different sort of undertaking in mind. No one who looked intelligently at its working, whether an Englishman or a foreigner, could fail to see that it challenged accepted notions at many points and raised large questions, exciting or vexatious, for the future.

Though most visitors were impressed by the power of the new railway, many of them had reservations on its management: not only about the arrangements for travelling on it (cf. p. 22) but also about the place it had been allowed to assume in the economy and society of the district it served. It at once began to show some of the characteristics of a monopoly; and monopoly was an evil itself to most Liberals – in private hands especially evil to the *Etatistes* of the Continent. The critical conclusions drawn in Lancashire were reflected almost at once in Belgium. There a new state established itself, by revolution, in 1830–1: separated from Holland, and ambitious to develop its economy at the expense of that former partner. One of the ablest men in the new government, Charles Rogier, had been interested in tramways for some time past and was well abreast of what was going on in England. He quickly conceived the idea that railways might become a vital instrument to Belgium in her struggle.[5] A number of young engineers were sent immediately to England to study them, and from their work and the politicians' discussion there emerged a plan not merely for one railway but for a system, like the Liverpool & Manchester in its technology but utterly unlike in its management.

The Belgian system came into being as a deliberate act of the State and, at the outset, fully controlled by it. Even when, in later days, private enterprise was permitted to engage in the business, it was always restricted, to a degree quite unknown in Britain. As other systems evolved during the next generation, all over Europe and across the Atlantic, they came to differ very widely. To some extent at least, it would be possible to classify them by types, in their relations with the

5. *Biographie Nationale*, xix (Brussels, 1907), 719.

State, their management, their economic and social policies, their technology in matters such as gauge and motive power. But no British type appears as such – except in Britain. In each of those matters Britain evolved her own solutions to the problems (which had generally arisen there first) and then stuck to them, or changed them only very slowly. It would not be true to say that she refused to learn lessons abroad, though Mr Podsnap spoke for some British railway managers, as well as for many of the rest of his countrymen, when he remarked that other countries 'do – I am sorry to be obliged to say it – *as* they do'. The Belgians' promotion of third-class travel in early days was noted earnestly in London[6] and may have had some effect on the legislation of 1844. French and Belgian systems of communication between passengers and train crews were examined by the Board of Trade in the 1850s.[7] Much later, towards the close of the century, there was a good deal of movement across the Atlantic to study American management and operation – with notable profit here and there.[8] But the British system set into a mould very early. It suffered the disadvantages encountered by most pioneers: the difficulty of changing what had become established at the beginning, often at the expense of very large investment, and a timidity in the face of large investment to come. Again and again the British railway manager's cry was a more sophisticated and reasonable version of Mr Podsnap's: things might be done differently elsewhere, and done well, but the conditions in Britain were special, and she must retain her own peculiar ways of meeting them. We have noted a number of such arguments, in which there was blind conservatism and hypocrisy, as well as others in which there was sound sense. All these considerations combined to keep the British system apart from those of the rest of the world.

At the close of the nineteenth century English writers began to note that foreigners were coming less and less to observe and learn from the railways of their country, that the intercourse was now chiefly in the opposite direction.[9] There was truth here, but some exaggeration too. The *Bulletin* of the International Railway Congress included a great many contributions dealing with British railways. And it found space to

6. Cf. G. R. Porter in *Journal of the Statistical Society* 7 (1844), 177–8, and Samuel Laing in PP 1844, xi. 621–4.
7. PP 1852–3 xcvii. 329.
8. Neele describes a visit he paid to the United States with a party of London & North Western directors in 1881, and adds notes of the frequent visits Americans paid to his company too (*Reminiscences*, 249–64); Herbert Walker was sent there by the same company in 1902 (C. F. Klapper, *Sir Herbert Walker's Southern Railway*, 1973, 24, 37). The visit of Col. Yorke, on behalf of the Board of Trade, has already been mentioned (pp. 211).
9. Acworth RE, 470–1.

print, from 1895 onwards, an annual review of British train performance and locomotive practice written for it by Charles Rous-Marten – something it never did in respect of any other country. The series came to an end in 1907 solely on account of Rous-Marten's death. It is worth recalling too that whilst Churchward learnt much in designing his locomotives for the Great Western Railway from French, American, and German examples (cf. p. 182–3), the outstanding French locomotive engineer of the next generation, André Chapelon, acknowledged the greatness of Churchward in turn.[10]

So even in current practice, at the end of the years considered in this book, the British railway system stood apart as something peculiar, but also worth study and observation. And when people in other countries looked back into history, towards the origins of that system and of their own, they were never in any doubt where those origins were to be found, nor did they hesitate to recognise the railway as one of the cardinal achievements of the nineteenth century. It was summed up perfectly at Munich, when the Hall of Fame in the Deutsches Museum was hung with portraits of German men of science, Humboldt and Liebig and Helmholtz and a score of others who had done much for their country and the world. Only two men were chosen to appear there who were not Germans. They were Euler, a German Swiss; and George Stephenson.

The early development of the railway in Britain, then, was unique: one of the chief contributions she has made to the civilisation of the world. Having fashioned this complex instrument, and given it all its essential parts, she made use of it in her own style. The railway came to serve her special purposes: purposes that might be different from other people's, or if they were the same were attained by another route. We have seen something in this book of the way in which the railway evolved in Britain, the changes in its character that took place over these three generations. It is now time to consider the uses to which it was put and some of the consequences it entailed. The consequences were not always those that had been intended. Some of them passed unperceived at the time, though we can discern them now. They cannot easily be shaped into generalisations: for things happened differently from time to time, and from one place to another. It is best to range widely over the whole field, looking at cases, taking soundings, before trying to reach any broad conclusions. The first such exploration must be one of the country itself and of the societies within it. So the volume succeeding this one will

10. H. C. B. Rogers, *G. J. Churchward* (1974), 209.

examine the place taken by the railway in London, the cities and towns large and small, villages and the rural world. Since transport was vital to the whole community, that inquiry will involve, in some degree, an anatomical investigation of Victorian England and Wales.

Appendix I   A note on train services

Inadequate attention has been paid in the literature of railways to the services they offered to the public – save, to a limited extent, in respect of express passenger services from the 1880s onwards.

The Liverpool & Manchester Railway ran at first four trains a day over its line; a service presently increased to 10–12, according to season. The journey of 31 miles seems to have taken about 1¾ hours, though when they announced the times of departure the directors always abstained from disclosing the expected times of arrival at the other end. On Sundays no trains ran between 9 a.m. and 1 p.m., to avoid interference with religious services. The fares charged were 5*s.* first class and 3*s.* 6*d.* second, approximately half those of the coaches; and they were entirely free from the surcharge for tips to guard and driver that on the coaches were virtually obligatory.

When the main trunk lines started work, from 1837 onwards, the services they provided were less frequent than these. In 1840–1 the London & Southampton provided six trains a day, the London & Brighton five. The Great Western, when it was completed between London and Bristol in 1841, offered a more generous service of eight trains, together with two goods trains carrying third-class passengers. The fastest of these averaged 28.4 m.p.h., the slowest 11.6. Short-distance trains ran also: so that, with this addition, there were 15 services daily from Bath to Bristol, 17 from London to Slough.

When suburban railways developed in London they provided frequent services from the start. The London & Greenwich Railway began with an hourly service in February 1836; by December there were four trains an hour, and in March 1839 (though for but a short time) six.[1] Only then did the railway match the coach services in frequency,[2] though of course

1. R. H. G. Thomas, *London's First Railway* (1972), 86.
2. Coaches ran every ten minutes in 1838: *Robson's London Directory* (1839), 787.

it always enjoyed the advantage of speed. The London & Blackwall afforded a quarter-hourly service on its opening in 1840. Ten years later the North London did likewise, maintaining the same practice for over 60 years.[3]

Such were the most liberal services provided in these early days: the most liberal, indeed, that were possible with safety in the era of hand signalling, before the development of the telegraph[4] and the block system. At the opposite extreme, many railways offered what seems to us well below an acceptable minimum of service. The Hartlepool Company ran only two passenger trains a day.[5] The Taff Vale, connecting two of the three largest towns in Wales, did likewise in 1841–4; it then added a third, and at that the service stuck for a long time.[6] Some companies did not trouble themselves with passengers at all: the Hayle Railway in Cornwall, opened in 1838–9, provided no service for them (though some used it informally) until 1843.[7]

The variety of passenger services was much enlarged in the 1840s by the provision of Parliamentary trains, under the terms of the Act of 1844 (see p. 37), and of excursion trains, run on particular occasions, at very cheap rates. The second of these developments will demand a chapter to itself in a subsequent volume of this work. At the same time express trains also emerged, first on the Great Western Railway in 1845 and then elsewhere. They did not maintain their early promise. They were slowed down soon after 1850 and developed little in speed over the succeeding 20 years, until the force of competition was brought to bear on them. The number of trains – the total service – gradually increased. The volume of travel grew relentlessly.[8] In approximate terms it happens to form a pattern that is almost exactly symmetrical. Between 1850 and 1869 the number of railway passengers in England and Wales (excluding season-ticket holders) multiplied four times over; in the 1870s and 1880s it doubled again; in 1890–1909 it increased once more by half. To accommodate this enormous growth, trains became heavier (see p. 200) and more numerous. By the 1880s very few lines were supplied with only two or three a day; four or five was now, for most of them, the minimum.

3. M. Robbins, *North London Railway* (4th edn, 1953), 16–17.
4. The London & Blackwall Railway, however, employed the telegraph throughout from its inception.
5. PP 1842.
6. D. S. Barrie, *The Taff Vale Railway* (2nd edn, 1950), 11.
7. MacDermot, ii. 157.
8. Though not without occasional brief interruptions. The number of passengers travelling fell very slightly in 1869 and 1909; more substantially (by 2.2 per cent) in 1912, but the reduction then may be accounted for largely by the coal strike of that year.

Here and there an individual station might be scantily served; but the vast majority enjoyed something much more than the statutory single train in each direction.[9] In and around London and some of the great cities an intensive service was beginning to develop, though the process was fitful, varying from one company to another, and from place to place. On the Inner Circle line in London, trains ran every 10 minutes; but as it accommodated other services too, the average interval on most of the Circle was little more than five. The Mersey Railway, under the river from Liverpool to Birkenhead, also offered at this time a ten-minute service throughout the day, with trains running every six minutes during the rush hours. Such provision as that was exceptionally lavish. The busiest provincial suburban services, like Newcastle-Tynemouth or Manchester-Altrincham, comprised about 35–40 trains in each direction, and that could mean a few gaps almost an hour long between services in the middle of the day. Elsewhere things were quieter. In Birmingham the railway service was curiously sparse.[10] The Harborne line, constructed as a suburban branch in 1874, had one train an hour, with two extras thrown in at the peak time; and the same was true of the Stour Valley line to Wolverhampton. On the old London & Birmingham line, running eastwards, the first station was Stechford, nearly 4 miles out, until Adderley Park was opened in 1860. The purpose of this new station was to serve a suburb; but it got only nine trains a day.

There were other important factors in railway travel, from a passenger's point of view, besides frequency and speed. The services now began to grow more convenient, in a different sense: through the provision of cross-country trains, to eliminate the necessity of changing.[11] In early days they had been rare. By the 1880s, however, a whole group of them were running: two each from Liverpool to Hull, Scarborough, and Newcastle, for instance; two through services from Birmingham through Hereford to Swansea; a 'Scotch Mail', conveying passengers, every night from Bristol to Glasgow.

9. A few commanded less – did they escape the eyes of the Board of Trade, usually so sharp? At Penter Rhiw, for example, on the Brecon & Merthyr Railway, for many years one train stopped a day, in one direction only (cf., e.g., *Bradshaw*, Apr. 1910, 463). Scafell on the Cambrian had several trains, calling on request, but again in only one direction: R. W. Kidner, *The Cambrian Railways* (1954), 20.
10. The development of railways in Birmingham is summarised, with a useful map, in VCH *Warwicks.*, vii. 37–41.
11. This was a convenience that came to be insistently demanded. John Hawkshaw, the engineer, who had much experience of travelling in Belgium, thought that although travelling there might be cheap, it would be found intolerable by Englishmen on account of the frequent changes involved; but he allowed that the provision of through carriages increased the cost of the service. PP 1867 xxxviii (i), 808–9.

A different means of providing through services had also been developed: the slip carriage, released from a moving train at a station *en route*. The apparatus for this purpose had two essential elements: a device for uncoupling the carriage to be slipped and a brake that could be controlled by a guard to bring the vehicle to a halt.[12] The first such services appeared in 1858, on the Brighton main line at Haywards Heath, and then before the year was out at Canterbury, Slough, and Banbury.[13] The practice came to be widely adopted, though not universal.[14] It had the drawback that it could work in one direction only; there was no corresponding appliance for attaching vehicles to a moving train. Moreover the carriage (or carriages) usually remained an isolated unit; when dining cars became general, the passengers in slip carriages did not, as a rule, have access to them. Nevertheless, the invention did enable some services to be provided that would perhaps not have been offered without it. Small towns, lying on a main line or just off one, might get through services from London in this way: like Stamford,[15] East Grinstead, or Bridgwater.

It was all one more means of saving time. On the Continent, where time perhaps seemed to be less precious, the slip carriage was very little employed, though it was known in France and Holland. In England it proved useful; and, it may be added, made its contribution in safety, for no serious accident ever arose that was attributable to the practice.

In the 1870s and 1880s the English express train[16] comes to stand out as something of a model to the rest of Europe. Increasing public attention was paid to it, by economists and statisticians, by a growing band of interested amateurs – like the Eton master who told the court of inquiry into the Wigan accident of 1873 that he was in the habit of

12. It is carefully described in T. B. Peacock, *Great Western London Suburban Services* (1970), 28–9.
13. H. Ellis, *British Railway History* (1954–9), i. 396–8.
14. The North Eastern never employed it, the Lancashire & Yorkshire only from 1889 (Marshall LYR, ii. 236), the London & South Western discontinued it in 1902 (Williams LSWR, i. 240). It was little used in Wales or in Scotland, though there were at one time or another slip-carriage services to Carmarthen and Lanark.
15. See Acworth's comments: RE, 235.
16. The definition of an express train is that put forward by Foxwell and Farrer (3–4, 93), applicable to the late nineteenth century: in Britain, one running at a minimum speed of 40 m.p.h. throughout (including stops), on the Continent one at 29 m.p.h. They explain the reason for adopting these two different standards. By 1914 the 40-m.p.h. standard can be used for all alike. In the United States conditions differed too widely to make generalisation useful; but on many railways east of Chicago the standards were as high as those in Britain, or higher. *Ibid.*, 77–87.

'timing the speed and taking observations of the gradients during his journeys'.[17] A cardinally important book emerged at this time as a result: *Express Trains English and Foreign* by E. Foxwell and T. C. Farrer (1889). From the analysis here and from *Bradshaw* useful information can be gleaned concerning the time taken in travel and the nature of the services provided. It needs to be seen historically, to be compared with the services given by the horse-drawn coach established before railways entered the business. Table 10 summarises a little of the information we have, indicating the fastest services provided between London and 18 of the largest towns in Great Britain at five points in time between 1836 and 1914.

How far are these to be considered good services or bad? To answer that question one must look at the Continent, in order to make it more fully comparative. Table 11 sets out the services provided between London and eight provincial towns, together with six services in France and Germany that may be regarded as fairly comparable, in distance and in the importance of the towns concerned. It also takes the extraordinary case of the Liverpool-Manchester services (uniquely liberal, owing to the force of competition) and shows them against those between Brussels and Antwerp, perhaps the closest parallel to them in Europe.

One thing here is self-evident. In the nineteenth century Britain stood far above any other European country in the speed of travel its express trains afforded. Foxwell and Farrer demonstrate this in a table in their book, reproduced on p. 272 as table 11.

Table 11 also seems to show something else: travel in Britain looks relatively expensive. Only in France were third-class fares higher. But on that simple basis alone the comparison is misleading. To begin with, the British railways, from very early days, carried a generous quantity of their passengers' luggage free. Then, supplementary fares for travelling by express trains had ceased to be levied anywhere north of the Thames by the mid-1880s, whereas on the Continent they were universally charged. Third-class passengers had access to a much larger proportion of express trains than in any other European country, except Denmark. And from 1875 onwards they had come to travel a good deal more comfortably in most respects than their fellows on the Continent. The Midland had set a decisive example when it abolished second class and upgraded third-class accommodation to the old second-class level. The result of this was that by the end of the century many middle-class

17. PP 1874, lviii. 772.

TABLE 10. FASTEST SERVICES FROM LONDON, 1836–1914

The towns included here fall into four groups: the ten largest in England (increased to 11, since Nottingham overtook Plymouth in size at the census of 1881); three other large towns, in areas of the country unrepresented in the first group; the two towns that had become the largest in Wales by 1914; and the two chief cities of Scotland, Edinburgh and Glasgow. The source used for all the train times is the August issue of *Bradshaw* (regular service, Mondays-Fridays). In column 3 blanks appear where no service by railway throughout was available. These times are prefixed, in column 2, by those of the fastest coach services in 1836, as shown in A. Bates, *Directory of Stage Coach Services* (1969).

1	2	3	4	5	6	7
Town	*Coach 1836*	*1844*	*1854*	*1876*	*1900*	*1914*
Birmingham	11hr 00m*	3hr 55m	3hr 00m	2hr 45m	2hr 15m	2hr 00m
Bradford	23 00†	—	6 30	4 45	4 03	3 46
Brighton	5 15*	1 30	1 15	1 10	1 05	1 00
Bristol	12 14	4 20	3 00	2 36	2 15	2 00
Cardiff	17 23	—	4 31	4 58	3 17	2 50
Hull	18 00‡	11 05	5 50	5 20	4 10	3 52
Leeds	21 21	8 45	4 50	4 35	3 49	3 25
Liverpool	21 15	8 15	5 45	5 00	4 15	3 35
Manchester	18 30*	7 45	5 30	4 45	4 15	3 30
Newcastle	30 20	12 15§	7 25	6 05	5 32	5 20
Norwich	11 00	—	3 15	3 30	2 31	2 28
Nottingham	12 54	5 30	3 50	2 50	2 23	2 15
Plymouth	22 26	—	7 10	6 10	5 07	4 07
Portsmouth	9 00*	3 25‖	2 48	2 10	2 00	1 51
Sheffield	16 49	6 50	4 44	3 40	3 09	2 57
Swansea	21 48	—	6 05	6 45	4 45	4 00
Edinburgh	42 53	—	10 50	9 00	8 25	8 15
Glasgow	42 30	—	11 25	10 30	8 25	8 15

* In these cases the fastest service was not provided by mail coach.
† Approximate time, allowing for change of coaches at Wakefield or Leeds.
‡ Approximate time, by Royal Mail to Barton-upon-Humber and thence by ferry.
§ To Gateshead.
‖ To Gosport.

TABLE 11. EXPRESS SERVICES IN BRITAIN AND EUROPE, 1888 AND 1914

1 Journey	2 Distance (miles)	3 Number of express trains		4 Number admitting third class		5 Average speed of trains (mph)		6 Speed of fastest train (mph)	
		a 1888	b 1914	a 1888	b 1914	a 1888	b 1914	a 1888	b 1914
*London – Birmingham	113	14	44	all	all	40.6	52.6	43.7	56.5
– Bristol	118	9	17	5	all	43.2	48.8	45.4	59.0
– Cardiff	154/145†	none	12	none	all	none	48.3	36	51.5
– Glasgow	401	6	12	all	all	42.3	45.4	44.6	50.1
* – Leeds	186	23	37	all	all	43.4	47.1	46.4	54.4
* – Manchester	184	29	33	all	all	42.5	45.2	43.3	52.6
– Newcastle	269	9	18	7	all	43.9	47.3	47.2	50.4
* – Nottingham	124	13‡	34‡	all	all	49.3‡	45.1‡	51.3	55.9
Paris – Bordeaux	365	10	16	4	6‖	33.2	46.1	40.0	54.5
– Lille	154	7	12	2	4¶	35.8	49.1	40.5	53.4
– Lyon	318	6	10	none	3	31.3	42.8	35.7	47.6
Berlin – Cologne	367	6	9	2	2¶	34.4	43.8	37.7	46.2
– Hamburg	178	4	17	2	13	36.0	49.4	39.7	55.1
– Leipzig	101	6§	18	2	14	31.0	47.0	33.7	52.2
*Liverpool – Manchester	32	57	93	all	all	44.1	45.6	48.0	48.0
Brussels – Antwerp	27	17	30	all	all	30.6	46.3	33.8	47.6
Average speed of British trains						43.7	47.3	45.1	53.2
Average speed of Continental trains						33.2	46.4	37.3	50.9

* These services are competitive.

† 154m. in 1888, via Bristol and the Severn Tunnel; 145m. in 1914, via Badminton.

‡ These figures relate only to the through services by the Midland Railway. The Great Northern also ran a service, by which it was usually necessary to change at Grantham.

§ Strictly speaking, 4 (one 3rd-class); but 2 more (one of them 3rd-class) have been included since they miss the 29 m.p.h. average by only one minute.

‖ One more of those in col. 3(b) conveys 3rd-class passengers more slowly, but still at express speed.

¶ Two more of those in col. 3(b) convey 3rd-class passengers more slowly, but still at express speed.

Source: Bradshaw; Bradshaw's Continental Railway Guide

TABLE 12. EXPRESS TRAINS: FARES, MILEAGE, AND SPEEDS, 1888 (EUROPEAN EXPRESS TRAINS)*

Countries of Europe arranged in ratio of express miles per day to population

Express fares in pence per mile approximately Classes			Country	Population taken from Whitaker's Almanack 1888 (000)	Express mileage Third class	% of third class to total	Total	Average speed (mph) incl. stops	excl. stops	One express mile per diem to following no. of inhabitants
1	2	3								
2.00	1.25	0.95	Great Britain†	32700	57207	93	62574	41⅔	44	525
1.60	1.30	0.80	Holland	4390	6475	81	8000	32½	35	540
1.48	1.09	0.73	Belgium	5910	4133	59	6919	31¾	33½	850
1.91	1.43	1.05	France	38000	11263	27	41130	32	36¼	920
1.70	1.31	0.94	North Germany	32180	18657	72	25798	31¾	34½	1250
1.66	1.18	0.85	Switzerland	2906	157	7	2285	24	26	1270
1.70	1.31	0.94	South Germany	11713	2567	28	9085	31	33	1290
2.30	1.75	0.95	Ireland	4800	1646	58	2818	33	35	1700
1.50	1.07	0.69	Denmark	2030	845	100	845	30	32	2400
1.80	1.33	0.90	Austro-Hungary	39000	6297	46	13852	30	32	2820
2.23	1.66	0.95	Roumania	5000	—	—	1207	29¼	32	4500
2.00	1.33	0.85	Italy	30000	1213	26	4705	29½	31¼	6400
1.80	1.30	0.90	Sweden	4644	—	—	632	29	31½	7350
1.85	1.23	0.74	Egypt	6000	—	—	520	36	37	11500
2.37	1.72	0.81	Russia (European)	85000	—	—	3060	29	31⅔	27700

Average fares in Europe and Egypt:

1	2	3
1.85	1.36	0.86

* Taken from Foxwell and Farrer, 95, with the addition of the average fares.
† At 40 miles per hr; all others at 29 miles per hr.

No express, i.e. trains whose speed, including stops, is 29 miles an hour or over, in Algeria, Asia Minor, Bulgaria, Greece, Montenegro, Norway, Portugal, Servia, Spain, Tunis, or Turkey.

people in Britain travelled third, where the same sort of people travelled second in Europe. In other words, while they paid on average 0.95*d.* a mile for their journeys, the comfortable *bourgeoisie* on the Continent paid 1.36*d.*, or 43 per cent more.

At the same time one other conclusion must also be drawn from table 11: that Britain's lead in the provision of express train service was rapidly diminishing by 1914. Whereas, on average, the trains analysed in 1888 were 10 m.p.h. faster in Britain than on the Continent, by 1914 that differential had shrunk to less than 1 m.p.h., and there was no great difference in the speed of the fastest expresses. On the other hand, the old European practice of excluding third-class passengers from the best trains was still widely followed. For many reasons – political as well as economic – the British express train had become a democratic institution, which it never was on any of the large national systems of the Continent before 1914.

Such were some of the services that were offered, provided in the time-tables. They were not always adhered to in practice. Some railways – the Midland among the great trunk lines, the South Western, the Brighton, and the two companies serving Kent – had an unsavoury reputation for their unpunctuality. It would be beyond the scope of this note to examine that, though there is a great deal of material for the purpose. The Midland Company's board set up a committee to examine the matter in 1870[18] and a Commission of Inquiry into Train Delays, which produced 82 reports in 1891–3; statistical returns on unpunctuality were presented to Parliament from time to time, notably in 1890.[19] We can only remind ourselves that the services described and analysed here are what the companies professed to afford; they are not necessarily what their customers actually got.

Finally, it must be added that no comparable analysis can ever be made of the services provided up and down the country for freight traffic. *Bradshaw* has nothing to say of them; the only source of information is the companies' working timetables, and of those only very incomplete series survive. Some analysis can be made; but it is too fragmentary, and requires too much complicated explanation, to be suitably presented in a brief note such as this one.

18. BTHR RAIL 49 1/20, min. 8511. If the committee presented a report, it does not seem to have survived; BTHR RAIL 491/740.
19. PP 1890, lxv. 797–825.

Appendix II Statistical summary of the growth of the system 1860-1914

The figures given in this table are those printed in the *Railway Returns*, included annually among the *Parliamentary Papers*. Those in respect of passenger and goods traffic were required under the Regulation Act of 1840. Though many of the others shown were asked for by the Board of Trade, and furnished, it does not appear that the Board had any statutory authority to do so until 1871. The Regulation Act of that year (sects. 9 and 10) prescribed the form in which they were to be made. This, amended by the Regulation Act of 1873 and by the Railway and Canal Traffic Act of 1888, continued to be the practice until 1913, when for the first time returns were made on a new basis, set out in the Railway Companies (Accounts and Returns) Act of 1911. Thus the figures for 1860–70 form one group, those for 1871–1912 another; those for 1913 stand on their own, on a different basis, which perhaps accounts for the reductions shown in columns 6 and 7. Although some figures are available for earlier years, they reveal so many deficiencies and inconsistencies that it has seemed best to begin the series at 1860.

These figures ordinarily indicate growth. On the few occasions when a decline appears in columns 2–7, the figure for the year is printed in italics.

STATISTICAL SUMMARY 1860–1914

1	2	3	4	5	6	7	8
		Passengers conveyed (excl. season-		Receipts			
Year	Miles open	ticket holders)† (000)	Passenger traffic £000	Goods traffic £000	Total from all sources‡ £000	Working Expenditure £000	Col. 7 as % of Col. 6
1860	7583	136959	11059	12413	23473	11258	48.0
1861	7821	145797	11246	12775	24022	11802	49.1
1862	8176	152438	11834	*12695*	24529	12051	49.1
1863	8568	173605	12262	13950	26213	12660	48.3
1864	8890	197162	13268	15400	28668	13536	47.2
1865	9251	216694	13981	16185	30166	14561	48.3
1866	9701	238137	14754	17521	32275	15895	49.2
1867	10037	250599	15208	18190	33398	16765	50.2
1868	10200	269257	15634	18446	35227	17135	48.6
1869	10774	*268896*	15935	18764	36105	17504	48.5
1870	11044	288633	16332	20359	38122	18228	47.8
1871	*10850**	328553	17450	22392	41383	19387	46.8
1872	11136	372450	18877	24499	45039	22065	49.0
1873	11369	401465	20187	26875	48857	25799	52.8
1874	11622	423522	21178	27014	50210	27535	54.8
1875	11789	451541	21825	27947	51726	28220	54.5
1876	11989	481285	22162	28342	52476	28466	54.2
1877	12098	492404	22486	28578	53057	28597	53.9
1878	12229	503983	22788	*28282*	53143	*28059*	52.8
1879	12547	504050	*22072*	28365	*52479*	*27070*	51.6
1880	12656	540669	23141	30458	55795	28536	51.1
1881	12807	558676	23346	30994	56643	29339	51.8
1882	13052	587230	24528	32068	59093	30876	52.2
1883	13215	616402	25105	32873	60522	31768	52.4
1884	13340	621131	25584	*31973*	*60099*	*31680*	52.7
1885	13612	622170	*25387*	*31318*	*59321*	*31423*	53.0
1886	13678	641502	25771	*30818*	*59278*	*31170*	52.6
1887	13825	647775	26077	31693	60503	31719	52.4
1888	13982	654173	26274	32887	62006	32340	52.2
1889	14034	684422	27774	34916	65676	34455	52.3
1890	14119	722279	29208	35976	68273	37018	54.1
1891	14156	747862	29907	36765	69836	38818	55.4
1892	14242	764143	30358	*36283*	69852	39305	56.1
1893	14440	770803	30505	34341	68253	39261	57.4
1894	14536	805215	31025	36867	71934	40663	56.5
1895	14651	818004	31688	37015	72792	41126	56.4
1896	14708	861225	33248	38959	76585	43153	56.3
1897	14818	898061	34461	40396	79760	45668	57.3
1898	15007	922171	35587	41484	81781	48121	58.8
1899	15044	959602	37226	44187	86708	51866	59.8
1900	15195	992426	38634	45340	89393	55826	62.5

1	2	3	4	5	6	7	8
		Passengers conveyed (excl. season-		*Receipts*			
					Total	*Working*	*Col. 7*
	Miles	*ticket*	*Passenger*	*Goods*	*from all*	*Expen-*	*as % of*
Year	*open*	*holders)†*	*traffic*	*traffic*	*sources‡*	*diture*	*Col. 6*
		(000)	*£000*	*£000*	*£000*	*£000*	
1901	15308	1021179	39609	*44895*	90704	58293	64.3
1902	15358	1041263	40414	46306	93369	58661	62.8
1903	15501	1047142	40875	46658	94556	59257	62.7
1904	15626	1052390	41264	46892	95397	59873	62.8
1905	15731	1054416	41565	47782	96931	60700	62.6
1906	15859	1093398	42635	49569	100289	63064	62.9
1907	15897	1110614	43549	52226	104230	66435	63.7
1908	15999	1139577	44290	*50225*	*102950*	*66409*	64.5
1909	16045	*1133320*	*43920*	50647	103149	65116	63.1
1910	16148	1171676	45261	52335	106347	66392	62.4
1911	16200	1188204	46309	53921	109190	68196	62.5
1912	16223	*1161993*	46653	54587	110500	70411	63.7
1913	16401	1292819	48883	56593	*106566*	*67965*	63.8

* This decrease puzzled the Board of Trade, which tentatively explained it by a discrepancy revealed through the adoption of a new method of collecting the figures. See PP 1872, lii. 509.

† The figures in col. 3 are fundamentally unsatisfactory. What we want chiefly to know is the number of passenger journeys, the total volume of travel. But these figures exclude 'holders of season or periodical tickets' (whose numbers are shown separately). No accurate count could be made of such passengers, since they did not give up a ticket at the end of each journey. It was a common rough practice to assume that every season-ticket holder made 300 double journeys a year, and therefore to multiply the number of season tickets by 600 to get an approximate total. This method cannot be satisfactorily adopted in the present case, however, since there is much confusion in the reckoning of these passengers. In 1869, for example, the number of season-ticket holders suddenly drops by 40 per cent, compared with that for 1868; one major company, the South Eastern, inexplicably omits to furnish any return of them. In 1876 a drastic reduction occurs again, owing to a new and stricter method of reckoning (PP 1877, lxxiii. 83, 165). Down to 1912 workmen's daily tickets were included individually, as if they had been ordinary third-class passengers, whereas workmen's weekly tickets were reckoned as seasons (PP 1914–16, lx. 651). Only for the last year of the series, 1913, can we get something like a reliable figure for passenger journeys. It is:

	(000)
Ordinary passengers	1004092
Workmen (calculated on a single-journey basis)	288726
Season-ticket holders (× 600)	392320
	1685138

In that year, therefore, the total of passenger journeys was about 30 per cent greater than that of 'passengers conveyed', as given in col. 3 of the table.

‡ Including miscellaneous receipts, e.g. from hotels.

Conversion tables

Table of £ s. d./£p equivalents	£	s.	d.	£p	£	s.	d.	£p
			1d.	½p		6s.		30p
			2d.	1p		7s.		35p
			3d.	1p		8s.		40p
			4d.	1½p		9s.		45p
			5d.	2p		10s.		50p
			6d.	2½p		11s.		55p
			7d.	3p		12s.		60p
			8d.	3p		13s.		65p
			9d.	4p		14s.		70p
			10d.	4p		15s.		75p
			11d.	4½p		16s.		80p
			12d. (1s.)	5p		17s.		85p
		2s.		10p		18s.		90p
		3s.		15p		19s.		95p
		4s.		20p		20s. (£1)		100p
		5s.		25p				

Table of weight equivalents	
1 oz.	28.35 g
1 lb	0.4536 kg
1 stone	6.3503 kg
1 cwt	50.802 kg
1 ton	1.016 tonnes

Table of distance equivalents	
1 in.	2.54 cm
1 ft	30.48 cm
1 yd	0.9144 m
1 mile	1.6093 km

Index

Index